ORGANIZED LABOR AND THE CHURCH

REFLECTIONS OF A "LABOR PRIEST"

Msgr. George G. Higgins
with William Bole

PAULIST PRESS
New York   Mahwah, N.J.

Acknowledgments for Photographs:

Cover photo, Ch. 1 photos of Msgr. Ryan, Bishop Haas, Ch. 2 photo below Gibbons statue, Ch. 3 photo w/Cesar Chavez, Ch. 6 photo of Corn Mill strikers: Courtesy of CNS (Catholic News Service) Washington, D.C., used with permission.

Chapter 1 photo of Msgr. Hillenbrand: Courtesy of the Archives & Record Center, Archdiocese of Chicago, used with permission.

Chapter 1 photo of Charles & Anna Higgins: Courtesy of the Higgins family, used with permission.

Chapter 4 photo of NACST Reception: Courtesy of Msgr. Higgins, used with permission.

Chapter 5 photos of Walter Reuther and George Meany: Courtesy of RNS (Religious News Service) New York, used with permission.

Chapter 7 photo of Lech Walesa and Chapter 8 photo of Solidarity flag: Courtesy of the AFL-CIO News, Washington, D.C., used with permission.

Copyright © 1993 by Msgr. George G. Higgins

Library of Congress Cataloging-in-Publication Data

Higgins, George G., 1916–
    Organized labor and the Church: reflections of a "labor priest"/
George G. Higgins with William Bole.
        p. cm.
    Includes bibliographical references and index.
    ISBN 0-8091-3374-1
    1. Higgins, George G., 1916– . 2. Church and labor—United
States. I. Bole, William. II. Title.
HD6338.2.U5H54 1993
261.8'5—dc20   92-36139
                                                                          CIP

Published by Paulist Press
997 Macarthur Boulevard
Mahwah, New Jersey 07430

Printed and bound in the
United States of America

Contents

Foreword

A few years ago, in a lecture at the New York Public Library, the historian David McCullough reflected that one of the most interesting things about autobiographies is what the autobiographers leave out. McCullough said, "Look at what the author is not telling you."

So it is with this fascinating book by Monsignor George Higgins (which is how I always refer to him, even though he characteristically disdains the honorific and identifies himself as Father Higgins). What he does not tell you directly—what you comprehend only by reading between the lines—is the utterly unique role that he plays in the church and the trade-union movement.

For many years he has been a kind of translator who knows the subtle dialects of Catholics and of trade unionists, and he has a remarkable gift for translating the dialect of each group into terms that the other can understand.

In a sense this is a perfectly natural task, since the humane values of the church and trade unions have a common philosophic base: both institutions define themselves through their commitment to the dignity of the individual, and each has a solid tradition of social action meant to ensure the recognition of that dignity.

But Monsignor Higgins' mission has never been simple. As you read of his encounters with representatives of one side who know nothing (or, even worse, know just a little) about the other, notice the great sensitivity and patience that he shows when he is doing his work of translation.

Some of the more daunting projects he has taken up involve disputes arising from the organizing of workers in Catholic hospitals, schools, and

1

other institutions. The managers of such institutions know perfectly well about the church's teaching that workers have a moral right to be represented by trade unions. But when their own employees show an interest in bringing unions into the workplace, some of these managers react with a smooth adaptation of the "not in my backyard" position. (As a Catholic, a trade unionist, and the son of a parochial school janitor, I must confess a personal interest in this kind of thing.)

You will notice as you read this book that George Higgins has handled many such cases with great tact and without losing sight of church doctrine. Indeed, the responsibilities of "the church as employer" and those of the union as "responsible representative of workers' interests" have occupied a good deal of his time and attention through the years.

But the relationship between church and trade union, and Monsignor Higgins' part in it, has a thousand other aspects. Most are harmonious. A few are not. One of the most remarkable passages of this book is in the chapter, "Religion and Labor: Then and Now," where he offers advice to those who are working for more cooperation between church and trade union: learn more about each other, accept the similarities and differences between the two sides, don't try to convert the other side to your agenda. This is the advice of one who has a generous measure of common sense and good humor, but also, in the words of the philosopher Isaiah Berlin, "possesses antennae of the greatest possible delicacy."

Some people make their mark on the world primarily because of the position they hold. That is not true of George Higgins. He has, of course, had impressive job titles and credentials, but in the hands of someone of lesser ability, they would have counted for little. It is because of his personality and his commitment to the rights of working people, nothing more and nothing less, that Monsignor Higgins has accomplished so much.

For people like myself—Catholics seeking validation of their efforts (however effective or ineffective) to improve the conditions of workers— he is a giant figure whose place in the pantheon of the social thinkers and social activists of the church has long been secure. For those of us who came to maturity in the 1950s and 1960s, his was the voice we wanted to hear speaking out for our church. He was the writer, lecturer, and guide we all sought and from whom we took strength.

Throughout the last thirty years he was the activist supporter of farm workers and hospital workers, of the forgotten workers of America. As a member of the United Auto Workers' Public Review Board for over thirty years, he has been an arbiter of one union's conduct toward its members, and the guardian of due process and democratic values within our institutions.

He has been the defender of our rights and of our unions; but he has never been slow to criticize any union's conduct that fell short of the moral goals he insisted we share.

Monsignor Higgins leaves out of this memoir any mention of a small, brief tussle with a church bureaucracy that sought to retire him prematurely as part of an "administrative reorganization." It is interesting only because of the speed and intensity with which his outraged friends and admirers, led by the late Father Geno Baroni, rose in indignation at the mere hint that George Higgins was not central to the church's social mission. Suffice it to note that the bureaucracy beat a hasty retreat.

Monsignor Higgins writes that one of his moral predecessors, Monsignor John Burke, was "the right man in the right place at the right time." For more than fifty years, that has been just as true of George Higgins himself. But whatever his place and time might have been, he has been and remains the right man.

Scholar and activist, researcher and doer, writer and advisor, exemplar and individualist, George Gilmary Higgins defies easy classification. A man of great personal charm, with a zest for life and a love of people, he is a person of extraordinary talents.

The pages of this book only hint at the positive effect he has had on the "social church" and on the lives of countless Americans who are the unknowing beneficiaries of his impatience with casuistry and his intolerance of injustice.

What a shame it is that the church doesn't have a thousand more like him!

> Thomas R. Donahue
> Secretary/Treasurer of the AFL-CIO

Preface

Long ago I made up my mind never to turn down an invitation to offer a prayer at a trade union gathering. I felt then, as I do now, that in and through prayer for God's blessing, the church makes visible its presence in the labor movement. In so doing, the church signals its support for the legitimate aspirations of working people.

Some would say that at this point, prayers are all that the American labor movement has going for it. I take a different view. No doubt the movement finds itself on a downward slide. But I prefer to look upon labor's moment of decline as a period of transition. All across the country, unions are finding new ways of dealing with new workplace realities. Further, the crisis of organized labor and erosion of working conditions in the United States have led many people outside of unions to rediscover "the labor problem."

Not only labor, but the Catholic Church and other faith groups have arrived at a turning point. During the 1930s and beyond, the American labor movement drew timely support from churches and synagogues. The Catholic Church in particular blessed the struggles of workers to form independent unions and secure a living wage. After labor gained recognition in many industries, religious groups began to lose interest in the labor cause, generally speaking. More recently, with a revival of anti-unionism by employers, religion and labor have slowly begun to renew their ties.

Will the Catholic Church, my church, reclaim its heritage of support for the organization of average working people? I am afraid I cannot say for sure. In fact, the church stands in danger of losing forever its tradition of

5

cooperation with organized labor. It is for that reason, above all, that I wrote this book.

With the possible exception of the first chapter, I do not offer this as an autobiography. God knows there are more than enough of those to go around. When I draw on personal experience, I do so simply to illustrate a given time and place in the religion-labor encounter. These pages hardly amount to a history or a comprehensive study. My goal is more modest: to relate some of what I, as a Catholic priest, have seen and heard during nearly fifty years of involvement in the labor movement. I also wish to argue for the enduring relevance of organized labor—to the cause of social justice and the church's social mission in the modern world.

To acknowledge all who contributed to this book, I would have to name, among others, the many hundreds of people I have known in organized labor and the Catholic social action movement—throughout the United States and to some extent in western Europe, Poland, Latin America, and southeast Asia. Suffice it to say that I could not have written it without them. In more practical terms, I and my co-author, William Bole, would like to thank the Paulists, especially Father Kevin A. Lynch, for his confidence in this project, and our diligent editor, Father Richard C. Sparks. Our thanks also to the rank and file of Paulist Press—the people who type, proofread, design, print, and deliver the books, and otherwise make it all possible.

Msgr. George G. Higgins
Washington, D.C.
May 15, 1992

Charles and Anna Higgins

Msgr. Reynold Hillenbrand

Msgr. John A. Ryan

Bishop Francis J. Haas

1

The Formation
of a "Labor Priest"

A Blue-Collar Intellectual

In Chicago during the Depression we had something that would be hard to find anywhere today, even in New York: a real Jewish ghetto. The ghetto was where Jews from the old world had settled and set up their shops and outdoor stands. Occasionally, on a Sunday afternoon, Charles Higgins would lead his four children out of the shell of our placid suburb and venture into the Near West Side of Chicago. There we would find the Jewish settlement bustling with the trade of small things, a pound of smoked salmon here, a pair of socks there, and maybe a radio or two. A commuter ride from our overwhelmingly Protestant town, closed for the day of worship, the Jewish settlement had the charged atmosphere of a bazaar. And on what might have been a slumbering suburban afternoon, the scene was enough to make a young Gentile shake with excitement.

I am not exactly sure where or how my father developed his warm feelings toward the Jews. I do know he worked with Jews at the post office in Chicago (he was a clerk), and he always counted a number of friends among them, usually young, aspiring intellectuals who sorted mail at night so they could go to school by day. What impressed him the most was the great value they seemed to place on books and studies, greater than, at least, the Irish.

Mind you, this was decades before the ecumenical and interfaith conversations now expected as a matter of course, long before people like Arthur Goldberg and Charles Higgins' son would explore the terrain of Catholic-Jewish relations. (Goldberg, the late Supreme Court Justice,

United Nations Ambassador and labor lawyer, came from the Jewish ghetto.) The word "ecumenical" had not yet entered the working vocabulary of the faithful of La Grange, Illinois. In our town of about ten thousand people, there stood about a dozen Protestant churches and a single Catholic parish, one of the smallest and poorest in town, and no synagogue. (As I recall, La Grange had one Jewish family, which owned a jewelry store in the tiny business district.) With a lopsided majority of WASPs, there seemed little call for dialogue among the faiths. And in any event, ecumenical activity was not a familiar part of religious experience in those days, even in the more pluralistic neighborhoods and towns. The only whisper of ecumenism in La Grange came when our pastor, Father John Henry Nawn, had tea with the Episcopal church vicar. When it happened, the tea parley was the talk of the town. That was the extent of ecumenism in the 1930s. (I would wager that today the town has a ministerial council that meets monthly and comments on everything from Tiananmen Square to Timbuktu.)

I would be stretching a point if I were to say that my father tried, in his own way, to further interreligious cooperation with his excursions into the Jewish ghetto. This was not his exact purpose, and yet nor was it to pick up a few ounces of smoked salmon. The outings were more in a spirit of education in the school of life, a venture into the unknown. "This is another part of the world," he would say. "You ought to know about it."

For a postal clerk with an eighth grade education, Charles Vincent Higgins took his children far and wide. Not literally, of course. My father never traveled (he didn't have the money to travel) and never owned a car. Before visiting me years later in Washington, his longest journey came when he and my mother left their home in south-central Illinois, logging a grand total of one hundred and seventy-five miles.

In Springfield my father and his brothers worked as machinists, firemen and engineers on the railroad. They were one hundred percent Irish, with both parents from the old country. It always seemed, though, that they were not of the Irish of Boston and New York. There was never much Irish lore in my father's family or any ersatz Irish nationalism. They did not dwell in the Irish-American subculture, with its ritual bashing of the British and that unmistakable feeling of inferiority, the sense that the Brahmans were ruling over them. Undoubtedly, this owed much to their midwestern perspective. The Higgins family looked not to the Irish lore but to the lore of Abraham Lincoln.

The Higgins brothers did have one thing in common with the eastern Irish: dedication to the union. Each of my uncles took his place in the active ranks of organized labor. My father, too, became a strong union man, but his interests ran wider. And—how this came about, I do not know—his deepest pursuits were intellectual. While still in Springfield, he met Anna Rethinger, a strong and decisive woman whose father had emigrated from Alsace-Lorraine when it was a German holding. In 1912, four years before I was born, he and my mother pulled up stakes and headed north, opening up a new world for them and their family.

My father had a virtual obsession with getting his children interested in serious things, and in an urban center like Chicago, the possibilities were numberless. In the days before television and before most people owned a radio, lectures were big business, much bigger than today. They were the only way to see or hear the great writers and thinkers of the time, and my father rarely missed a major lecture in Chicago. If the circuit brought around a G. K. Chesterton, a Hilaire Belloc or a John A. Ryan (big names then, particularly in the American Catholic sub-culture), he would go to hear them and take me with him.

I was barely a teenager when Chesterton came to town. There we were, high up in the gallery of Orchestra Hall, and I could understand hardly a word the man was saying. I could hear him well. The content, however, flew way over the head of an eighth grader. Undaunted, my father would tell me: even if you don't understand, you should know that Chesterton is an important person and that this is an important event. In my father's mind, it was an exposure, and one that came at no small sacrifice. The Chesterton lecture probably cost him three or four dollars, a lot of money in those days, especially for a postal clerk.

Although my father's intellectual interests gravitated toward literature and the arts, he exposed us to the political world as well. I was in the seventh grade when Al Smith, the man who would have been the first Catholic president, came to town in 1928 and gave a speech at a huge public park miles and miles from where we lived. In a ride that seemed to go on forever, we took the commuter train and two streetcars to reach the Far South Side of Chicago. Although I remember the event distinctly, I haven't the faintest recollection of what Al Smith said. But, once again, I wasn't there for a lesson in American politics; my father simply wanted to expose me to something important. A unique opportunity to do so came in the next season of presidential politics. Through his cousin, a minor player in the Democratic structure of downstate Illinois, my father wangled a ticket to the 1932 Democratic convention at Chicago Stadium. I spent a couple of days there, as Franklin Delano Roosevelt accepted the first of his four presidential nominations.

A little before that, the lecture circuit brought around a person as closely identified with the social reforms of the New Deal as anyone besides Roosevelt. "You may not understand a whole lot, but he's a great man," my father told me. "You ought to be exposed to him." In all likelihood he had read articles by Msgr. John A. Ryan but never any books. Nonetheless my father, like many others, was committed to what Ryan stood for. We went to see the greatest of American Catholic social action- ists. Three decades later, I would be with Ryan on the last trip of his life.

Charles Higgins may not have been a public person, but he did enjoy a small measure of celebrity, in his way. Some of the more attentive readers in Chicago and elsewhere were familiar with the name of C. V. Higgins— the signature he affixed to hundreds of "letters to the editor." He held forth on many and various subjects, from the New Deal and League of Nations to liturgical arts and literary criticism. The media of his message were usually daily newspapers in Chicago, *America* and *Commonweal* (two Catholic intellectual journals) and *The New World* (published by Chicago's Catholic archdiocese). My father mastered the art of letter-writing, and practiced it not only on editors. While in seminary I got a letter from him every week, and he wrote as often to his family in Springfield. The letters were never personal in the sense of relating if a neighbor had died or if someone had broken a leg. They were all commentary, his thoughts on what he was reading and what was otherwise happening in the worlds of literature, public affairs, the arts and religion.

When my father wasn't writing, he was reading. He could never have dreamed of higher education and yet was infinitely better read than anyone in the family, including nieces, nephews, children and grandchildren who would later go on to college. If he were alive today, he would be appalled at how little his great grandchildren, or any others, for that matter, read in college. For someone who never reached secondary school, my father was a persistent and systematic reader. Reading was almost a religion to him. Even when his eyesight began to fail, he insisted on reading at least two hours a day (a lifelong habit, almost an addiction, that I picked up from him).

Because of his failing eyes, he had to be somewhat selective. He re- ligiously read magazines like *America* and *Commonweal* (two of his favor- ites) cover to cover. He read literature, poetry, journals of the arts. When I got old enough, he would have me read aloud, for relief when he was too tired as well as to further my own education. He worked the nightshift at the post office and was always home for lunch, so I would rush home at noontime from the parish school and take my place at the kitchen table to read from the small-print columns of *America* and *Commonweal*. To under- line the educational point of this, he would have me look up all the words I didn't know (an exercise that I have appreciated more in retrospect than I did at the time).

My father had a way of measuring the value of education outside the classroom. "The investment I've made in your education," he often said, "will be worthwhile—if you're impatient whenever *Commonweal* or *America* is late in the mail." That was his way of saying that formal education was a waste of time and money unless it led to a taste, preferably a thirst, for at least a modicum of serious reading. (During the intervening years, both magazines have had their ups and downs, but I, for one, couldn't get along without them. And, though I don't always agree with them, I still get impatient when they arrive late—which, given the sad state of the U.S. postal system, happens more frequently than it used to in days gone by.)

My father was conversant in the works of Belloc and Chesterton and read virtually all of Jacques Maritain and Christopher Dawson. Though lesser known than the others, Dawson left a special impression on me. The British Catholic historian and philosopher wrote eloquently on the concept of vocation, the sense of calling that must be discerned by not only the priest but the civil servant, labor leader, business executive and all others. In Dawson's words, "the need for a restoration of the ethics of vocation has become the central problem of society." Written a half-century ago, his words seem more timely now than ever.

For as long as I can remember, my father had a peculiar interest in the *Divine Comedy*. I was too young to even wonder why, but he pillaged Dante's classic, reading it over and over, perpetually (in translation, of course). He would take it with him on the train for the commute to work, and after reading the newspaper, he would take out his old, dog-eared copy of the *Divine Comedy*.

My father also had a passion for the visual arts. Whenever he could spare the time, he would take us to the Art Institute, a museum-school in Chicago. He tried to instill this passion in his children, though he succeeded only with my late, younger brother, Eugene, who would go on to study at the Art Institute. My father, however, did not love art simply for art's sake. He was interested in the way art comes alive in a community. And so he subscribed to *Liturgical Arts*, an attractively illustrated magazine that passed on long ago but in its day did much to raise the interest of Catholics in modern art and its possibilities for religion. The magazine concerned itself not so much with the aesthetic in and of itself but with the aesthetic conditions of a vital worship and, indeed, religious and ethical life. On this, my father and other enthusiasts of liturgical arts proved many years ahead of their time. And their enthusiasm reflected only part of a larger, incipient movement to draw connections between the liturgy and social life.

A name that loomed above all others in that field was Virgil Michel, a monk and founder of the American liturgical movement. With uncanny anticipation of what would come, Michel called attention to the link between the performance of liturgy and our human performance in daily life—in more familiar terms, the connection between spirituality and social action. He wanted to bring the social gospel into the liturgy and the liturgical spirit into social reform.

This monk was hardly silent when it came to his opinions, usually expressed in a straightforward manner that appealed to an informed layman like my father. Never one to shy away from a debate, Michel joined in critical conversation with some prominent figures, among them his fellow Minnesotan, Msgr. John A. Ryan. Michel believed that the Catholic social action movement symbolized by Ryan had concerned itself too much with reform of social and economic institutions and not enough with moral and spiritual reform. More to the point, he believed activists of his time paid far too little attention to the liturgy, which, he constantly insisted, is the indispensable basis of Christian social action. It has served as a constant reminder throughout my own social ministry.

(In retrospect, I think that Michel to some extent exaggerated the weakness of the social action movement in this regard and understated the failure of too many liturgists to relate the liturgy in a meaningful way to contemporary social and economic problems. In any event, the monk of St. John's Abbey in Collegeville, Minnesota, sounded a prophetic alarm. Now, although much work remains, the familiar slogan of both the liturgical and social-action movements is "keeping things together," a great step forward that would have gladdened the heart of Virgil Michel.)

*   *   *

My father was anything but private in his intellectual pursuits; he shared almost everything on his mind and in his books, even before we could fully understand. On the questions of the day, his thoughts were our thoughts. Yet in my thoughts about the formative institutions in my life— the church and the labor movement—I wasn't necessarily my father's son. Although a strong union man, my father rarely, if ever, attended a union meeting. The fact that he worked the night shift would have been enough to keep him from the union hall. But more important than this, my father was, by temperament, never much of a "joiner." I was not raised on the union.

As far as church goes, my father went to mass but was not especially pious and, indeed, was capable of irreverence toward the reverends. At one time we had a pastor whose views on social issues clashed with my father's. The pastor had served as a seminary dean, and people thought of him as quite the intellectual. He told his parishioners in a sermon once that the only two books they'd ever need to read were the Bible and the *Imitation of Christ*. My father went along with that to a degree. "Maybe," he said. "But

I wish he'd keep his mouth shut about political problems." My father was, however, friends with an earlier pastor, John Henry Nawn. A one-time Shakespearean actor from Massachusetts, Nawn was a first-rate preacher with a flair for the dramatic. One of the memorable scenes of grade school was Nawn coming in to relieve the nuns every now and then and regaling us with a Father Brown mystery or some other story. He would act out the parts as though in a performance of Hamlet; we were all spellbound.

He and my father, when they met on the street or in front of the church, would talk about a new book by Belloc or Chesterton or someone else. And as usual with my father's intellectual pursuits, I was drawn into the conversation. More and more, my after-school hours were taken up in Nawn's library at St. Francis Xavier's parish. It was a good library, for those days, and Nawn encouraged me to borrow books whenever I wanted. In due time, without any particular prompting by him and certainly no pressure, the question of priestly vocation came up at home and rectory. By the end of grade school it had become an easy decision. It seemed like the natural thing to do.

Mundelein, Illinois

In La Grange during the 1930s, a young person could grow up without a sharp sense of the fact that the country had fallen into economic depression. It's not that all was well. In our neighborhood, where most of the Catholics lived, families struggled to keep their heads above water. But the community as a whole was rather well-to-do, with the more affluent Protestants working as bankers and lawyers in Chicago. And while my father's salary was nothing to write to Springfield about, he always had a steady, government job; we never went hungry. In our town there were no soup lines or shantytowns, nothing of the squalor so visible where I live now, in Washington, D.C.

Wanting to be a priest meant that I would pass up high school in La Grange. It meant that every day, for five years, I would take a train and two streetcars to downtown Chicago, near the North Side. Notwithstanding our family day-trips to the urban jungle, I really did not know the city. My commutes to Quigley Preparatory Seminary of the archdiocese of Chicago were an unfiltered exposure to the big city, in the middle of the Great Depression, as well as to the children of the Depression. Quigley was of a size that church leaders today, faced with a diminishing pool of seminarians, could only dream about. We had eastern Europeans, Irish, Germans, and others of just about every ethnic group imaginable at the time, in all about a thousand young men. A large city parish would have as many as fifty students in seminary at any given time. For me, it was a new world.

Yet, while exposed to the sights and sounds of urban life during the Depression, I heard little of this behind the high walls of the seminary. We did what all high school students preparing for the priesthood did—Latin, Greek, algebra and the like. We had only a vague awareness of social ferment of the time, the battles of organized labor and experiments of the New Deal. We knew even less that our own cardinal, a princely and somewhat mysterious figure, was figuring in some of the more intriguing of these events. Even to this day, there remain many unanswered questions about the Roosevelt-Mundelein alliance, lasting literally up until the last hours of the cardinal's life.

Cardinal George Mundelein, archbishop of Chicago from 1915 to 1939, had a keen interest in seminaries and seminarians. On a twenty-five hundred acre tract of land in Area, Illinois, he constructed more than a dozen buildings that would make up the largest major seminary (that is, college-level and beyond) in the country. It was such an achievement that the city fathers changed the name of the town to Mundelein. To us the cardinal was a distant figure, and yet he was close to his seminarians, in his way. He knew all of our names (quite a number to keep in mind) and monitored the progress of each and every one of us. He even knew about our families, once asking me, in a surprise encounter, how my father was doing at the post office. This quiet yet engaged style of leadership carried over into his public life. Although public speeches and high-profile appearances did not appeal to him, Mundelein was a strong F.D.R. supporter, a social-minded prelate who supported the New Deal agenda.

They knew this in Washington. On the way to give one of his most memorable and controversial speeches—the so-called "quarantine" speech in which he announced a naval blockade of Germany in 1939—the president made a widely publicized stop at the cardinal's residence. The visit with Mundelein was nothing if not political, a crucial part of Roosevelt's strategy that day. At the time Roosevelt was walking a tightrope over the smoldering issue of war in Europe. While he claimed to have no interest in war, the public—including a large bloc of his New Deal coalition, the ethnic groups—believed otherwise. The Germans wanted nothing of war with Germany, and he had to tread lightly with the Irish, who generally detested our would-be allies, the British. Every step of the way Roosevelt had to keep one eye on the ethnic vote. To have in his corner a cardinal, one held in high esteem by millions of ethnics, was understandably of great importance to him.

Given Mundelein's low-key and undramatic manner, it seems fitting that his best-known intervention on behalf of Roosevelt took place behind closed doors. In a talk to a regular gathering of clergymen in the archdiocese, Mundelein remarked, "Adolph Hitler is nothing but a paper-hanger, and a poor one at that." Admittedly it was not the cleverest of comments, but it made an impact at the time. Somehow the statement immediately hit the world press with headlines like "Cardinal Slams Hitler."

To this day no one seems to know if the cardinal himself leaked the statement to the press or if someone else did. In either case, Mundelein must have known what he was doing. The monthly gatherings of clergy were not the place for statements on social or political issues. They dealt strictly with church business. And how Mundelein managed to bring in the issue of Hitler, I do not know. It was, in any event, the most famous quote ever attributed to Mundelein, one that appears in books about the years leading up to American involvement in World War II. And for Roosevelt, who badly wanted to get on with the war, it could not have come at a better time.

In his maneuvers with the church, however, Roosevelt made a classic error in the wake of Mundelein's death in October 1939. One of those who, theoretically, stood in line to succeed Mundelein was Bishop Bernard Sheil, a great orator and leading social progressive. Though controversial, he was well liked—particularly by Jews, because of his progressivism as well as his relentless support for the establishment of a Jewish state. Sheil was Mundelein's auxiliary in Chicago and, when it came to manner and style, the near opposite of his archbishop. Sheil always seemed willing, if not eager, to pick a fight, the more public the better. In spite of these differences of style, Mundelein encouraged his auxiliary—or, should I say, he let him loose. And Sheil, a masterful speaker, ran with the opportunity.

In one of his most dramatic interventions, Sheil teamed up with John L. Lewis, the toughest labor leader of the time, if not the century. At a rally in the Chicago stockyards, Sheil and Lewis stood side by side, delivering impassioned speeches in support of the packinghouse workers and their right to organize. At a tense and pivotal moment of labor history, the event made headlines across the country. Sheil had already been dubbed "the red bishop" by his detractors, and allying with Lewis, leader of the militant Congress of Industrial Organizations, did not win him any friends among the powers that were.

Meanwhile, on the Near North Side of Chicago, the students of Quigley Preparatory had little idea of the political stew their auxiliary bishop was stirring. Among the seminarians, Sheil was known as the "CYO" bishop who worked with the Catholic Youth Organization as well as the Catholic Golden Gloves. But some years later, at the height of the McCarthy era, I did get a chance to hear Sheil give the most famous speech of his stormy career. The United Auto Workers gathered in Chicago that year, and Sheil, invited to address the convention, delivered a monumental blast at red-baiting Senator Joseph McCarthy. Because of McCarthy's following among Catholics, the speech attracted wide media attention. To help spread the word, the UAW published a million copies of his speech (drafted, as we now know, by John Cogley, the late *Commonweal* editor and *New York Times* religion writer).

Sheil was, in short, Roosevelt's kind of bishop. And when Mundelein passed away, Roosevelt had a successor in mind. In a rare display of political ineptitude by the Roosevelt White House, the president plunged himself into ecclesiastical politics, getting word to the Vatican, through his emissaries, that he would like to see Sheil in the archbishop's seat. It was, not to put too fine a point on it, a dumb move. For one thing, Sheil had little or no chance of getting the nod. He had a volatile personality that made him an unlikely administrator of a major archdiocese. Moreover, anyone who knew the church could have told the White House that the Holy See would resent such intervention. It was foolish and counter-productive. The appointment went, instead, to an outsider, Samuel Stritch, the archbishop of Milwaukee. (While it was hard to tell exactly where Cardinal Stritch stood on social matters, he followed Mundelein's way of letting things happen in the area of social action.)

If the particulars of Mundelein's own alliance with the president are not altogether clear, the political machinations on the last night of his life only deepen the mystery. Mundelein lived on the grounds of the archdiocese's major seminary, St. Mary of the Lake, in the town that bears his name. We would see him only from a distance, except for an occasional mass that he would come over to celebrate. But I vividly remember one Sunday in October of 1939. Like every other Sunday, we held solemn vespers—our high liturgical event of the week, with stately processions and marvelous music—at five o'clock, just before supper. We had never seen the cardinal at solemn vespers. But on this particular Sunday afternoon Mundelein took a seat in the back row of the church along with his priest-secretary and a layman. No one recognized the layman, though we were not especially curious. We assumed the cardinal simply wanted to show off our magnificent choir.

The next morning brought word that Mundelein had died in his sleep, and the layman, who stayed overnight, turned out to be Tommy Corcoran, one of Roosevelt's closest advisors. You do not have to be a student of diplomatic history to know something was cooking. Corcoran was a classic inside operator, a fixer, a wheeler-dealer of the first rank. I assume Roosevelt used him as, among other things, his Catholic contact. Although he lived up until the mid-1980s, Corcoran never wrote about the exact purpose of his mission that night. Yet we may assume that an operator like Corcoran had not flown to Chicago for a briefing on trends in liturgical reform. He undoubtedly went there on business for Roosevelt, perhaps having to do with the war, some message he wanted to get to the Vatican.

Years later, Corcoran would say he made two telephone calls upon learning of the cardinal's death—one to Roosevelt, the other to Auxiliary Bishop Francis Spellman of Boston, then at the early stages of his meteoric rise in the American Catholic hierarchy. No one knows for sure why the White House would have put in an immediate call to an auxiliary bishop. Yet we do know that Spellman, who spent years in Rome as a priest, had his Vatican connections. And Roosevelt had his political tightrope act. The president was continually deflecting charges of dragging us into war, while at the same time casting us out toward the allies. Through it all, he was preoccupied with what the Holy See was saying about Germany and, more to the point, with Catholic opinion in the United States.

That was Roosevelt's genius. The president had galvanized a coalition —the ethnic groups, mostly Catholic—that barely existed before the New Deal. To lead the nation into war, he had to have his most loyal supporters, the Irish, Germans, Italians, Poles and other ethnics, marching behind him. I can only assume that Corcoran's mission had something to do with Roosevelt's delicate balancing act. We would never have known about it if not for the fact that the cardinal died that night.

*   *   *

Among those encouraged by Mundelein was a young, quiet priest named Reynold Hillenbrand. An English teacher in the minor (mainly high school level) seminary, Hillenbrand took students seriously. He would enter the classroom with a briefcase full of books and empty it out onto the desk. Those interested could take the books and bring them back whenever they wanted. At the time I assumed that Hillenbrand's main interests were in literature and related subjects, not knowing of his social outlook. Less than two years into my major seminary studies, Cardinal Mundelein took the rising professor out of Quigley Preparatory and (after an appointment to the diocese's "mission band") made him rector of the seminary in Mundelein, Illinois. That move would have a far-reaching effect on priests of my generation.

A reflective, soft-spoken and deeply spiritual man, Hillenbrand had a quiet sort of German determination about him. He had a tremendous influence on people, and, in short order, ushered in an ecclesiastical New Deal at Mundelein. In those days, seminaries were insular environments, much more so than the seminarians today, with their cars and easy mobility, could even imagine. We never left the seminary; we hardly ever read the newspaper. Hillenbrand, however, opened the windows of seminary life. He called attention to social problems and the labor problem in particular. With a crowded seminary curriculum, he started evening courses in Catholic social teaching and related subjects. And though his experiment would be short-lived, Hillenbrand had a lasting effect on his seminarians. He helped us realize that social action was not an extra-curricular activity, not a hobby that we may or may not want to pursue outside of our "real" priestly work. It went to the heart of our mission.

Those were exciting days in church and society, and Hillenbrand brought them home to us. As my friend and seminary schoolmate, Msgr. John Egan, has put it, "We had not only the influence of Hillenbrand at the seminary, but so many things happening outside: Msgr. John Ryan in Washington, Dorothy Day and the Catholic Worker movement, and all of the things that were going on with organized labor and the New Deal. The papers were full of this, day after day: the Wagner Act, the NRA (National Recovery Administration), the sit-down strikes." And then there were the so-called "labor priests."

They did not call themselves labor priests. Other people put the label on them, either in high or low regard, depending on their point of view. By any name, labor priests made the unions their parishes. They were not blind to the faults of organized labor or prejudiced against employers; in fact, some would go on to inspire movements against racketeering and corruption in unions. They became known as labor priests because, in season and out, they supported the God-given right of workers to organize and bargain collectively. Moreover, they vigorously supported the exercise of this right.

Labor priests saw unions as a moral and economic necessity not only for workers but for the economy as a whole and the common good. In places like Detroit, Chicago, New York, Pittsburgh, and Boston, they would set up "labor schools." These were not schools in the traditional sense. Their "students" came out of the rank and file, a mostly immigrant work force that wanted to learn more about the labor movement. In the evenings and on weekends, workers received training in the nuts and bolts of organized labor, rudiments such as public speaking, parliamentary procedures, and democratic elections. They also got a dose of American labor history and Catholic social teaching.

Hillenbrand built all of this, and more, into our priestly formation. In doing so, he always saw himself as following the lead of the pope. Yes, he was a "papalist." Yet, in certain respects, this counted as something progressive in those days. It signaled support for the papal encyclicals on social teaching, regarded as strongly progressive. To this extent, papalism stood in the Catholic avant-garde. (Later on, Hillenbrand earned more papalist colors by pushing Pius XII's encyclical on the liturgy, which provided new space for liturgical innovation.)

Hillenbrand's Talmudic readings of the encyclical letters were the order of the day among social-minded people in the church. The papalist approach found a wide audience through Father John Cronin, who wrote a useful series of popular expositions on the encyclicals. In those days they called it social "doctrine," not merely teaching. The young church in America looked to the pope to proclaim definitive truths and denounce errors on nearly every conceivable question. No wonder it was considered a triumph for progressives when Pius XI, in May 1931, issued his social encyclical, *Quadragesimo Anno* (the English title of which is "On Reconstructing the Social Order"). The encyclical endorsed the aspirations of labor and the idea of government intervention into the economy. At the time, the rector of Catholic University proclaimed, "This is a great vindication for John A. Ryan."

It should come as no surprise, then, that the Catholic social action movement placed a high priority on instructing people in the encyclicals. During summer vacations, Hillenbrand brought priests from around the midwest to Mundelein for two-week seminars on the modern social encyclicals. In those days there were two: Pope Leo XIII's May 1891 encyclical, *Rerum Novarum* ("New Things," in Latin, or "On the Condition of Workers," as it is known in English), which inaugurated modern Catholic social teaching; and Pius XI's *Quadragesimo Anno* (which literally means "In the Fortieth Year," in commemoration of the anniversary of Leo's encyclical). Not terribly sophisticated or scholarly, these courses were geared to practical results. At the time the labor problem was paramount in the social field. Since the crucial issue facing mass production workers was a simple one, the right to organize, classes in Catholic social teaching usually emphasized what the encyclicals had to say about labor. Students of the encyclicals grabbed hold of the pro-labor teaching and ran with it. At a time when the labor movement was frequently branded as communist and anti-religious, social-minded Catholics would respond, encyclical in hand, "No, unions are a good thing." This was the heart of the matter.

Even labor leaders, Catholics and non-Catholics alike, dabbled in the rhetoric of papalism. While relatively few in the labor movement actually read the encyclicals, they knew that the papal teachings were on their side. Further, labor knew it could use the documents to bolster its demands for recognition. Typical was a remark that became legendary in Mundelein. In the summer of 1938, Hillenbrand brought together about one hundred priests for a gathering on the social encyclicals. The program featured talks by national leaders in Catholic social action, among them Fathers Ryan, Francis Haas and Raymond McGowan—and a Chicago area labor leader named Joe Keenan, who died in the mid-1980s. Keenan was a wonderful man, a well-liked and effective leader of the electrical workers' union who probably never went beyond the seventh grade. During a discussion of the labor movement, someone asked Keenan how he would relate his comments to the encyclicals. "The *ensikiers?*" Keenan replied. "Labor's for 'em."

It was not the temper of the times in American Catholicism to engage in critical study of papal encyclicals. In Europe, the release of Pius XI's encyclical set off a storm of intellectual debate over the document's view of socialism (which it condemned) and its seemingly ambiguous statements on separate Christian labor movements. In the United States, social-minded people took a more pragmatic view of the documents. They tended to quote from the parts of the encyclicals that lent support to labor and an activist government. At the same time, they steered clear of arguments over the concept of private property and Christian unions (of the European variety). While this method of interpretation was sufficient for a struggling, immigrant church, the approach also helps explain why, in later years, the social encyclicals lost much of their appeal to Catholics.

After the Second Vatican Council, Catholics looked for new ways of approaching the social question and found little use in the old papal documents. John Cronin's books went out of print, Catholic universities ran dry of course offerings in the subject, and the social encyclicals receded in the consciousness of American Catholics. In more recent years, however, people have taken a second look at the church's social teachings and realized there was more in that tradition than they had thought. The rediscovery of this tradition finds expression in the title of a popular study guide, *Catholic Social Teaching: Our Best Kept Secret* (published by the Center of Concern in Washington). With the much-celebrated centenary of Pope Leo XIII's 1891 encyclical, *Rerum Novarum*, the social teachings have made a comeback, though in new and different forms.

Today, students of Catholic social teaching look for a more sophisticated, critical analysis of the encyclicals. They examine the presuppositions and "methodologies" at work in the documents. They look to see if the documents employ a more inductive approach, one that appears sensitive to historical development and human experience. They question whether Leo XIII correctly interpreted Thomas Aquinas' doctrine on property when he elevated the right of private property to the status of absolute principle, giving it a rather unmixed blessing in *Rerum Novarum*. (Many respected scholars say he missed the Thomistic mark on this.)

Some have concluded that the documents present a basically conservative program. On this point, however, I think it is the critics who are being rather a-historical. In their time, the encyclicals of Leo and Pius were widely looked upon as radical, if not revolutionary. Even in Europe, aside from debates over socialism, most commentators saw the documents as staking out new, progressive ground for church and society. And in the United States, as Joe Keenan succinctly observed, labor was "for 'em."

All this could easily give the impression that Catholics of the immigrant era embraced the encyclicals more out of political expediency than religious devotion. And, to be sure, socially progressive Catholics did use the encyclicals as a papal shield against conservative attacks. In other words, with Pius XI calling unions a good thing, the Hillenbrands of the church had something to fall back on when accused of communism or heresy, or both. The encyclicals provided them with an opening to advance their social concerns. Yet Hillenbrand was no cafeteria-style papalist, picking what he liked from the documents and passing up what he didn't. He and so many others took the papal teachings a la carte; they believed the papacy guided the church on this and all matters. So much was this the tenor of the times that many people believed we would never need another Vatican Council. "Who needs a council," they would say, "when you have a pope?"

Hillenbrand never lost his papalist colors. Years after his rectorship, he paid a visit to Washington, where I caught up with him and another priest for what started out as a pleasant dinner conversation about Dorothy Day and the Catholic Worker movement. The conversation soon turned into a heated exchange, between Hillenbrand and the other priest, over the question of Dorothy Day's pacifism. I should make it clear that Hillenbrand was devoted to the saintly founder of the Catholic Worker. But he disagreed with her pacifism because it went against the teaching of Pius XII. At one point in the exchange, the other priest said, "Oh, to hell with Pius XII." Hillenbrand was, to put it mildly, unhappy with the suggestion.

In the years leading up to Vatican II, some of his fellow priests would poke fun at Hillenbrand's papalism. On one such occasion, in the mid-1950s, I joined him at a priests' conference in Worcester, Massachusetts, where he delivered an impassioned talk on the Young Christian Workers, a youth movement that came under the general heading of "Catholic Action," or social action. After he declared that Pius XII had pronounced the Young Christian Workers as the definitive form of Catholic Action, a rather skeptical Jesuit got up and said, wryly, "I find that very encouraging because we only had one hundred and sixty-one statements from the pope on what is the definitive form of Catholic Action, and you've just added one more."

Hillenbrand may have been a papalist, but his progressive brand of papalism proved too radical for some clerics. In the summer of 1944, while I was studying at Catholic University in Washington, word came that

Cardinal Stritch had removed Hillenbrand from his job as seminary rector and assigned him to a parish in the suburbs. It came as shock to all who knew and admired Hillenbrand, for Stritch was not a conservative on social matters. Although no one really knows who pulled the trigger and got the cardinal to move against Hillenbrand, there are those who believe (and the matter still comes up in conversations with Chicago priests) that Hillenbrand's innovative ways did him in. This is probably true to some extent. There were pastors who could not put their finger on what they did not like about Hillenbrand but knew that whatever it was, it was new. Maybe some of them were upset because their new priests from the seminary spent their evenings at the union hall rather than the church hall.

Yet the move against Hillenbrand probably had as much to do with personalities and internal church politics. He had no political instincts, none whatsoever. He was never the gregarious sort who would go around the diocese making friends among the pastors. As a result, he never really gathered support for his programs at the seminary. As Tim Unsworth wrote in *Commonweal* (June 1989), "Hillenbrand had no time for the small change of priestly interaction. If he went to a wake, it was to pray for the dead, not to embalm the deceased in gargle or spend the evening wallowing in clerical gossip. Superb in the front of the church, he never learned how to work the vestibule." This could not have made things easier for Hillenbrand. Afterward, Hillenbrand remained an important figure in the Young Christian Workers and Christian Family movements, though he was burdened in later years by repeated operations resulting from a terrible auto accident. Long before then, however, the quiet reformer had engraved his legacy on a generation of seminarians. They would go on to influence Catholics in Chicago and beyond.

"The Right Reverend New Dealer" & Co.

At Hillenbrand's recommendation the archbishop sent a dozen seminary graduates to Washington, D.C., for further study at The Catholic University of America. Our arrival on campus in August 1940 took many by surprise. Chicago had never assigned priests to full-time graduate studies there because Mundelein, for reasons known only to himself, was out of sorts with the university. But his successor, Samuel Stritch, saw things differently. Hillenbrand, not knowing that his time as rector would be short, had a long-term plan to shore up and diversify the seminary faculty. My assignment was to pick up a degree in economics.

In those years, a Catholic University student could hardly avoid a sense of history in the making. It was the era of the New Deal, and the air was charged with a feeling of social reform. Catholic University, though established a half century before as what its founders termed "the Catholic Harvard," was admittedly not in a class with its imagined rival in Cambridge, or, for that matter, with Yale, Princeton, Berkeley, Stanford and a good number of other institutions. But two things made this Catholic outpost in northeast Washington the place to be, for myself and many others.

For one thing, it was a congenial place for a young priest. With the onset of World War II, American priests could not travel to Europe for graduate studies, and so there were scores of priests on campus, far more than ever before or since. The situation presented an opportunity to form lasting friendships with peers from around the country. In addition, Catholic University was the right place to study labor-management relations. In our time a number of priests on the faculty had national reputations in the field of labor relations and social reform. Because of its reputation in the social field, the university was able to secure the personal and official papers of well-known labor leaders, among them Philip Murray, the late president of the Congress of Industrial Organizations. (Honesty, though, compels me to say that in more recent years the university has tended to rest on its laurels, letting a tradition of social reform slip away.)

My stay in Washington did not end with the four years it took to earn a doctorate in labor economics. As I was finishing up my studies, Father John Hayes—a fellow Chicago priest on staff at the bishops' conference downtown—contracted a serious illness and had to leave Washington for an extended period of recuperation. His supervisor, Father Raymond A. McGowan, said to me, "You're just about finished with school now. Why don't you come and spend the summer with us?" I had yet to receive my assignment in Chicago, and so I joined the conference on a temporary basis. As things turned out, I stayed on until Labor Day, thirty-six years later.

Being young and innocent, I had accepted McGowan's invitation without a letter of appointment either from the National Catholic Welfare Conference, as it was known then, or from the archdiocese of Chicago. I never did get one. It was not until about ten years later that my archbishop made reference to this unusual situation. It was November, when the U.S. bishops hold their annual meetings in Washington, and I paid a social visit to Stritch in his hotel suite. With me were the cardinal's secretary, Msgr. James Hardiman, and another Chicago priest then working at the bishops' conference, the now-retired Bishop William McManus. As we left his suite, the cardinal, typically a very gentle and courteous person, asked rather sharply, "Higgins, what diocese do you belong to?" I said, "Well, I've been working on the assumption it was Chicago, and I was kind of hoping that you had the same assumption." He said, "Well, I'd think we'd see more of you; we never see you." I answered, "Well, I work here."

Afterward I got to wondering what this was all about and decided to take a trip to Chicago. A week later, when I entered his office, the archbishop was holding his head in his hands, obviously distraught by a pastoral crisis of one kind or another which had reached his desk. In short, I never even sat down. I said, "Your Eminence, I was just passing through and I thought I'd say hello." Without even raising his head from his desk, he said in a distracted way, "Yes, Father, come in anytime; we're always glad to see you." I walked out, and that was the last time I ever set foot in the chancery (although I enjoyed a close, personal relationship with the archbishop for many years afterward).

*   *   *

During those years in Washington, three priests, natives of the midwest, stood above all others in the field of social reform. The contributions of John A. Ryan, Francis J. Haas and Raymond A. McGowan are incalculable, though church authorities would at times show their appreciation in curious ways.

By the time I arrived at Catholic University, John A. Ryan had retired as professor of moral theology and social ethics. But while still a student, I met him for the first time at a small dinner in New York with some priest friends. I can hardly remember anything about the evening other than how impressed I was to be in his company, conversing with the intellectual architect of American Catholic social action. It was clear, though, that this was a scholar of a different kind.

He was an Irish-American farm boy, born in 1869 and raised on a small Minnesota dairy farm that had been settled by his immigrant grandparents. Throughout his life Ryan remained very much the farm boy. His manner was down-to-earth, with a ruggedness that showed in the rough features of his face. There was nothing elusive about Ryan's manner. Ask him a question, and you got a swift and direct answer. His conversation was often laced with an earthy, farm-boy sense of humor. Blunt, gruff and quick to speak, Ryan was anything but the effete scholar.

In 1906, eight years after his ordination, he won worldwide attention with the publication of his first book, *A Living Wage*. Written as his doctoral dissertation in moral theology at Catholic University, the book advocated legal protection of the right to a living wage thirty-two years before the federal government got around to enacting the Fair Labor Standards Act, which initially provided for a minimum wage of twenty-five cents per hour and a maximum work week of forty-four hours. It was one of the first publications in any language to advocate the establishment of a minimum wage by law. And even to this day, his example in fashioning one of the earliest state minimum wage laws—Minnesota's—has yet to be followed in some states.

His most important book, *Distributive Justice*, which systematically applied the principles of moral theology to a wide range of industrial and economic problems, appeared in 1916. I would agree with his biographer, Francis L. Broderick, that with its publication Ryan had had his say as a scholar. Although he never stopped writing, after 1916 he spent most of his career on the active apostolate for social justice. Ryan's main thrust during this extraordinarily active apostolate was the urgent need for adequate socio-economic legislation. He also regarded organization—particularly the organization of workers—as crucial to resolving social and economic problems. But he looked to legislation as the main remedy, saying in *A Living Wage* that "the majority of the underpaid workers cannot be lifted out of that condition within a reasonable time except by the method of legal enactment."

At that time, people who so much as intimated such things were often tarred with a "red" brush. And Ryan got his share of smears, usually from industry leaders and conservative churchmen. Of course, the insinuations of Bolshevism were preposterous. Ryan was as anti-communist, even anti-socialist, as the day was long. But if the critics were looking to target an unapologetic progressive, they had the right man. Ryan's ideas "were more radical than the program of a good many moderate, dues-paying socialists," Broderick writes in his 1963 biography, *Right Reverend New Dealer: John A. Ryan*. "Not technically enough of a socialist to draw the formal censure of his ecclesiastical superiors, but too radical for most of his co-religionists," Broderick says Ryan's own view was simpler: "He was about as radical as Leo XIII."

An early triumph was the adoption of his program by the Catholic hierarchy in the United States. Ryan was the architect of the 1919 "Bishops' Program of Social Reconstruction," an ambitious statement that endorsed a minimum wage, subsidized housing, labor participation in industrial management, child labor laws, social insurance for the jobless, sick and old-aged, and other reforms—basically, the New Deal program, thirteen years before the New Deal. When issued in November of that year, the program was denounced by one industry leader as "partisan, pro-labor union, socialistic propaganda under the official insignia of the Roman Catholic Church." It remains the best short summary of Ryan's legislative program.

Ryan was sixty-three years old and seven years from his forced retirement at Catholic University when Franklin Delano Roosevelt promised a new deal for all Americans. On the question of New Deal liberalism, Ryan was a realist. He was mindful of the New Deal's flaws, compromises, and halfway measures. Yet he also believed that Roosevelt had set a course for far-reaching social reform, cutting the nation's ties to what he had described as the "baneful heritage of the eighteenth century," the doctrine of economic individualism. It was in his twilight years that Ryan entered into the most publicized battles of his career.

After decades of articulating a reformist agenda, Ryan was not going to let advancing years keep him out of the ring when critics began to pounce on the New Deal. It was nevertheless with considerable reluctance that Ryan went to the mat with one of Roosevelt's most influential and charismatic foes, the Rev. Charles Coughlin. The best-known cleric of his time, the "radio priest" from Royal Oak, Michigan, had a following of millions through his Sunday broadcasts over CBS. In the early 1930s, Coughlin took the side of liberal social reformers. He made scathing attacks on Herbert Hoover and enjoyed the patronage of senators and congressmen as well as, after Hoover's election debacle, the newly elected FDR. Coughlin interpreted the papal encyclicals as teaching that workers had not only a right to join unions but an obligation to do so. He excoriated the American Federation of Labor for ignoring the masses of industrial workers. And when attacked by conservative prelates, the likes of Dorothy Day and John A. Ryan came to his side.

But the powerful cleric became increasingly erratic in his social views and started sliding down an authoritarian path. Later on, Coughlin claimed that he was not a fascist or anti-semite, but during the 1930s he nonetheless praised Hitler and Mussolini, condemned democracy as an unworkable form of government and issued vague warnings of Jewish domination. At first Coughlin applauded the social reforms of Roosevelt's first "hundred days." But by the mid-1930s Coughlin had turned on the president, linking him to imagined Jewish and communist conspiracies. The priest put on a major show of strength in January 1935, blocking U.S. Senate approval of a key foreign-policy initiative—the proposed adherence of the United States to the World Court. Coughlin won the day with a last-minute radio appeal for popular pressure on the senators.

Ryan, meanwhile, had spoken out in favor of the World Court, and the defeat engineered by Coughlin helped put the two priests on a collision course. The Democratic National Committee, fearful of Coughlin's clout during the upcoming 1936 presidential elections, began to prod Ryan. The Democrats wanted him to go on radio and refute Coughlin's charges against the Roosevelt administration. Ryan, at first, demurred. He, as Broderick notes, had no desire to compete with Coughlin on his demagogic terms. (On those terms, Ryan—not much of a speaker and certainly no rhetorical match for Coughlin—would have lost hands-down.) But Ryan's main worry was the embarrassment that a dogfight between two priests might cause the church. Nonetheless, three weeks before the 1936 election, Ryan boarded a train to New York to deliver his famous radio speech, "Roosevelt Safeguards America."

During the live, evening address to the nation, Ryan denied that Roosevelt or any of his principal advisors were communists. He denounced authoritarianism on the right and the left. And he moved to dispel any impression that the radio priest from Michigan spoke for the Catholic Church. Ryan said Coughlin's economic theories and proposals "find no support in the encyclicals of either Pope Leo XIII or Pope Pius XI," adding: "I think I know something about these encyclicals myself." Ryan urged the working people of America to stand by Roosevelt and others who were "your tried and competent champions in public life." Ryan made his speech within a half hour, caught a train to Washington, and was home at Caldwell Hall (his Catholic University residence) by 2:00 A.M.

In his afternoon radio broadcast the next Sunday, Coughlin abandoned his earlier politeness toward Ryan. In what Broderick describes as a voice dripping with sarcasm and contempt, Coughlin taunted the "Right Reverend spokesman for the New Deal." He chided the "Right Reverend Democratic Politician" for making a radio broadcast paid for by the Democratic National Committee. Ryan probably did not win over many followers of Coughlin. Of the twelve hundred letters that poured in, only twenty-five of them, by his own estimate, were expressed in courteous language. Nonetheless he had scored a direct hit with his speech. He woke up the next day to a banner headline in the *Washington Post* and an editorial heaping praise on the Right Reverend. He enjoyed similar treatment in the *New York Times* and, via an Associated Press story, newspapers across the country.

Shortly afterward, Linna Bresette, the field secretary for the Social Action Department of the bishops' conference, was in Detroit to help prepare for a meeting on labor sponsored by the department. Detroit's archbishop and later Cardinal Edward Mooney asked her why Ryan, who headed the department, had not requested permission for such an involved political maneuver as taking to the airwaves for the Democrats. Bresette told the cardinal that the answer seemed obvious: no one would have given him permission. Indeed, if Ryan had gone to the bishops before time, they would have probably said, "Oh, don't do that. That's getting us too involved." And in a sense, they would have been right. When I worked at the conference, I, too, would have balked at the idea of staff members entangling themselves in party politics. Ryan, however, had grown into such a larger-than-life figure that no one in the church (at least at that point) could touch him. Three months after his broadcast, Ryan gave the benediction at the 1937 presidential inaugural, the first of two that he would give for Roosevelt. Ryan asked that the Almighty grant "our Chief Magistrate . . .

the light and the strength to carry through the great work he has so well begun, and to pursue untiringly his magnificent vision of social peace and social justice."

*   *   *

Ryan was not the only New Deal reverend in Washington. One of his disciples was Msgr. Francis Haas, a priest from Milwaukee and master of the art of labor arbitration. Haas had the look of a St. Bernard dog, big and shaggy-haired. They called him "Red Haas" long before some conservative businessmen would do the same for reasons having little to do with the color of his hair. Haas, who served as dean of Catholic University's School of Social Science, was very close to his large, extended family in Racine, Wisconsin. During hard times, he would send them his pay and then borrow from priest-friends for his own needs.

When I arrived on campus, one of the most popular events was Haas's extra-curricular seminars. On Sunday mornings after mass, dozens of students would pack a classroom to hear him talk about the latest in labor-management relations and related issues. During the week I would tag along with Haas at labor gatherings, and through him I had some valuable introductions to people in the movement. I still meet people in labor who talk about Haas. One of them is J. C. Turner, a Protestant who attended Catholic University on a boxing scholarship and never missed a Haas seminar. After graduating with honors, Turner (with help from his mentor) took a minor post in the labor movement and worked his way up to become president of the International Brotherhood of Operating Engineers. Whenever I see Turner, now retired in the Maryland suburbs of Washington, he talks about Haas and the priest's lasting influence on him.

The government called on Haas during some of the most bitter and violent labor disputes, including the Minneapolis truckers' strike of 1943 and the New York, New Jersey and Pennsylvania textile strike of 1943. In Minneapolis, Haas came under criticism for working with radical officials of the Teamsters' Local 574. One businessman wrote to the rector of Catholic University to ask if it was true that Haas "has been thrown out of several Catholic schools in which he taught because of strong Socialistic and Communist tendencies, etc., and that he is not in good standing with the Ecclesiastics of the Church."

Father Maurice Sheehy, who was the rector's assistant and a good friend of Haas, replied that Haas was one of the nation's most respected educators. Sheehy asked the businessman to kindly deny the "calumny" about Haas if he heard it spoken again. Haas, in Minneapolis, received copies of the correspondence with Sheehy's wry note: "I called up

Comrade McGowan [second-in-command at the Social Action Department] who is the only good Communist I know and he assured me that you were not a Communist in good standing, that he hadn't been able to collect any dues for months from you." As the strike wound down, the joke was picked up again by the president of the Teamsters' local, William Brown, who said he was "practically convinced that the rumor that Father Haas is a paid Communist agent is greatly exaggerated."

Haas did not look upon strikes merely as something to be settled. He likened them to medical operations needed for a diseased condition. In Minneapolis, the disease developed from the industrial condition of substandard wages and hostility toward collective bargaining. It took Doctor Haas thirty-six days to complete this surgery, but when he left the operating room, management was satisfied and the truckers rejoiced. In this way—his biographer, Thomas E. Blantz, estimates—Haas settled or assisted in the settlement of fifteen hundred strikes from the start of the New Deal until his death twenty years later.

His appointment in 1943 as the first director of the federal government's Fair Employment Practices Commission, a program long advocated by John Ryan, illustrates how the two men complemented each other. Ryan originated ideas, while Haas put them into practice. Haas had a unique ability to bring people together, and considering his unapologetically pro-labor stance, his success at mediation was all the more remarkable. Haas, however, did more than simply apply Ryan's principles. As Blantz notes in his 1982 biography, *A Priest in Public Service: Francis J. Haas and the New Deal,* Haas and Ryan had somewhat differing approaches to social and industrial reform. Haas placed his deepest hope in a strong labor movement. Like so many other priests of his time, he believed that workers had not only a right to join labor unions but a sacred obligation to do so, in view of our nature as social beings. Ryan, too, was a reliable friend of labor. But his ideas had taken shape long before the movement arrived as a major social force. Thus Ryan believed that progress would come principally through legislation. Their friend and collaborator, Raymond McGowan, pointed to yet another way.

*   *   *

By the time I joined the Social Action Department in 1944, Ryan was semi-retired. He would come in two or three times a week to answer his mail and prowl around for a couple of hours. The department was, for all practical purposes, run by his assistant, Father Raymond McGowan. Warm, lovable and funny, McGowan was disorganized yet effective, and always far-seeing. For years he wore the same unpressed suit, with cigarette dust on it and papers stuffed in his pocket, a pair of old, worn shoes and a very likeable old hat. In his disheveled way, the priest from Missouri's railroad country got a lot done.

As a young priest just beginning his distinguished career in Catholic social action, McGowan was asked to come to see a grand old man who was rapidly approaching the end of his own career as the dean of the American labor movement. In the early winter of 1923, McGowan had just established the Catholic Conference on Industrial Problems. A garbled news release on the proceedings of the organization's first meeting in Chicago was a little disturbing to Samuel Gompers. It seemed to Gompers that McGowan and company had set up the Conference as a separate Catholic union or federation to compete with the affiliates of the AFL for the loyalty of Catholic workers.

The idea was not as far-fetched then as it may seem now. In Europe the movement had split into rival Christian and secular (usually Marxist) labor federations. Gompers was keenly aware of this and disposed to do all he could to avoid it. The old man summoned McGowan to the American Federation of Labor—then only four blocks from the American bishops' former headquarters on Massachusetts Avenue in Washington. When McGowan arrived, Gompers was with the entire Executive Council of the AFL. In short order, McGowan managed to clear up the misunderstanding. He went on to explain that the long-range program of the industrial conference was an organized system of labor-management-government cooperation in American life. This was, in a nutshell, the program of Pope Pius XI's 1931 *Quadragesimo Anno;* McGowan was pushing it almost ten years before publication of the papal encyclical. As McGowan related it to me years later, Gompers appeared sympathetic to the idea—something that might have brought on a significant turn in industrial relations. Unfortunately, Gompers died before he could do anything about it.

The Catholic Conference on Industrial Problems was characteristic of McGowan's ability to move the work out of the bishops' conference and into the field. The organization held about half a dozen conferences a year in different parts of the country, always with local sponsorship, bringing labor, government and some management people together to address industrial problems. (As might be expected, employers were often repelled by the pro-labor slant.) At the bishops' conference, McGowan was always hatching new ideas and projects, more in the free-flow of conversation than in any formal way.

The bishops' conference of McGowan's time was almost the opposite of today's U.S. Catholic Conference, a highly structured agency with a large professional staff. McGowan had a handful of people working under him. Someone who walked in would likely find him with his feet up on the desk, telling stories about railroads and small-town life. Outside the Conference, he had a wealth of friends in the press. He loved to go downtown and sit at the bar at the National Press Club, where he would exchange stories with reporters. (This was not Ryan's style. Ryan could take a good drink, but he was never one to make the rounds with any but a small circle of friends.) All the while, McGowan's mind was operating. He was looking ahead.

Surely it took rare vision to establish the Catholic Conference on Industrial Problems in the so-called "golden" 1920s. It took even greater vision to establish, a few years later, the Catholic Conference for International Peace, a pioneer in Catholic social action on the international level. Before practically anyone else, McGowan saw the importance of the Latin America issue; he set up some of the first contacts between Catholic social reformers in that region and the United States. These and other efforts by McGowan got off the ground at a time when few Americans were even remotely interested in the application of moral principles to domestic economic life and international relations. It is doubtful that any of them would have come along at such an early date if not for the initiative and vision of Raymond McGowan.

If McGowan was a pioneer organizationally speaking, he was even further ahead of his time in the realm of Catholic social theory. Few, if any, of his contemporaries were as quick to see the logical necessity of an organized system of labor-management-government cooperation in American economic life. Because he had the idea of *Quadragesimo Anno* years before the encyclical appeared, he was one of the first to grasp the full significance of its program of social reconstruction and one of the first to begin thinking realistically about how to apply it to the American economy. To this day, two or three of his articles stand up as among the most valuable commentaries on the papal encyclical.

While breaking new ground, McGowan deliberately worked in the shadows of John Ryan. He ran the programs and day-to-day operations of the department so that Ryan might have the leisure to pursue his apostolate of scholarly writing and lecturing. Like Haas, McGowan worshiped the ground on which Ryan walked. He never called Ryan by his first name. It was always, "Dr. Ryan." (For Ryan's part it was always "Father McGowan," and in his autobiography Ryan wrote that a bad word never passed between the two in their twenty-five years of work together.)

Yet McGowan had a distinct agenda. He took an interest in social legislation, but only as a secondary means of social reform. Temperamentally, as well as intellectually, his primary concern was organization, especially the forms of labor-management-government cooperation that have only recently appeared on the nation's industrial agenda. And thus it seems appropriate that, even as a young priest, he should have been consulted by the elders of the AFL. His meeting with Gompers in the early 1920s was the first of literally thousands of formal and informal conversations with representatives of not only labor organizations but employers' associations as well.

*   *   *

The church could not have hoped for servants of greater dedication than Ryan, Haas and McGowan, and yet their experiences with church authorities were bitter-sweet.

Francis Haas had brief tenure at the Fair Employment Practices Commission. Within months of his appointment to the post in May of 1943, Haas was named bishop of Grand Rapids, Michigan. At the time, many suspected that the church had removed Haas because of the political nature of his work and his close association with the Roosevelt administration. And, to be sure, more than a few bishops did not like what Haas was doing. Rumors were so widespread that Haas begged reporters: "Please do not say that the Catholic Church took me out of this job."

In addition, as Blantz points out, a change of ecclesiastical climate had taken place since the heady days of the 1930s when Haas and Ryan were named monsignors and Haas was made a dean at Catholic University. The papacy of Pius XI, author of *Quadragesimo Anno,* gave way to the more conservative Pius XII. Cardinal Spellman of New York, no fan of Ryan-Haas progressivism, had arrived at a position of unsurpassed authority in American Catholicism. Yet I have always suspected that if any one person wrote Haas' ticket to Grand Rapids, it was the progressive archbishop of Detroit, Edward Mooney. Grand Rapids was a suffragan, or subsidiary, diocese of Detroit, and given all that Mooney had to contend with—the radio tirades of his priest, Charles Coughlin, and arguments over the church's involvement in the labor issue—Mooney probably wanted someone like Haas in his camp.

In any event, Haas should never have been made a bishop. There was no shortage of qualified candidates for the position of Grand Rapids bishop, but Haas had a special talent, and I doubt that he ever aspired to the episcopacy. He certainly did not seek out the job. (His response was less than enthusiastic when one reporter approached him after the announcement: "In the organization to which I have devoted my life, we are good soldiers. We do what we are told.") Although I stayed in touch with Haas for some time afterward, completing my dissertation with him by mail, I am not sure how he performed as a bishop. I suppose he did as well as the average. It was, in any case, a waste of his talent.

Like any other bishop, Haas spent much of his time on administrative detail, never his strong suit. Yet in that last decade of his life, the bishop did have a few opportunities to exercise his genius. He was called on by state and federal officials to mediate several industrial and labor disputes. In 1947 he served on President Truman's Committee on Civil Rights. In the eyes of those who knew and admired him, Bishop Haas remained, as the title of the book says, "A Priest in Public Service."

Brunswick, Maryland is not nearly as far from the bishops' headquarters as Grand Rapids. But it is far enough. Ray McGowan never drew attention to himself and consciously stayed in the background of John Ryan. Because the two worked as a team, critics tended to train their fire on McGowan's boss. But one exception to this was Archbishop Michael J. Curley, head of the archdiocese of Baltimore, which encompassed Washington, D.C., and who believed himself to be McGowan's bishop. In June of 1937, Archbishop Curley (the namesake of CU's Curley Hall, where I live) abruptly assigned McGowan to the pastorate of St. Francis Church in rural Maryland.

Shortly before the move, Curley had fired off a letter to McGowan asking if he was "fully responsible" for an article that appeared in the Washington *Daily News*. Curley was referring to the "Father McGowan Says" column, syndicated nationally by the news service of the National Conference of Christians and Jews (now known, under different auspices, as Religious News Service). In this particular column, McGowan endorsed Roosevelt's plan to enlarge, or "pack," the Supreme Court. McGowan also attacked business interests and said the legal system existed for their "special and main benefit." As for the legal profession, he said it was in dire need of "an intellectual and moral conversion." The column seemed to cross the line set out by Curley, whose archdiocesan newspaper had run an unsigned, front-page editorial titled, "Hands Off the Supreme Court."

The Right Reverend New Dealer was not indifferent to the move against his second-in-command. As Pastor McGowan tended to the flock in Brunswick, Ryan set a modern indoor record for end-runs around a bishop. There are differing versions of the story. One is that Ryan somehow managed to have McGowan "excardinated" from the archdiocese of Baltimore and "incardinated" in the archdiocese of St. Louis, whose archbishop had nothing against McGowan. Another is that, upon checking, McGowan turned out to have never been officially received into the Baltimore archdiocese—so Curley had no effective authority over him. Whatever the case, the machinations took seven months, but McGowan was fully restored to the department. In March of 1938, Curley wrote to Ryan: "I wish to place myself on record as opposing most emphatically the presence of your Assistant Director, Father McGowan, within the limits of the

Archdiocese of Baltimore." Yet while never elevated to the rank of domestic prelate (monsignor), McGowan stayed on the job and was allowed to go forward with his distinguished career in social action. He became head of the department after Ryan's death in 1945.

Unlike Ryan and Haas, McGowan is completely unremembered today. I doubt if his name would mean anything to more than two or three people, if that many, at the U.S. Catholic Conference. There is no book or doctoral dissertation about his life and work, though a couple of students have written Master's theses on him at Catholic University (and, for my recall of some details, I am indebted to Mark A. Miller and his 1979 thesis, "The Contribution of the Reverend Raymond A. McGowan to American Catholic Social Thought and Action: 1930–1939.")

McGowan's obscurity is probably no one's fault but his own. Humble and self-effacing, McGowan was allergic to flattery or merited praise; he was not the sort of fellow who left papers or records of his accomplishments. His weekly column in the Catholic press (syndicated by the Catholic News Service, as it is now known) is one source, yet he even shied away from that, asking me at one point to take it off his hands for a couple of weeks. That was 1945, and I have written the "Yardstick" column ever since. Because of poor health, McGowan retired as director of the Social Action Department in 1954 (thus leaving me with something else to do). Eight years later I was attending the first session of the Second Vatican Council when word came that my mentor had died. My feelings toward McGowan remain as they were when I wrote to his sister shortly afterward:

". . . I owe him more than I could possibly calculate, and I know I don't have to tell you that my indebtedness to him extends far beyond the field of Catholic social action. His priestly qualities of mercy, kindness, and compassion and his almost child-like confidence and trust in the Providence of God were an inspiration to me at all times as well as to countless other priests who were privileged to know him intimately."

A year after retrieving McGowan from his rural pastorate, Ryan met with bitter disappointment at Catholic University. In April the board of trustees set sixty-five as the normal retirement age for faculty, with the understanding that a professor might be invited to stay on past sixty-five but not after seventy. Although the full purpose of the decision will never be known, Francis Broderick reflects the sense of many at the time. "Though expressed in general terms, the regulation applied only to Ryan in 1939, and, coming six weeks before his seventieth birthday, it appeared to be directed specifically at him." Ryan asked for but did not receive an exception. The trustees gave him a pension, but there were no expressions of gratitude, not even the honorific title of professor emeritus. A few months later he was told to give up his rooms in Caldwell Hall.

Ironically, this blow at CU came as Ryan was triumphing in the secular world. Six hundred people, including scores of congressmen, gathered at the Willard Hotel to throw Ryan the biggest birthday bash of his life. Supreme Court Justice Felix Frankfurter, an old friend, said the evening would be remembered "as testimony of our gratitude and as proof of a life greatly lived." Greetings came from the White House. "With voice and pen," Roosevelt said, "you have pleaded the cause of social justice and the right of the individual to happiness through economic security, a living wage, and an opportunity to share in the things that enrich and ennoble human life."

Ryan still had his most devoted students, the women at Trinity College—a small, liberal arts college where he taught for many years, near Catholic University—and he was able to hold on to his post at the Social Action Department. Though plagued by colds, dizzy spells, and fatigue, Ryan kept himself on the firing line. There were more skirmishes with the Coughlin forces over Roosevelt, war and anti-semitism, more sparring over the air waves.

There were many joyous moments in those final years. In 1940, the U.S. bishops affirmed nearly every major legislative reform pushed by the Social Action Department for almost two decades. The White House called on Ryan, once again, to give the benediction at Roosevelt's 1945 inaugural (both great men would not survive the year). And Archbishop Curley extended an olive branch. There was no doubt about it—the lovable, gruff monsignor had mellowed. He went out to dinner more often, read mystery novels and visited friends out of town; where there was a so-called "Trinity girl" (Trinity College alumna), there was a household eager to welcome the old professor.

On a lovely morning in May, a group of priests drove out to National Airport, where Ryan and I were to catch a plane for St. Paul, Minnesota. Ryan's health had deteriorated more than he realized. And his friends wanted to get him back to St. Paul where he could be with his family at the end. So they cooked up a story that I was flying out there on business: Why don't you, Monsignor, go along with Father Higgins so you could spend some time with your family?

As it was, the story seemed improbable, and the presence of friends and colleagues made it even more so. The other priests who had come to see him off felt they had to go to rather elaborate lengths to camouflage their real reason for being at the airport, which was to say goodbye to John Ryan for the last time. There was a great deal of studied casualness and awkwardly contrived cheerfulness and good humor about our conversation as we waited for our plane to be called. But the gruff old monsignor, never one to wear his feelings on his sleeve, must have seen through the charade, for there were tears in his eyes as he boarded the plane.

In any event, the old man quickly regained his composure, and for most of what turned out to be a slow and tedious trip to St. Paul, he read from a tome on economics, marking up the pages with a big pencil and taking notes as if he were preparing for a lecture. When not reading, he was gulping down a piece of apple pie and glass of milk or commenting, with his usual bluntness and clarity of thought, on the headline stories in the morning paper.

Four months later, Ryan died in a Catholic hospital in St. Paul, surrounded by brothers and sisters and nieces and nephews, and fortified by the sacraments of the church he loved so dearly.

Years Later

I did not know what I was getting myself into when I arrived on the campus of St. Xavier College in Chicago, in the summer of 1968. I went there for the annual meeting of the National Catholic Action Conference, which was to address the future of religiously oriented social action in the United States. Upon arriving, I learned that representatives of the "old breed" (as the program committee chose to identify them) would be mercilessly paired off at two seminars with the ultra-hip spokesmen for the "new breed."

As the reluctant lead-off man for the old-timers I was tempted at first to try to buy (or, if you will, lie or soft-soap) my way out of the lion's den by flamboyantly playing up to the under-thirty crowd. (I was at the dinosaurian age of fifty-two.) If you want to get out of this place alive, I said to myself, why not cater to their vanity? Flatter them, butter them up, tell them what they obviously want to hear. What difference does it make? Tell them they're the pioneers of social reform, boldly going where none had gone before. Tell them that anybody over thirty is hopelessly square (this *was* the 1960s) and shouldn't be trusted. Maybe this would soften them up and persuade them to go easy on me during the question-and-answer period.

On second thought, I decided that this would hardly make for a very interesting or lively seminar. So I mustered up enough courage to begin my presentation on the future of Catholic social action by lavishly praising some of the giants of yesteryear—men and women whom many of the so-called new breed seem never to have heard of. I suggested that the current crop of social actionists, in spite of their protestations to the contrary, tend in many cases to be more churchy and more clerical in their approach to social reform than they are willing to admit, and more so, incidentally, than many of their forerunners.

For good measure, I also suggested—at the risk of being locked up on charges of senility—that some of the new breed tended to put too much stock in the efficacy of March on Washington-style demonstrations, which are here today and gone tomorrow. I intimated that they tend to be cynical about long-range programs of social education and reform that may not produce measurable results in the immediate here and now.

Needless to add, I also praised the new activists very sincerely and enthusiastically for their many courageous and constructive innovations in the field of social reform. I wasn't kidding, though, when I suggested that the old pioneers, in spite of the fact that they lived and died before the new theology of the lay apostolate had been adequately formulated, were, in many cases, less churchy and less clerical in their approach to social problems than some of today's new breed who have had the advantage of living through the Second Vatican Council.

By that I mean that the Ryans, McGowans and Haases tended to emphasize the layperson's independent and autonomous role, as a citizen and a member of secular organizations, in solving social problems. Witness the labor schools and industrial conferences. On the other hand, many of the new breed tend to stress the role of the church as an institution—and, specifically, the bishops. Both approaches, of course, are valid and usually intertwined. There is, however, a distinction between the two. And I, for one, find it rather intriguing that the latter approach, in many cases, is being more heavily emphasized after Vatican II than it was by some of those who had gone to their reward before the council started.

Be that as it may, the moral of the story is that one cannot talk intelligently about the future of the social action movement without reference to its past. Having looked at the record, we can say, if we will, that the performance of those who went before us wasn't very impressive. Maybe not. For my own part, however, I happen to think that, given the obstacles against which they had to contend, our forerunners in the Catholic social action movement turned in a very creditable performance indeed, and one which, in many respects, was more impressive than our own.

In any event, I wasn't joking or looking for an argument when I told the audience in Chicago that we have much to learn from these social pioneers—men and women of the stature of John A. Ryan, Francis J. Haas,

Raymond McGowan, Peter Yorke, William Kerby, John Maguire, Frederick Kenkel, Philip Murray, John O'Grady, John Brophy, Linna Bresette, John Monaghan, Sister Thomas Aquinas, John Boland, Mary Synon, Harry Read, George Hunton, and many others, long since forgotten—who patiently planted the seeds that we, in a more favorable climate, were only beginning to harvest.

Secretary of Labor Arthur Goldberg, Communications Workers President Joseph Beirne, Bishop Phillip Hannan, Msgr. George Higgins standing below statue of labor champion Cardinal Gibbons

2

Religion and Labor: Then and Now

An American Experiment

Cooperation between religion and labor is uniquely American—at least from an historical standpoint. To this day, what many of us would regard as rather ordinary forms of cooperation, such as national church-labor conferences, would come off as spectacular events in most countries. Let me illustrate the point with an example from my own experience.

In November of 1988, I was invited to deliver a paper at an international labor conference sponsored by the Metal Workers Federation of West Germany, the largest union in the world with two and a half million members. It was an extraordinarily interesting and productive gathering. Yet a few weeks before it convened, I learned through the grapevine that the German Catholic bishops' conference (which parallels the U.S. bishops' conference), had sent a telex to our conference in Washington. The Germans were perplexed: they wanted to know who I was and why I would speak at a German labor meeting. By coincidence a German theologian was living at Catholic University and taking his meals with us at Curley Hall, and I mentioned the incident to him. "Well, I'm not surprised," he said. The German visitor said that with the exception of the late Jesuit Father Oswald von Nell-Breuning (the John A. Ryan of Germany), "I can't think of any other priest in my lifetime who has ever addressed a trade union meeting in Germany."

This is a remnant of the very unhappy relationship that existed for many years between religion and labor in Germany and throughout most of Europe—and, especially, between the Roman Catholic Church and

Marxist-dominated labor movements. Like our German guest at Curley Hall, I was not surprised by the curiosity of his bishops. It was entirely understandable, given their history.

My first exposure to the church-labor rift in Europe came in 1949 when I spent six months in Germany, working on a study for the U.S. military government there. At the time the need for a united German government was uppermost in the minds of U.S. and British officials. They believed that the deep polarization and factionalism in pre-war German politics had made it possible for a Hitler to rise to power. In light of this, our government and the British had serious concerns about the German labor movement and its unity. Before the war, conflicts between Marxists and Catholics in Germany had produced a divided labor movement, as it had in the rest of Europe: a socialist federation on one side, a Christian federation of Protestants and Catholics on the other. The Allies believed that labor unity would help ensure the future of democracy in Germany.

It was an arguable point, and they asked me to prepare a study of whether a united labor movement—in effect, one without a separate Christian federation—was feasible in post-war Germany. In August of 1949, I submitted a fifty-one page report to the military government, taking a reasonably optimistic view of this prospect. As it turned out, the German Christian Federation of Labor was not resurrected after the war. To some extent, this was a conscious choice on the part of Christian unionists. But some in the movement felt that the Allied governments had placed unwarranted pressure on church authorities to keep the Christian federation out of business.

During my assignment I had ample opportunity to travel in my spare time, and I began developing contacts with labor and church people in Europe. I made my first trip to Rome and, in Switzerland, attended the 1949 meeting of the International Labor Organization (ILO). During the ILO conference I became entwined in a minor instance of the larger disunity between religion and labor in Europe.

I was traveling with the late Father Francis Flanagan, a former AFL-CIO intern who was studying philosophy in Rome, and we ran into George Meany and his wife in the lobby of the hotel near the ILO headquarters. Meany, who was then secretary-treasurer of the old American Federation of Labor, asked if we had anything planned for the evening. We did. But we also wanted to learn all we could about international labor. "Nothing special," I said. He told us, "Well, the Swiss labor movement is having a big dinner for the labor delegates. Why don't the two of you come as our guests?" We arranged to meet in the hotel lobby at six o'clock. A half-hour before that, Meany called on the telephone. "I'm very sorry, very unhappy about this," Meany said. "I've been told by our hosts, the Swiss labor movement, that it would not be proper for them to invite a priest to their dinner."

It was a harmless misunderstanding but indicative of the mood in those days. Then and for many years afterward, there was a cleavage in many parts of Europe between the labor movement and religion. Many of the dominant nineteenth century labor unions on the continent (and some south of our border) were Marxist in the fullest sense of the word, not only collectivist in their economics, which is less to the point, but all too often vigorously anti-clerical and even at times anti-religious in their official ideology. As a result, many sincere Christians—Catholics, especially, but Protestants as well—found it difficult if not impossible to participate in these unions. Their fear, however well- or ill-founded, was that they would compromise the essentials of their own religious faith. On the other side of the coin, many sincere, militant workers, not only Marxists, looked upon the church and organized religion in general as bastions of reaction.

This may reveal an American bias on my part, but what the Europeans seemed to lack was a concept of labor-union neutrality—that is, neutrality on religious and moral questions that have little to do with trade unionism. Labor unions as well as churches tended to theologize the labor movement. In other words, they seemed unwilling to let unions be unions and keep to the core issues, such as collective bargaining and distribution of property; they also felt called upon to bring in questions of ultimate meaning and reality.

This led to more than a few ridiculous arguments. The polemics between religion and labor became so far-fetched that in some places noisy debates erupted over the question of cremation. Some of the socialist unions saw it as a symbolic issue. At the time, the Catholic Church was speaking out against cremation, so the unions decided that they would draw public attention to the cremations of some of their members as a way of sticking it to the church. (As usual, the church went for the bait.) Of course, outlandish debates of this kind had nothing to do with the trade union problem and only brought on further division.

In Holland, any Catholic who belonged to any union except the Catholic union did so under pain of excommunication. The Dutch labor movement had split along both denominational and ideological lines, with separate trade union federations for Protestants, Catholics, socialists and communists. There, as in other parts of Europe, the church's feelings toward the labor movement were more or less the same as they were toward the wider culture. That is to say, they were distant, and Holland had the most ghettoized Catholic Church in all of Europe. If you were a Dutch Catholic, you went to a Catholic doctor, read a Catholic newspaper, listened to a Catholic radio station—and you joined a Catholic trade union.

Today the situation of the Catholic Church in Holland appears to have shifted to the other extreme. There is no Christian trade union in Holland nor, for that matter, no overwhelming presence of Catholic institutions of any other kind. The Dutch church is in disarray, at least from an institutional standpoint. The change is striking. When I arrived in Holland, a first order of business was to acquire a copy of the so-called "Mandatum," the document in which the Dutch bishops decreed that Catholics should belong to Catholic unions and no others. One of the signers of the decree was the young Bishop Bernard Jan Alfrink. Less than two decades later, at the Second Vatican Council, Cardinal Alfrink emerged as a leading liberal voice for the church's opening to the modern world.

In more recent years, church-labor relations have taken a significant turn for the better on the Continent, although the German inquiry as to why a priest would go to a labor gathering, in 1988, showed the lingering bad will between the two groups. (If the bishops of Germany think the metalworkers are radical, they haven't looked recently at the number of banks and other capitalist enterprises owned by the union.) Still, the European experience tells us much about the uniqueness of the American situation. There has long been a good working relationship between organized labor and organized religion in our country—so much so that European labor representatives who visit for the first time often point to this as one of the most striking characteristics of our national tradition.

A Belgian labor leader passing through Washington in 1989 asked the very question: How did labor and religion get on such good terms in the United States? This fellow is an officer of the Christian federation of labor in Belgium, one of several European countries that still have divided labor movements. I started off by telling him a story about a nineteenth century cardinal from Baltimore who intervened with the Vatican at a critical moment in the history of church-labor relations.

*   *   *

When I go to Rome, I try, if possible, to visit the fourth century Basilica of Santa Maria in Trastevere. I do so not for aesthetic but for nostalgic historical reasons. It was in that basilica that James Gibbons of Baltimore, upon his elevation to the rank of cardinal in 1887, spoke in defense of religious liberty in the United States. This was generations before Rome would come around to endorsing the concept of religious liberty as a universal value. Gibbons' faith in the American experiment and openness toward American institutions would, within a few years, lead him to head off a Vatican condemnation of the labor movement in this country.

"For myself, as a citizen of the United States, without closing my eyes to our defects as a nation," he said in the basilica, "I proclaim, with a deep sense of pride and gratitude, and in this great capital of Christendom, that I belong to a country where the civil government holds over us the aegis of its protection without interfering in the legitimate exercise of our sublime mission as ministers of the gospel of Jesus Christ." For the great progress which the church in the United States has made "under God and the fostering care of the Holy See, we are indebted in no small degree," he added, "to the civil liberty we enjoy in our enlightened republic."

Gibbons was not the first American bishop to voice these sentiments, not the first to display an openness to what the modern world, within reason, had to offer. Seven years before the principle of religious freedom was legally guaranteed by the First Amendment to the Constitution, the first bishop of the United States, John Carroll of Baltimore, declared: "We have all smarted heretofore under the lash of an established church and shall be on our guard against every approach toward it." He made this declaration despite the fact that the twenty-five thousand Catholics committed to his pastoral care suffered under severe legal disabilities. Such was the state of the church in all of the original colonies except Pennsylvania—even in Catholic-founded Maryland, where Catholics were disenfranchised in 1654. But, in 1776, Maryland followed Virginia's lead with a grant of religious freedom, and Pennsylvania reiterated its standing promise of religious liberty. Thereafter the Declaration's inalienable right of "liberty and the pursuit of happiness" became meaningful for Catholics.

Carroll was thus prompted to say that "the United States has banished intolerance from its system of government. Freedom and independence, acquired by the united efforts and cemented by the mingled blood of Protestant and Catholic fellow citizens, should be equally enjoyed by all." Bishop Carroll's guarded optimism proved somewhat premature. Intolerance toward Catholics persisted, in varying degrees, for many generations. And yet the American Catholic community never muted its applause for the political system of our country and never hesitated in its belief in the promise of American democracy.

In the latter part of the nineteenth century, it was the American labor movement that held out hope of advancing the American experiment. The only organization at the time that even remotely resembled what we would today recognize as a union was the Knights of Labor. By modern standards, it was not much of a labor movement. It was, however, all we had, and many of the new Catholic immigrants rallied behind it. The Knights were unlike trade unions of today in that they welcomed, as the saying had it, "everyone but bankers and bartenders." In other words, the Knights took in non-salaried workers such as self-employed craftsmen and shopkeepers. They did as much fraternizing as collective bargaining. And the Knights shrouded themselves in secrecy, having all the paraphernalia of a secret society—passwords, ceremonial vows of secrecy, and the like.

This was the rub for the Catholic Church, which harbored a deep suspicion of secret societies, mainly as a result of the church's experience with the Masons and other societies with anti-religious overtones. It was inevitable, then, that the Knights would become a point of contention in the church. In Quebec, the French Canadian bishops had prevailed upon the Vatican to condemn the Knights in Canada and, for all practical purposes, forbade Catholics to belong to the union. In Rome, church leaders were ready to extend the ruling to the United States.

The prospects of condemnation alarmed Gibbons and the American bishops, particularly the liberal-minded "Americanists," as they were known. Unlike their Canadian counterparts, the U.S. bishops did not look upon the Knights of Labor as a danger to the faith of their people. They knew that the secret nature of the organization pertained not to religion or ideology but to the need for protection against enemies. Aside from this, the bishops were shrewd enough to know that the idiosyncratic Knights would not become the permanent labor movement in the United States. Indeed the organization would soon fade away, setting the stage for Samuel Gompers and the American Federation of Labor.

The bishops chose not to sit around and wait for word from the Holy See. In 1886 they drafted a memorandum signed by Gibbons, who, as the only cardinal and spokesman for the Catholic Church in the United States, sailed off to Rome to make their case. In their memorandum, the bishops argued that at a time when American workers were struggling for their rights, an organization such as the Knights of Labor was indispensable. They told Rome that a condemnation would lead to disaffection among Catholic workers, at least some of whom, they warned, would leave the church. In short, the bishops urged the Holy See to drop the matter, and they prevailed. There was no condemnation of the Knights of Labor in the United States.

The Gibbons memorandum is one of the neglected classics in the histories of American religion and labor. Certainly it is required reading for anyone who would hope to understand the tradition of church-labor cooperation in this country. Perhaps the following excerpt from the memorandum will suggest the flavor of the cardinal's thinking:

> Since it is acknowledged by all that the great questions of the future . . . [are] the social questions, the questions which concern the improvement of the condition of the great masses of the people, and especially of the working people, it is evidently of

supreme importance that the church should always be found on the side of humanity, of justice toward the multitudes who compose the body of the human family. . . . In our country, especially, this is the inevitable program of the future, and the position which the church must hold toward the solution is sufficiently obvious.

My friend, the late Msgr. John Tracy Ellis, a first-rate historian, viewed the cardinal's memorandum as perhaps the single most important document ever issued by the American bishops. For had the Vatican gone the other way and condemned the Knights of Labor, as the French Canadian bishops had urged, a split would have occurred in the American labor movement, as it had in Europe. In that case, some Catholics would have remained loyal to the church and joined an inconsequential Catholic union, while others would have fallen away from the church to one degree or another. This would have proved disastrous for not only the church but the workers, who needed solidarity. But the American labor movement was never divided along religious lines, and there has never been a serious attempt to organize a national Catholic or Christian or Protestant union.

Although the American bishops stood up for the Knights and rejected the sectarian option, they did not extend the argument by saying their European counterparts should do the same. To do so would have been not only unwise from a tactical point of view but, perhaps, bad sociology as well. The Americans knew that whatever social and political conditions had prompted the European church to cultivate a separate Christian labor movement, those conditions did not exist in the United States.

For one thing, in contrast to Europe, no atheistic or anti-religious or anti-clerical movement had ever and would ever take hold in the American trade union movement. The United States, like most European countries, did embrace the concept of separation of church and state. But our variety of church-state separation differed fundamentally from theirs.

As it developed from the French Revolution, the European doctrine of separation of church and state aimed at keeping religion out of the social realm. In the United States, on the other hand, the founders who drafted the First Amendment wanted to keep the government out of religion. So, unlike the case in western Europe after the French Revolution and up until fairly recent times, our government never took an anti-religious stand. This gave the Catholic Church some breathing space in the secular order. And as a result, Catholics could join the labor movement with the full blessing of their church, and, in fact, they became extraordinarily active in the movement, more so than any other religious or ethnic group. Despite the many changes in religious, cultural, social, ethnic and political life, that still holds true today.

Closing Ranks

The Gibbons intervention might have made for a good start in American Catholic social action, but no movement of any consequence appeared for at least a generation afterward. The church had other things on its mind. In those years, millions of immigrants arrived on the shores of the United States, and the larger burden fell on the Catholic Church to settle and assimilate these new Americans. Bishop Carroll's scattered band of twenty-five thousand Catholics was augmented by the influx of millions of Europeans during the second half of the nineteenth century and the first quarter of the twentieth century. This massive movement of impoverished people from the Old World to the New confronted the church with a pastoral problem of staggering proportions.

During the early waves of immigration, the institution of American Catholicism, as we know it today, began to take shape. The church went about the business of building schools, parishes, hospitals, orphanages and homes for unwed mothers, assimilating millions of poor and penniless workers. This became a total preoccupation, and little time remained for serious consideration of the larger issues of social justice (although individual Catholics labored in the social field). The church, as an institution, had yet to make social reform an integral part of its mission.

This hardly means, however, that the Catholic Church was irrelevant to the processes of social change in America. The church's response to the immigration problem, with all its strengths and weaknesses, has only recently begun to receive the degree of scholarly attention it so richly deserves. In any event, it is clear even now, as the distinguished (non-Catholic) historian Henry Steele Commager has written, that the Catholic Church was during the immigration period "one of the most effective of all agencies for democracy and Americanization. Representing as it did a vast cross section of the American people, it could ignore class, section, and race; peculiarly the Church of the newcomers, of those who all too often were regarded as aliens, it could give them not only spiritual refuge but social security."

It is easy by hindsight to criticize the church's manner of dealing with the problem of mass immigration (some historians believe the church should have been more critical of the "melting-pot" process of assimilation). Yet it can hardly be denied that the church helped millions of immigrants become acclimated to their new and strange surroundings and adapt to American social and political institutions—on their own terms. One of these institutions, in due course, would be the labor movement. Underlying the church's response to the new Americans was a communitarian ethos that would help sustain the very notion of collective bargaining.

During the early immigration period, the Social Gospel movement in American Protestantism provided leadership in the arena of religious social action. The movement worked to apply biblical teachings to the economic realm. (One of its more memorable battle cries was against "economic atheism," that is, economics as if God and moral principles did not exist.) I think many of my Protestant friends, however, would agree that the Social Gospel movement amounted to little more than a sideshow in American Protestantism. It caught the interest of intellectuals and some socially minded people in the upper classes. But the movement, partly due to its elitist character, never reached deeply into the grass roots. It had little connection to working people and organized labor.

Nonetheless, Social Gospelers helped awaken the consciences of certain elite segments in America, forming the soul of a Progressive movement that achieved early victories in the area of legislative reform. And the movement came to exert an indirect influence on American Catholicism in the person of John A. Ryan, born and bred on progressivist soil in Minnesota. Ryan, one of those moved by the preaching of midwestern Social Gospelers, believed that the American experiment (particularly its reformist strands) and Catholic tradition could be reconciled. The enduring testimony to this belief is the bishops' *Program of Social Reconstruction,* issued in 1919 and drafted by Ryan. The program served as the vehicle of American Catholicism's formal entry into the social arena, at once embracing and going beyond the progressive agenda of social reform.

Those who believe today's church leaders go too hard on business should listen to the words of the bishops in 1919. After pointing out that laborers should put in an honest day's work for an honest day's pay, the *Program* ended with these words:

> The capitalist must likewise get a new viewpoint. He needs to learn the long-forgotten truth that wealth is stewardship, that profit-making is not the basic justification of business enterprise, and that there are such things as fair profits, fair interest, and fair prices. Above all, he must cultivate and strengthen within his mind the truth . . . that the laborer is a human being, not merely an instrument of production; and that the laborer's right to a decent livelihood is the first moral charge upon industry. The employer has a right to get a reasonable living out of his business, but he has no right to interest on his investment until his employees have obtained at least living wages. This is the human and

Christian, in contrast to the purely commercial and pagan, ethics of industry.

The *Program* marked a turning point for the Catholic Church in this country, signaling a new desire by the church's hierarchy to compete in the marketplace of social ideas. (The bishops even enlisted the services of a public relations specialist in New York to promote the document, which drew extensive notice when first released.) In terms of official Catholic social action, the statement helped set a progressive tone for the bishops' national organization, which came into existence a few months later, in November.

It was hardly pre-ordained that the bishops' Social Action Department (from its beginning, under the leadership of John Ryan) would push a basically progressive agenda. Nor, for that matter, was it so ordained that the bishops' conference itself would amount to much more than a paper organization. On both counts, a large part of the credit (or blame, depending on one's viewpoint) goes to a Paulist priest who served as the conference's first general secretary. By most Vatican II standards, Paulist Msgr. John Burke was admittedly conservative or, at best, very moderate in his approach to a number of theological and secular issues. But by the standards of his own generation he was significantly ahead of his time across the board.

The bishops' conference, a significant element of any Catholic social action movement, almost died on the vine. For those accustomed to having an activist organization representing the bishops at the national level, it may be difficult to understand how unique and controversial it was at the beginning. Previously, during the First World War, there was an organization called the National Catholic War Council, set up to oversee war-related activities in the church. The agency coordinated, among other things, assignments of Catholic chaplains and what later became known as U.S.O. work among Catholic soldiers. As a voluntary organization, the bishops did not have to belong to it, much less follow its lead on social issues. With the close of World War I, the bishops decided that their experiment with a national coordinating body had been reasonably successful, and they decided to form a permanent organization called the National Catholic Welfare Council.

The new organization came under fierce attack from a small but vocal group of bishops who feared that it might come to exert authority over them and their dioceses. They saw a kind of legislative authority implied in the very word "Council." The Vatican agreed and ordered that it be dissolved, not only suppressing the young organization but banning annual meetings of bishops as well. Yet as they had done a generation earlier with regard to the Knights of Labor, the bishops rallied together. Burke played an important, behind-the-scenes role in arranging for Bishop Joseph Schrembs of Cleveland to argue the conference's case in cliff-hanger negotiations with Vatican authorities in Rome.

In the end, the bishops succeeded in their effort to reverse the Holy See's ill-advised suppression of the organization. Rome's only demand was that the bishops drop "Council" from their name, and with this minor concession, the National Catholic Welfare "Conference" (NCWC) was born in 1922. (Today, once again, this debate is being played out in the back-and-forth arguments between U.S. Catholic leaders and Rome over the status of national bishops' conferences. Much like the curia of Burke's day, Vatican officials such as Cardinal Joseph Ratzinger have questioned the teaching authority of national organizations of bishops.)

With the bishops' conference firmly in place, Father Burke's never-failing support of progressive social action programs made it possible for John Ryan's agenda to become the NCWC's. Msgr. Burke was the right man in the right place at the right time; for this the Catholic Church in the United States has every reason to honor his legacy. One shudders to think of what might have happened, what direction the NCWC might have taken, if its first general secretary had come from a more hidebound or conservative theological and political tradition. Be that as it may, the only thing that matters now is that the conference—whose uniqueness, in its time, has yet to be fully appreciated—got off to a basically progressive start under Msgr. Burke's far-sighted and resourceful leadership.

Notwithstanding Burke's support and Ryan's renown, the Social Action Department might have labored in relative obscurity if not for its assistant director, Father Raymond McGowan. Working deliberately in the shadow of his illustrious superior, McGowan gave the department its distinctive character. For all practical purposes, he directed the department while Ryan pursued his apostolate of writing and lecturing on social concerns.

In 1922 McGowan spawned, from the side of the Social Action Department, the Catholic Conference on Industrial Problems, which he once described as "a kind of traveling show of Catholic social teaching." Assisted by Linna Bresette, the department's field secretary, McGowan staged conferences around the country, bringing together labor leaders, government officials, employers and exponents of Catholic social teaching to discuss industrial issues. McGowan's organizational activities were a prototype of his industrial vision—that of genuine cooperation between labor, management and government. In McGowan's vision of a cooperative society, employees worked as full partners in business enterprises; unions participated in decisions not only about wages and work conditions but about prices and profits as well.

McGowan's efforts at reform came during a dry period of social action in the church and wider society. In her advance field work for the conferences on industrial problems, Bresette encountered a recurring skepticism (notably among employers and well-to-do Catholics) about the need for such an organization during a supposedly prosperous era. Furthermore, after early advances in the organization of skilled workers, the labor movement went into a period of steep decline during the 1920s, in large part because of renewed resistance by employers. In this conservative climate, McGowan promoted such reforms as a mandatory minimum wage, recognition of labor unions and the right to strike, and the establishment of consumer cooperatives. The labor-management-government conferences, while lasting into the 1950s, made their most distinctive contribution by sounding an industrial wake-up call during the complacent 1920s.

In the 1930s, when social action was still of questionable centrality in the church, the bishops' conference quietly nurtured a constituency of priests dedicated to social ministry. My predecessor at the Social Action Department, Father John Hayes of Chicago, had begun to circulate *Social Action Notes for Priests,* written for what was intended to be, at most, a few hundred priests with an interest in social problems. The newsletter paid special attention to the labor problem. It reported on the activities of priests and lay people in this field and carried excerpts from some of the more useful articles and documents that touched on organized labor. Its distribution was based purely on demand in the sense that every priest who received the newsletter had specifically asked to be placed on the mailing list. By the time it went out of publication, approximately six thousand priests had written in for subscriptions.

When Father Hayes took sick and had to leave the conference (in what turned out to be only a brief interruption of his long and fruitful ministry of social action), this part of the department's work fell to me. The assignment put me in contact with thousands of priests, some of whom would later become leading social-minded bishops of the 1960s and 1970s. In those fluid and formative years of Catholic social action, I seldom knew what I would be doing from one day to the next. I would arrive at my desk in the morning and find a stack of letters from priests with questions about the Taft-Hartley Labor Act of 1947 (which outlawed such union practices as the closed shop and secondary boycotts) or any other aspect of the labor problem. As the one whose job it was to involve clergy, I answered every one of them.

In the front ranks stood the so-called labor priests, those who made the working person their apostolate. In many places where workers struggled to organize, the priests opened "schools" for the rank and file, sometimes as an extension of colleges and universities run by the Jesuits. Numbering in excess of one hundred at their peak in the 1940s and 1950s, the labor schools represented an early and somewhat raucous form of what we know today as "adult education." They arose in a context of struggle and confrontation, a time when millions of workers asserted their rights of free association in the workplace. After quitting time, many of these workers (who tended to know as little about unions as former Soviet citizens today know about free markets) would come together for basic education in the workings of labor. One of the more ambitious undertakings was in Connecticut, where Msgr. Joseph Donnelly oversaw the establishment of nearly two dozen labor schools. He went on to become chairman of the state's labor mediation board, a post that he held for twenty years before being named auxiliary bishop of Hartford.

One of those who remain active in local affairs is Msgr. Charles Owen Rice, a well-known figure in Pittsburgh who emerged as the industrial city's leading labor priest during the Depression. In 1936 he and Father Carl Hensler formed the Catholic Radical Alliance, which had its roots in the Catholic Worker movement. "I am a radical, a Catholic radical," Rice said on many occasions. "I believe that the present social and economic system is a mess and should be changed from top to bottom." A native of New York City who spent seven years of his boyhood in Ireland, living among relatives after his mother died, Rice was never one to run from a fight. In fact, he deliberately and almost gleefully started many a good fight himself. Rice personally took part in strikes by the Congress of Industrial Organizations. He joined with workers on the picket line during such actions as the 1937 strike against the Pittsburgh-based Heinz corporation. He spoke to many an overflow crowd in churches, union halls and immigrant meeting houses.

Unlike most other labor priests, Rice plunged himself into the internal politics of the labor movement, fighting communists in the leadership ranks of CIO unions, especially during the late 1940s and early 1950s. He became one of the leaders of an anti-communist movement in the United Electrical Workers, then a communist-controlled union with a big local in Pittsburgh, home of Westinghouse corporation. (On this point, Rice has openly voiced some regrets in recent years, a matter to which I will return presently.) Yet during the CIO's formative years in the 1930s, Rice's name was virtually synonymous with the movement of industrial unions, so much so that he became known as "the chaplain of the CIO."

Although labor priests generally kept to matters of local concern, there is at least one whose name and cause became known all across the country. John "Pete" Corridan, a Jesuit priest, was one of the most color-ful and effective opponents of labor racketeering. A rough-and-tumble New Yorker, Corridan inspired author and screenwriter Budd Schulberg's 1953 movie, *On the Waterfront*, based on events during the 1940s and 1950s, when Corridan led a crusade against racketeering in New York's maritime industry. The "waterfront priest," as he was known, worked through the Xavier Labor School, headed by his fellow Jesuit, the late Rev. Philip Carey.

In the early 1940s the school directed its attention to unions con-trolled and influenced by communists, including the Transit Workers of New York City. Carey believed that the communists did not have the interests of the unions at heart and, unless opposed, would hijack the unions for their own ideological ends. His strategy, he always said, was to train workers in "union democracy," with a view toward fair union elec-tions. When Corridan came on board in the late 1940s, the focus turned to racketeering, and the two Jesuits made for an ideal combination. Gentle, though shrewd, Carey was the man on the inside, overseeing the day-to-day work of the labor school, which trained longshoremen who wanted to clean up their union. Corridan, tough and street-smart, was the man out on the docks, going up against the triple alliance of crooked union leaders, employers, and politicians who looked the other way.

Corridan's swashbuckling manner was hardly the usual style of labor priests, and yet he was typical in the sense that he sought to apply the universals of social ethics to the particulars of concrete reality. The harsh, day-to-day reality on the waterfront was its outmoded hiring system. They called it the "Shape-Up"—the notorious system that required stevedores to line up or "shape up" for work twice a day before a hiring agent, who had the power to determine their economic life or death. Getting a favor-able nod from the hiring boss often meant having to go see the loan shark, who lent money at the usurious rate of twenty percent a week. This form of extortion came with a union seal of approval.

To those workers struggling against the system of the Shape Up, Corridan held out a deep and lively spirituality, a blessed assurance that they were not alone. "I suppose some people would smirk at the thought of Christ in the Shape. It's about as absurd as the fact that he carried car-penter's tools in his hands and earned his bread and butter by the sweat of his brow," he once said. "As absurd as the fact that Christ redeemed all men irrespective of their race, color or station in life."

Corridan was revered by the dockworkers. When they staged a wild-cat strike on the morning of November 8, 1948 (which quickly spread up and down the Atlantic Coast, lasting eighteen days) the Waterfront Priest was catapulted onto the national stage. His presence in the rebel movement required a shift of tactics on the part of the top union boss, Joe Ryan, president of the International Longshoremen's Association. Up until this point, Ryan could garner a certain amount of public sympathy by labeling the rebel dockworkers' movement and its underground publication, *The Crusader*, "a Communist production." But after Corridan's responsibility for the newspaper became known, Ryan began calling it "the work of a religious fanatic." Somehow the new scare words did not pack the same punch.

While excellent in many respects, the motion picture *On the Waterfront* could easily give a simplistic impression of good guys vs. bad guys. This may be expected of Hollywood, and yet it would have probably taken little more than a few lines to get across the bigger picture that Corridan always kept in view. He was more than a Jesuit gangbuster; he had a social critique. The problem, as he saw it, was not just a few crooks but an economic system driven purely by profit. Like other labor priests of his time, Corridan knew that individual moral reform alone was not enough. There had to be reform of economic institutions and structures, whether it was of the Shape Up on the docks or the Shake Down by any others who would deny workers a living wage.

Extremely affable, but fearless and tough as nails, Corridan risked his life to bring about needed labor-management reforms. But for the grace of God, he might have well ended up in the East River for challenging the gangster-controlled hiring system on the docks. In the end, Pete's efforts led to congressional hearings, labor-law reforms and the formation of the New York/New Jersey Watchdog Waterfront Commission. In a fitting tribute at the time of his death in 1984, Budd Schulberg said Corridan was about the "closest I ever came to feeling what true Christianity was about."

The labor school which served as Corridan's base would turn out to be one of the very last in the Catholic Church. At one time church-sponsored labor schools provided a source of hope for workers battling against great odds. If the schools accomplished nothing else, they lent a certain respectability to the union movement in an era of extreme resistance toward its campaigns. With representatives of Roman Catholicism teaching workers how to organize themselves and build institutions, labor's enemies found it harder to portray the movement as a wholly owned subsidiary of the Soviet Union. Yet many of them would keep on trying.

In New York ten thousand union members passed through the Xavier Labor School, which Carey operated for fifty years in Lower Manhattan. But when the Jesuit passed away in July 1989, so did the labor school. As Carey admitted to the *National Catholic Reporter* in 1988, his work at the labor school was not what it was when fifty thousand longshoremen worked New York's bustling ports. Today, only one thousand union members staff the docks, but Carey said he thought he still had a contribution to make. His death, at the age of eighty, signaled the end of an era of Catholic social action. In his time Catholic labor schools dotted the industrial landscape; now they have all but disappeared. As of this writing, Father Ed Boyle's Boston Catholic Labor Institute was the only one left. Yet as I will discuss later in this chapter, new circumstances have given rise to new efforts toward collaboration between religion and labor.

*   *   *

Since the heyday of church-labor cooperation, revisionist historians have looked for dark and cynical motives behind the Catholic Church's involvement in the labor movement. A common thesis is that if not for the Catholic Church's intervention, there might have been a socialist labor movement in the United States. It is worth clearing the air on this point, if for no other reason than that the ghosts of past quarrels appear now and then in dialogues between religion and labor.

Much of the revisionism has dealt with the now-defunct Association of Catholic Trade Unionists (ACTU). That's "unionists," not unions; the difference is between separate Catholic unions of the European variety and parallel organizations of Catholic union members—the ACTU model. Launched in New York City by former members of the Catholic Worker (notably John Cort, a Catholic convert and early organizer of the International Ladies Garment Workers Union), ACTU defined its mission as spreading the church's teachings on labor. The movement drew part of its mandate from Pope Pius XI's 1931 encyclical *Quadragesimo Anno* which encouraged Christian workers to form parallel (though not necessarily competing) associations of Catholic workers.

In practically no time, the movement branched out from New York and spawned independent chapters across the map of urban industrial America. ACTU published a number of first-rate newspapers. In Detroit, for example, *The Wage Earner* took an active role in promoting the legitimacy of industrial unions as ACTU leaders worked closely with Walter Reuther of the United Auto Workers. For better or worse, ACTU had no national coordination. So while in many places the movement rallied support for striking workers, in others it knocked heads with communists in the labor movement or tried to root out organized crime. It is the brush with Bolshevism that has driven so much of the historical investigation.

A fairly typical work of this genre is Douglas P. Seaton's *Catholics and Radicals: The Association of Catholic Trade Unionists and the American Labor Movement from Depression to Cold War*. In his 1981 book, Seaton argues tendentiously—almost ad nauseam—that "the partisans of the church" and specifically ACTU were a, if not the, crucial factor in determining the "conservative" direction taken by the industrial unions during the period between 1937 and 1950.

Undergirding this sweeping generalization is Seaton's recurrent charge, tinged with a note of personal pique and hostility, that Catholic social teaching (which ACTU, however effectively or otherwise, tried to put into practice) is hopelessly "conservative." In a telltale footnote, Seaton gives his hand away by defining his loaded terms. In short, "radicals" (the good guys) are those committed to class struggle and a socialist order. "Conservatives" (the bad guys) are, conversely, those who reject the philosophy of class struggle and do not belong to any formal school of socialism.

With his basic code words so defined Seaton has no trouble proving, at least to his own satisfaction, that the Catholic Church in general and ACTU in particular were conservative. Even John A. Ryan, in the author's mind, was only a half-hearted progressive. On the other hand, he locates the "radicals" more often than not in the communist leaderships of some of the old CIO unions. All this begs the question of whether the program pushed by these so-called "radicals" in labor's communist ranks represented the best interests of labor and the nation as a whole. It's not as if we're talking about Mikhail Gorbachev-style communists, much less democratic socialists of the Michael Harrington variety. These were Stalinists, and their virtually absolute allegience to the Communist Party was regarded by many, not unreasonably, as contrary to the idea of an independent labor movement.

Be that as it may, Seaton argues that ACTU's commitment to "conservative" Catholic social teaching and its reluctance to break with the church made it inevitable that an obsessive anti-communism would become "virtually the sole issue which occupied the organization." Seaton and other historians of his ilk are not alone in thinking that ACTU (or, more precisely, some local chapters of ACTU) went overboard with its anti-communism. One who has looked back on that period is Msgr. Charles Owen Rice, whose penitent reflections are captured in the title of his summer 1989 article, "Confessions of an Anti-Communist," published in *Labor History*.

Rice, who worked closely with ACTU through his Catholic Radical Alliance in Pittsburgh, says he is not proud of the crusades to remove communists from positions of influence in the labor movement. He still holds, quite rightly, that the primary loyalty of communists was to the Communist Party, not to the labor movement, and that their triumph would have been labor's disaster. In retrospect, however, he believes that the communists never had a chance. Most of all, he regrets that he (and other "actists," as they were known) at times employed tactics as ruthless and merciless, in his view, as those of their adversaries.

"Most of us ACTU people had been influenced by Dorothy Day in the direction of enthusiastic support for organized labor, but we lost Dorothy's serenity and positive spirit along the way," he wrote in *Commonweal* in 1984. "We were pro-labor and not merely anti-communist, but I for one wish there had been far less emphasis on the negative."

Misgivings about anti-communist crusades in labor have not only come after the fact. At the height of labor's cold war, the communist question provoked heated debates, pro and con, in ACTU circles around the country. The failure of many historians to report adequately on the ins and outs of this intramural ACTU debate is but one indication of their ideological bias. In Seaton's case the oversight stems not only from the apparently limited scope of his research (he appears to have relied much too heavily on the extant files of the New York ACTU, which, in the opinion of some, took its anti-communism too far). It also grows out of an almost compulsive desire to nail down his central thesis.

Other revisionists have attributed even darker motives to the church's interest in the labor problem. In his 1989 critical biography, *Rev. Charles Owen Rice: Apostle of Contradiction*, Patrick McGeever gives credence to charges that Rice and ACTU were primarily concerned not with social justice (nor even, for that matter, with anti-communism) but rather with having Catholicism prevail over all other religious groups. "Of particular note in this line of criticism," McGeever writes, "was the interest that the ACTU and its 'labor leaders' were at that time expressing in having the CIO establish relations in Europe not with the socialist trade union federation, the World Federation of Trade Unions, but with its Catholic rival, the International Confederation of Free Trade Unions."

While McGeever does not actually say he agrees with this "criticism," he does tailor the evidence to fit the thesis. In fact, the example that he relates is simply untrue. The World Federation of Trade Unions was then and up until its demise in 1990 a communist, not a socialist, federation; the International Confederation of Trade Unions was and still is a social-democratic federation and by no means a Catholic rival to the world federation. This spurious example betrays yet another flaw in many of these studies—the blurring of any distinction between "socialist" and "communist." At several points McGeever uses the two words interchangeably, as if to suggest that anti-communist equals anti-socialist (and therefore anti-progressive). In fact, not only is there a huge difference between the two, but ACTU and other Catholic activists often teamed up with democratic socialists in opposing labor's communist forces.

Still other revisionists have described ACTU as a plot on the part of the church's hierarchy to influence the labor movement. In other words, the bishops pulled ACTU's strings. This charge rankles in particular because it raises, once again, the myth of the monolithic church. During those years I happened to be the bishops' liaison to groups such as ACTU. I would have sooner attempted to infiltrate the Politburo or General Motors than insinuate myself into the politics of ACTU. The actists were fiercely jealous of their autonomy, guarding it against church authorities as well as other chapters of the organization.

More often than not, in a given city, ACTU got off the ground without any episcopal blessing and in some cases against the better judgment of the bishop. It would be hard to imagine that the New York ACTU was even remotely started up by the archbishop there. As it turned out, during a 1949 gravediggers' strike against cemeteries owned by the archdiocese of New York, ACTU sided squarely with the cemetery workers and opposed the archbishop. This could not have pleased Francis Spellman.

Did ACTU as well as other Catholic activists make mistakes in their dealings with labor? Undoubtedly. But being in a position to travel around at the time, I was about as close to ACTU as anyone else; and while I did not always like what I saw, the decisions were made, for better or worse, by actists on their own. They did not take their cue from the bishops. One exception to this determined autonomy was the situation in Detroit, where ACTU worked hand in hand with Archbishop Edward Mooney. Mooney, though, was a progressive, and it would be, at the very least, gross overstatement to call him a union red-baiter. Mooney's alliance with ACTU and organized labor eventually led him into a confrontation with his best-known priest, one that illustrates the church's encounter with the labor problem.

Father Charles Coughlin, the powerful priest of the nation's airwaves, was closely identified with the cause of organized labor because of his early support of the movement. But when the Congress of Industrial Unions arrived on the scene in the late 1930s, he turned into one of its bitter detractors. In radio sermon after radio sermon, Coughlin charged that the CIO—and its affiliate, the auto workers—had fallen into the hands of communists. John L. Lewis, the illustrious founder of the CIO, came in for especially harsh criticism for not expelling communists from CIO ranks. Coughlin went so far as to help organize a separate union of Ford workers that would be more agreeable to management, although this quixotic venture was short-lived.

At the time, ACTU chapters in Detroit and elsewhere were urging its members to rebut the anti-union broadcasts of Coughlin and his diatribes against the CIO in particular. While Mooney, too, lent his support to the

CIO, he was more cautious in his handling of Coughlin, a pastor in the Detroit archdiocese. For one thing, the archbishop realized that he could make a martyr out of Coughlin by coming down too hard on him. Furthermore, no one knew how the unsteady Coughlin, with his enormous and dedicated following, would react to a move against him by Mooney. (Douglas Fraser, former president of the United Auto Workers, once mentioned to me that when he was a boy, Coughlin's Sunday broadcasts were sacred in his family. When the radio priest came on, everything in his home came to a stop. Fraser recalls that this was true of his entire neighborhood.) The idea of Coughlin, directly or indirectly, stirring up a public outcry against his own archbishop was not unthinkable.

Mooney, however, found an opening at the time of a nationwide strike by Chrysler workers in 1939. Coughlin, who called for Chrysler workers to go back to work, made the mistake of quoting from *Quadragesimo Anno* —out of context. In describing the fascist system in Italy, the encyclical by Pius XI stated that strikes are forbidden. The encyclical did not say that strikes should be forbidden; it simply said that under the fascist system, they are forbidden. It was a declarative statement. Coughlin, however, took it as an admonitory statement—that workers should never strike—and he turned it against the United Auto Workers. This gave Mooney an opening because the matter involved not mere political judgment but church teaching, which he had to uphold as archbishop.

Mooney instructed Father Raymond Clancy, his social-action vicar, and Paul Weber, editor of the *Wage Earner,* to buy radio time to respond to Coughlin's attacks on the striking Chrysler workers. In his broadcast Father Clancy adopted ACTU's argument that Coughlin had repeatedly misrepresented Catholic social teaching. The message of disapproval sent by Coughlin's own archbishop amounted to one large step in the radio priest's eventual downfall.

Such an episode in the Catholic engagement with labor would be hard to find in the volumes of revisionist history. It does not fit neatly into the thesis of a "conservative" church that joined the labor struggle merely to oppose communism or, worse yet, to serve narrow, institutional interests. And yet, action for the genuine progress of labor was the rule rather than the exception in the Catholic social action movement. It defined the church's relationship to organized labor during the movement's formative battles for recognition.

A Tapering Off and Falling Out

During the days of the Mooneys, Corridans and Rices, religion and labor faced a relatively simple, moral issue—the right to organize. When the Congress of Industrial Organizations came on the scene, only a handful of independent labor unions had opened up in the major industries. With the masses of industrial workers unorganized, religious friends of labor could take a simple approach. Those in Catholic social action would say: unions are a good thing, the papal encyclicals say so, and the church ought to help this movement. The labor schools, in this respect, were unique to a period in which industrial unions conducted massive drives to organize the unorganized.

But with the great campaigns mostly behind them, religious leaders had considerably less to say about labor problems. Unions turned their attention to technical matters: negotiating and drawing up contracts and building their institutions. The tasks were somewhat removed from the basic principle of the right to organize, which provided the religious community's natural point of entry into the labor debate. From then on, collective bargaining became more and more complex. This is reflected in the union contract itself, originally little more than a statement of principle.

For instance, the first contract between General Motors and the United Auto Workers amounted to a page or two, in recognition of the union's right to represent the workers. These days the UAW contract runs about five hundred pages, with several volumes of supplementary material. After helping the UAW win its original contract, religious groups had no business telling the union how to write the fine print; and any cleric who presumed to do so would have looked rather foolish. The UAW's Walter Reuther (who benefited from church support as much as any other labor leader) did not need Cardinal Mooney's advice on how to run his union.

Not surprisingly, in the 1950s labor problems began to recede into the background of Catholic social concerns. Once the auto workers, for example, became a highly complex institution with a million and a half members, what was there for the church to do? By the same token, it makes sense that in more recent years, church involvement in the labor causes gravitated toward areas left untouched by the earlier industrial organizing campaigns. In the 1970s it was the agriculture and textile industries that demanded a religious response.

With the farm workers, the Catholic Church returned to first principles. The U.S. Catholic Conference and other church-related organizations became deeply involved in the farm labor problem. But we did not enter the dispute to tell Cesar Chavez or the growers how they should write their contracts. What we did tell the growers (and I think to some extent we helped the farm workers, merely through the respectability that comes with church backing) was that they had to recognize the right of these men and women to organize and bargain collectively. If the United Farm Workers had developed along the lines of the United Auto Workers, religious organizations would have long since moved out of the farm labor field. Unfortunately, however, the UFW has signed and held on to very few contracts. Chavez still has to call on church groups to endorse his boycotts and other union campaigns; he still struggles to organize the farm workers.

Likewise, simple moral principle drew religious organizations into one of the longest and hardest-fought labor disputes in recent American history. Throughout the 1970s, the name of the J. P. Stevens Company, one of the nation's leading textile-manufacturing firms, was synonymous with flagrant anti-unionism. Most of its competitors also opposed unions, but Stevens almost seemed to glory in its notoriety. At the time the company refused to recognize the right of its employees to bargain collectively through their union, the Amalgamated Clothing and Textile Workers. This was reason enough for intervention by the Catholic bishops of the southeast and other religious leaders. Their message to Stevens: We don't know how to run your business, but we do know these people have a right to organize. With this show of solidarity, church leaders bolstered the labor movement's boycott of Stevens products. They helped bring about eventual recognition of the Amalgamated union.

Religion and labor, however, were a coalition only for special occasions in the post-CIO era. When things started going fairly well for organized labor, after its major organizing drives, the movement began to lose interest in establishing coalitions with other organizations, churches included. For their part, many religious activists—who might have stepped into the labor arena a generation earlier—went off to fight other battles. During the 1960s they found new causes in the rise of the civil rights and anti-war movements.

How much did the tapering off of cooperation between labor and the Catholic Church, in particular, have to do with shifting demographics among Catholics in the United States? I will leave this question to the sociologists, except to note that in the past few decades, Catholics have moved rather rapidly up the economic ladder. Let me suggest one possible implication of this with an example from my own experience.

During this writing I received a letter from a frustrated labor leader. The letter seemed to bear out what some observers have seen as a disappearance of the working class from the consciousness of middle-class professionals, Catholic or otherwise. In the late 1980s my correspondent's local union in Connecticut decided that, because of a great lack of library materials pertaining to the labor movement in the senior high schools of his city, the union would fully fund the establishment of labor libraries in those three schools, one of which is under Catholic auspices. The union had already donated approximately fifty labor titles to each of the schools. It also provided the schools with a bibliography of four hundred and fifty titles to simplify the process of selecting new ones. (The union would periodically update the bibliography so as to make available to schools any newly published works.)

In negotiating with the three schools, the union discovered that not only students but the teachers themselves were sorely lacking in basic knowledge of labor studies. They were even uncomfortable with teaching from the materials on labor already in their regular curriculum. So the union decided to do something else. Together with the labor education center of a local university, the union put together a twenty-hour labor education course providing a certain number of required continuing education credits for teachers in the three schools.

The point of my correspondent's letter was that the principal of the Catholic high school refused to cooperate with the program. He explained to the union leader that his school was basically a college preparatory school and therefore he did not see any reason to teach about unions. The union leader, quite understandably, was dumbfounded. To him, the principal was taking a rather elitist view, out of character for a professedly "Catholic" school. In his letter the union leader said he hadn't realized that Catholics have come so far from their origins as blue-collar workers and the backbone of the labor movement. They had come so far that they no longer wanted to remember or reflect on the struggles of their forebears (struggles, I might add, that made it possible for their offspring to attend college preparatory schools).

I, too, was dumbfounded. Here was a Catholic principal unwilling to even consider the possibility of cooperating, at no cost to his school, with a labor education program. I could conceive of a high school principal declining the union's offer on strictly technical grounds and for arguably good professional reasons. But to do so on grounds that labor history has no place in a college preparatory school is something else again. It is evidence, unfortunately, of what social critic Barbara Ehrenreich has described as the growing provincialism of the professional class—living in its own social and restricted enclaves, hearing only the opinions of its own members (or, of course, the truly rich) and cut off from the lives and struggles and insights of the American majority.

If Gallup polls are any indication, the Catholic principal was not alone in his seemingly distant feelings toward working people. In their 1987 book *The American Catholic People: Their Beliefs, Practices and Values*, George Gallup and Jim Castelli report on the opinions and attitudes of Catholics toward a variety of subjects, including trade unionism. "While the new Catholic affluence has not caused a callousness toward the poor, it has contributed to a distancing of American Catholics from the labor movement—despite the fact that 23 percent of Catholics live in families with a member who belongs to a labor union and that 34 percent of all union members are Catholics," says the Gallup-Castelli book. "While Catholics remain more supportive of unions than do Protestants, the gap is narrowing."

This is mainly due, I suspect, to the thinking of many upwardly mobile Catholics. Many of them have bought into the idea that while unions may have served a useful purpose when their fathers, grandfathers, or great-grandfathers struggled to make ends meet, that is no longer the case. They seem to think, in other words, that in a society as affluent as our own, workers can readily fend for themselves in the so-called free market; workers have no need to organize.

Sad to say, they are wrong about that. Their own relative affluence has blinded them to the fact that, like their immigrant forebears, millions of today's workers struggle to maintain a minimum standard of living. Many of these workers are themselves recent immigrants, but not all by any means. A growing number of second, third and fourth generation American workers, who thought that they, too, were climbing up the economic ladder, now find themselves slipping back into poverty or near-poverty. All this, however, seems to have escaped the notice of many affluent Americans, Catholics included. During the 1980s they made much of the fact that millions of new jobs had appeared every year in the United States. They seem not to know, or at least not to care, that a sizeable percentage of these jobs paid poverty-level wages. For too many workers, economic growth meant twice the jobs at half the pay.

*   *   *

The loosening of ties between religion and labor had to do with more than just changing times and shifting priorities. With the tumult of the 1960s came a new cynicism toward unions. Many reform-minded people began to look upon organized labor as much less a movement than an institution (which, of course, is what all successful movements become). The image of the stodgy, conservative labor leader, embodying an "establishment" out of touch with the times, entered into the consciousness of social activists. These included the "new breed" of church activists. In the midst of the anti-war struggle, critics took a look around and noticed few labor unions on the battlefield (or at least on their side of it). And in the 1960s, if you weren't part of the solution, you were part of the problem.

In the religion-labor relationship, there came not only a tapering off but a falling out. The arguments, then and for a generation following, usually turned on international affairs in general and American labor movement's antagonism toward communism in particular. In the view of some critics, this anti-communism was so extreme that it blinded labor to the true causes of revolt, namely, oppressive poverty and under-development. The critics argued that in pursuing its foreign-policy goals, the American labor movement sometimes worked too closely with unsavory governments simply because of their stated anti-communism.

Religious activists had good reason to raise these issues with the labor movement, which at times made mistakes in its dealings overseas. Yet the issues were always more involved and less black-and-white than church critics were willing to admit. This appeared evident in the fractious debates between religion and labor during the 1980s.

At the time, Central America and Nicaragua in particular provided many of the sparks for religion-labor conflict. Church activists took special aim at the AFL-CIO's Latin American arm, the American Institute for Free Labor Development, known by its acronym, AIFLD ("A-field"). In some respects, the AFL-CIO and religious activists found themselves at opposite ends of the Nicaragua debate. The federation and AIFLD relentlessly bombarded Nicaragua's Sandinista government with criticism of its treatment of trade unions. Meanwhile, many religious activists sang an unending hymn of praise to the Sandinistas.

I heard the choir perform on many occasions, including once in Los Angeles, during a large Catholic social action gathering in 1985. At several points my remarks were interrupted with cheers and applause, once for condemning Chile's Pinochet regime for its suppression of labor, another time for praising the Solidarity labor union in Poland. Then I rather mildly criticized the Sandinista regime for restricting the freedom of certain Nicaraguan unions which had refused to affiliate with the official government-sponsored labor federations. Applause turned to dead silence. Afterward several people walked up to me to say I was playing into the hands of the Reagan administration.

This did not surprise me. Others before had taken exception with my comments on the matter. "Reverend: I am one of those dumbfounded by your remarks about Nicaragua and the Sandinistas," one correspondent had told me. "Certainly did not expect you to contradict the ideas of Maryknollers and Jesuits and the nuns, etc., who have gone to Nicaragua. I thought you were a liberated priest who understood that there are issues on which we do not break ranks. Shame." I would write back to the dumbfounded and assure them: "Yes, I oppose the Reagan policies in Nicaragua. Yes, I'm against aid to the contras. And yes, I think the U.S. economic embargo is a bad idea—but I also think that harassing free trade unions is inexcusable." That last point never went down well with the followers of Sandino.

It was this almost mystical attraction to the Sandinistas that helped set up a collision course between religion and organized labor in the 1980s. I never thought that the church critics fully understood the situation in Nicaragua or labor's position toward the Sandinista government. For labor, the critical issue was free trade unions, which were not free in Nicaragua under Sandinista leadership. Some church critics, however, were reluctant to admit this or simply allergic to any discussion of the matter.

When I visited the country, I met with officials of all of the country's trade union groups, including the ones under government control. It became clear to me that a number of non-government unions had to contend with constant harassment from the government. The Sandinistas tried to force the independent unions out of business by arresting, detaining and otherwise harassing their leaders. One conversation with the head of a major non-government union in Managua had shed particular light on the problem with some church activists.

I told this labor leader, whose union is affiliated with the International Confederation of Free Trade Unions, that church people made regular trips to Nicaragua. "Do they ever come to see you?" I asked. He said, "Never. You're the first one." It is not surprising, then, that a number of religious activists, hearing only one side of the story, knew or cared little about the situation of trade unions in Nicaragua.

Church activists tended more to excuse than categorically deny the suppression of free trade unions in Nicaragua. Some blamed it on the United States—the U.S.-financed war against Nicaragua (even though, in fact, the Sandinistas cracked down on labor before the arrival of Ronald Reagan in Washington). Others blamed it on the non-Sandinista unions themselves—allegedly "American-dominated" or "counter-revolutionary" (labels that the Sandinistas applied to everyone who disagreed with them). But in truth, too many of labor's critics simply placed little importance on freedom of trade union association. This accounted for at least part of the conflict between labor and religious activists, on Nicaragua and other international issues.

The question of labor's foreign policy is a ghost that haunted religion-labor coalitions until the last gasps of the cold war, and has so even since. I still hear complaints that George Meany, the late AFL-CIO president, and the people around him were so obsessed with anti-communism that it was the only issue on their minds. According to this view, Meany's obsession revealed itself in the AFL-CIO's adamant refusal to deal with government-run labor unions in communist countries. The AFL-CIO steered clear of the unions not because they were communist but because they were controlled by governments. Whatever one might think of this policy, the fact is that the federation applied it with equal force to government unions in anti-communist countries. Indeed, up until the death of General Francisco Franco, the AFL-CIO had a special antipathy toward the Franco unions in Spain.

During my years at the Catholic Conference, the labor attaché to Spain's embassy in Washington would occasionally drop by my office and tell of his frustrated attempts to get a foot in the door at the AFL-CIO. This Spanish official could not even get past the front desk there. I heard labor representatives of other countries express similar disappointment. One of them was the labor attaché to the Polish embassy (prior to the fall of the communist government there), a friend of mine with whom I had lunch every couple of months. When he first arrived in Washington, he asked me if I could assist him in making contacts at the AFL-CIO. I did not want to give him any false illusions. "Look, you haven't got a chance," I said. "You are never going to get inside the AFL-CIO building. If they see you coming, they'll tell the switchboard operator, 'Sorry, we're not in. We don't talk to people from government unions.'"

So even when exerting poor judgment in some areas of international policy, the labor movement has held to the principle of free trade unionism. What does this say about the debate over labor's international position? It suggests, at the very least, that the arguments are not all on one side, the issue not as simple as so-called progressives have framed it. Labor's foreign policy was not simply an anti-communist policy.

Yet even when labor's liberal critics in the churches were right, they were wrong about one thing: the nature of cooperation between different groups and institutions. They failed to draw a crucial line between mistakes by an institution and the essential purpose of that institution. Church critics could have dealt with mistakes by honestly and openly debating the issues while realizing that disagreements will happen. Mistakes and differences of opinion need not lead to disaffection, and yet this is precisely what happened in many areas of the relationship between religion and labor.

In the mid-1980s, officials of the AFL-CIO and national religious organizations began working toward a revival of religion-labor cooperation. This ambitious project had as its goal the formation of a national religion-labor organization, with representation by the major Protestant, Catholic and Jewish agencies. The effort, however, ran aground when some of the religious members of the dialogue started in with demands having to do with the AFL-CIO's foreign policies.

These church representatives (who, in this case, happened to be the liberal Protestant ones) wanted a quid pro quo. They wanted the AFL-CIO to formally condemn the Institute on Religion and Democracy (IRD), a small, neo-conservative group that was slamming liberal Protestant denominations because of their left-leaning stands on international affairs. The church participants also pressed the federation to discipline an AFL-CIO staff member who, as a Methodist layman, helped found the IRD. These liberal Protestant representatives were unyielding in their demands. And in the background lurked the whole issue of labor's foreign policy and Central America in particular.

While I had no particular affection for the IRD, I also had no desire to enter into a coalition on the basis of quid pro quo demands. It seemed to me that this way was doomed to failure, one reason being that two can play at that game. Suppose that the AFL-CIO had entered the dialogue saying, "Look, we can't deal with you. Look at the wage rates in your church office. Do you have a union there?" I would guess that the clerical staff in agencies represented by these church officials were not organized. In the game of quid pro quos, I could picture a hard-headed unionist telling his religious counterparts, "Well then, get out. When your people are organized, we can talk." That would be ridiculous, of course, but perhaps no more so than the demands issued by some on the religious side of the table.

Soon enough, I lost all interest in this religion-labor initiative. Shortly after another one of those insufferable quid-pro-quo sessions, I traveled to Miami to address the annual convention of the AFL-CIO's Industrial Union Department. Several of these church people sat at the table next to mine, so I went over to say hello. At that point I was told, rather frostily, that they weren't planning to stay for the dinner. "Why is that?" I asked. "Because Lane Kirkland is going to give the main address," was the reason —and they did leave before Kirkland spoke. As they left I thought to myself: What is wrong with this picture? These people want a coalition with a particular organization, and here they are walking out of a talk given by the elected leader of that organization. About then I decided that my life was too short to play along with this sort of dialogue between religion and labor.

Toward a New Solidarity

In 1965 a fledgling columnist for the *National Catholic Reporter* came up with what he considered a sure-fire way of telling "the older generation of Catholic liberals from the younger." Older liberals, said Garry Wills, who has since deservedly gained a national reputation as a distinguished author and scholar, "still think of labor unions as a sacred cause. Placidly mellowing monsignori, if they hear criticisms of the unions, still get red hot under their white Roman collars, and begin to froth the rhetoric of the 30s. The cause of labor was, for many of them, the Great Fight; and, like all victorious veterans, they get a bit misty-eyed and prosey on the subject."

That was a simple litmus test that one would have thought even a monsignor could apply without advance training. Try as I would, however, I couldn't get the hang of it. "Labor priests" aside, very few monsignori I knew personally had anything to say in public about unions; fewer still seemed to fit Wills' caricature. (Incredibly, one still hears this complaint—that priests have gone overboard with their support of organized labor—despite the fact that the number of labor priests has declined almost to a vanishing point.)

But time marches on and, behold, the labor problem which Wills apparently thought was old hat in 1965 is still with us today. In the mid-1960s, nearly a third of American workers were organized into unions. By 1992 that figure had shrunk to approximately seventeen percent—the lowest in any of the industrialized countries. (Union representation in the private sector stands at around twelve percent.)

As we near the final laps of a century that made great strides in the labor field, the labor movement is clearly on the defensive, and the right to organize is, once again, a live issue. The right itself is seldom explicitly or directly challenged as a matter of principle or theory. But in everyday practice, the right to organize faces a huge assault. Hundreds of thousands of workers struggle against great odds to achieve or hold on to the basic protection and benefits of collective bargaining shared by their fellow workers in other industries and other countries.

In their efforts to form new unions or hold on to ones that exist, workers have met with widespread and increasing employer opposition—which frequently violates the spirit and all too often the letter of the law. This led the American bishops in their 1986 pastoral letter on Catholic social teaching and the American economy to state that they "firmly oppose organized efforts, such as those regrettably now seen in our country, to break existing unions and prevent workers from organizing."

As the fortunes of organized labor have waned, so have those of America's working people. At the height of the so-called boom of the 1980s, economists Barry Bluestone and Bennett Harrison dealt with this problem very graphically in an article entitled "A Low-Wage Explosion: The Grim Truth About the Job 'Miracle.' " Their findings clearly demonstrated that those affluent Americans who look upon the labor problem in the United States as a matter of ancient history were, and still are, living in a dream world. Bluestone and Harrison reported, for instance, that since the early 1970s average wage and salary incomes adjusted for inflation had declined for nearly all groups within the population and in most industries. "Even more disturbing," they point out, "is the proliferation of low-wage employment. Between 1979 and 1985—the most recent years for which Government data are available—44% of the net new jobs created paid poverty-level wages."

There is no easy solution—surely no single solution—to this disturbing problem, but Bluestone and Harrison hit the mark when they concluded that "in the absence of a new wave of labor organizing in services and of government policies to expand high-value-added production, wage standards for a substantial fraction of American working people will likely continue to erode." (From the standpoint of Catholic social teaching, unions would remain essential—Pope John Paul II calls them "indispensable"—even if the vast majority of workers had adequate wages. For one thing, unions have an irreplaceable part in any credible system of labor-management cooperation, an idea that has gained currency during the age of lagging American competitiveness. Later on I will say more about this role—the representative and coordinating function of organized labor.)

Stirred by such harsh reality, many social-minded people in the religious community have rediscovered the labor problem. Religious activists may have had problems with unions, but few of them ever entertained the notion that we would be better off without a strong labor movement. This feeling of labor decline has led to renewed interest in union struggles on the part of some in the Catholic social action movement and its various counterparts in the ecumenical and interreligious communities. In my own reading of the situation, the danger is not that the labor movement may go out of business (although this is the prognosis of some labor-management experts), but that it would be rendered so weak as to be ineffectual.

Labor, too, is confronting this reality. For a long time labor leaders seemed uninterested in coalitions with religious and civic groups that lent the movement so much of its moral credibility in the early years. All this has changed. More and more the labor movement is calling on old friends, initiating coalitions and soliciting direct church involvement in labor-related causes. The new cooperation found dramatic expression in the 1989–1990 strike by mineworkers against the Pittston coal company in Virginia. The strike generated extraordinary solidarity, among unions as well as between labor and the churches. Leaders of the United Mine Workers gave the churches a large part of the credit for what could have been a union debacle but turned into one of labor's most dramatic victories in recent times.

For their part, religious organizations have looked more and more to the labor movement for help in pushing their social agenda. This amounts to an acknowledgment on the part of many church activists that they have seriously overestimated what they could accomplish on their own in the way of social reform. In the wake of the 1960s, a kind of euphoria took hold of liberal Christian activists. They managed to convince themselves that with enough position statements and "justice-and-peace" projects, they could change the world. By now, most of them know this is nonsense.

On the issue of health care, for instance, church activists would delude themselves by thinking they could lead the way in a movement for national health insurance. Such a step forward for America's working people will never happen without the active participation of working people themselves and their representatives in the labor movement. In other words, religious groups and organized labor need each another.

Furthermore, some of the pitfalls along the way to religion-labor cooperation have been covered up, happily, by the passing of cold war antagonism. This is not to say that quarrels over international affairs will go the way of the Stalinists and cold warriors. As two separate institutions with diverging interests and ultimate purposes, religion and labor will not always see eye to eye. Yet churches and unions find themselves drawing closer together around global concerns. Labor leaders debate the issues more seriously than they had in the past; church people recognize that some of their opinions may have been a little simplistic. In the future, differences over foreign policy are unlikely to be so great as to hinder serious efforts toward cooperation.

Indeed, mainstream religion and labor may be more likely in coming years to close rather than break ranks on international affairs. In the year following the demise of communism in eastern Europe, the nation's major unions and mainline religious denominations joined in opposition to high levels of American aid to El Salvador's military. Their common efforts contributed to a collapse of the Reagan doctrine as it applied to that country. It was but one indication of the new paths to cooperation opened up by shifting geo-political ground.

All this, however, does not add up to a new relationship between religion and labor. A revival of church-labor cooperation will require effort and determination on the part of many people. For those interested in forging this solidarity, I offer a handful of tentative but pointed suggestions on how and how not to go about it.

• Both labor and the churches and synagogues have much to learn about each other's organizational structure, mode of operation, chain of command, and so forth. My own experience leads me to suggest, and indeed to insist, that we both have a lot of homework to do in this regard. Ignorance of this kind can lead to false expectations and even disillusionment. I would suggest, therefore, that both sides start off by getting to know one another in our local and regional communities and by listening to one another before we plunge precipitously into programmatic cooperation: Find out what each side can and cannot do, and at what level.

I know from experience that many labor leaders haven't the faintest idea of the structure of the Catholic Church. Now and then I hear from a labor leader whose local has been tussling with a Catholic institution—very often, a hospital—over union organizing in the institution. One would think, from their attitude, that I was the pope. "Call the bishop; get him to take care of this," I've been told by more than a few labor leaders in these situations. More often than not, though, the bishop has no direct influence over the Catholic hospital. It is often the sisters who are in charge, and chances are that a bishop poking his nose into their business would be put in his place right away. "Go take a walk, Bishop. This is our hospital," sisters have been known to say.

In some cases, a little knowledge about church structure can be danger- ous. Most labor leaders do have a very rough idea of the levels of leadership in the Catholic Church, so they definitely know what they want when they come looking for a statement of support for a labor cause. They always want a cardinal, because a cardinal is presumably better than an archbishop, and an archbishop is better than a bishop, all of whom, of course, are better than simple priests. While this temptation to always "go to the top" may be understandable, it really doesn't go very far in the way of effective action. Usually it delivers only a superficial kind of support.

Yet this was precisely the kind that one labor leader tried to get when he met with a group of bishops in a Washington hotel at the time of the J. P. Stevens boycott. He wanted to leave the meeting with an official statement by members of the Catholic hierarchy on the Stevens dispute—but I threw a monkey wrench into the plan. As an individual, I had already endorsed the nationwide boycott of Stevens products. But I said that as long as I chaired the meeting, the bishops would not put out a statement on a matter about which they knew nothing.

What does the bishop of Rockford, Illinois, for example, know about the textile industry in the southeast? We decided that the bishops of the southeast should pick up the ball on this one, and they did. The southeast- ern bishops undertook a serious study of the issue, meeting with people on all sides. They wound up putting out a strong statement that proved quite effective, far more so than if the labor leader had gotten his way at the meeting in Washington. Their appeal rang out through the region, counter- acting the anti-union rhetoric of industry leaders and bolstering the case of the workers.

• Labor and religion, no matter how united, are two very different institutions. While labor and the religious community have much in com- mon, they may at times, inevitably, have conflicting agendas. Neither side should expect the other to agree on everything. By definition a coalition means that we agree to work on those things that we can work on, and quietly and in good humor go our own way on other issues.

• Don't try to convert the other party to your own agenda. This has been an unfortunate part of the relationship between religion and labor, much of it, in recent years, touching on matters of international policy. As earlier noted, organized labor has a somewhat different approach to some of these questions than do a number of church groups. This is a fact of life, and the changing geo-political climate, while lessening the problem, will not make it go away. I think we need to learn to live with these disagreements and talk about them amicably. To do otherwise would be to hold church-labor cooperation—and ultimately, the needs of working people—hostage to our own agenda.

Those in the churches, especially, need to keep this in mind. The labor movement has a long and unhappy history of outside groups trying to reform it or, worse, use it for their own ideological purposes. (I know of more than a few instances involving church people, stretching back to day one.) In light of this, church people should respect the internal procedures of the labor movement. We should keep in mind that unions are democratic organizations, however imperfect their structures may be. Much as I may disagree with the unions on certain aspects of international relations, I would have to admit that they are far more democratic than we in the churches. Their policy decisions are hammered out within the movement, and reform, if needed, must come from within the movement, democratically. It cannot come from church activists who claim to have the answers that the rank-and-file members are not smart enough to know.

Church people have found this lesson particularly hard to learn. Over the years a few bishops have asked how I could so strongly support the labor movement when it has refused to support Catholics on the issue of federal aid to parents with children in parochial schools. "What are you going to do about it?" one bishop called to ask. I said, "I'm not going to do anything about it. If somebody wants my opinion on the issue, I'll give it. But if you want the labor movement to change its position on federal aid to education, the way you start is to get people in the labor movement to bring it up on the floor. But don't call on a national representative like myself to go to a labor convention and try to change policies. That's not the way it works."

• Avoid like the plague anything that smacks of a quid-pro-quo approach. This is what derailed the initiative in the mid-1980s when some church representatives set forth demands relating to labor's foreign policy. On this and other matters, some church groups have refused to cooperate with the labor movement "unless"—whatever "unless" may be. That's the quid-pro-quo approach, and it's fatal. It will inevitably doom any attempt at church-labor cooperation in the future.

• Both as a practitioner and to a very limited extent as a teacher, I have noticed an appalling lack of knowledge in church circles (and U.S. society in general) about the history of the American labor movement. My own students, most of them seminarians, appear to suffer from a general amnesia with respect to the labor movement and its origins in the United States.

I would go so far as to say there ought to be a law against any church person getting involved in religion-labor cooperation unless he or she can certify as having read at least a few good books on labor history. A knowledge of labor history will help us to understand why and how the American labor movement has developed differently from the way others have—not necessarily better but, by the same token, not necessarily worse. In this regard, my experience in this and other countries has made me allergic to the more radical rhetoric of some labor movements, the ones admired by certain church people as more militant and more radical than the allegedly conservative American movement.

To these church people, I would recommend a trip to Latin America and a front-row seat at any one of the ideological sermons by certain so-called militant labor leaders. They would find that much of it is froth. In the mid-1980s I had an experience of this kind with a small American delegation that spent a few weeks in Brazil, visiting at one point with a young bishop in the part of São Paulo where the auto industry is based. He gave a great spiel about the conservativism of the American labor movement and seemed to think that the United Auto Workers, God help us, was somehow an agent of Wall Street.

I consider this bishop a great and wonderful man, a truly militant defender of the labor movement. But I had to say, "Bishop, I could cite some failures on the part of the Auto Workers, but I can say without fear of contradiction that you do not have a labor movement anywhere in all of Latin America that can even remotely compare to the Auto Workers in effectiveness in promoting the interest of workers." I could have said the same about the Steelworkers and some other international unions in the United States.

• Beware of stereotypes. Church and labor people come in all shapes and sizes, and so do their organizations.

That is the moral of a story told by Doug Fraser, former president of the United Auto Workers. In 1988 he gave a series of lectures at Columbia University's business school. After Fraser finished one of these lectures, a young man stood up and said, "Mr. Fraser, I owe you an apology." Fraser said, "Well, I don't know why. I've never laid eyes on you." The student said, "My stereotype of a labor leader of your rank is a man who is grossly overweight, who is wearing a very expensive but vulgarly flashy suit, who has big vulgar diamonds on his pinkies, who is smoking a very expensive and big cigar, and who is very vulgar and profane." Fraser said, "Young man, you have just given a perfect description of my good friend Lee Iaccoca."

I would suggest to our friends in the labor movement that they probably have some of their own stereotypes—about "conservative" prelates, for one. So I think we ought to take people as we find them. There is no monolithic group on either side.

• Go slow in dreaming about a national religion-labor organization. This was the goal of those conversations in the 1980s that foundered on the quid-pro-quo demands. Although I went along with these discussions, up to a point, my feeling was, and still is, that cooperation between religion and labor should start at the bottom, at the local and regional levels. Plow the fields and do the preparatory spadework that needs to be done. Then, eventually, if the need arises, a national organization will grow naturally and organically.

• Build relationships, and the issues will follow. The first order of business is to get to know and trust one another, and once this is done, someone from a church group may feel comfortable in asking, "Hey, can you tell us about the situation of race relations in your building trade unions?" Or a labor leader might say, "Look, you've got a labor problem in a number of your Catholic hospitals. Is there anything we can do together on this?" Once they have sufficient competence and structures of cooperation, religion-labor groups might also want to address the organization of women workers. This is a new frontier.

It seems that the time is long overdue for church-related groups interested in the labor field to begin concentrating heavily on women in the workplace. Women make up nearly half of all workers, yet only a minuscule percentage of them are organized into unions. In all honesty, I must say—speaking only of my own tradition—that relatively few Catholic women take part in the Coalition of Labor Union Women and in other associations dedicated to the organization of women workers and protection of their economic rights. Similarly, any working coalition of religion and labor will have to pay significant attention to the problems of immigrant workers, the lowest paid of our increasingly low-paid workforce. Without female and immigrant workers, the labor movement has no future in this country.

*   *   *

Some might ask: Is it all worth it? One school of thought says that in standing up for labor's right to organize, those of us in the church-labor movement are beating a dead horse, or that, alternatively, the labor movement is passé. No one doubts that labor has fallen on hard times. But as for myself, I have stopped counting the number of times the labor movement has been buried in my lifetime. I am glad I didn't waste time going to its funerals.

The labor problem is not a matter of ancient history. It is an ongoing problem that calls for active involvement on the part of those who believe in social justice. While organized labor is undoubtedly far from perfect—I even have intimations at times that my own church is far from perfect—no other movement in sight would enable American workers to protect their legitimate economic interests. No other movement would enable American workers to play an effective and responsible role in helping to promote the general economic welfare both at home and abroad.

At the height of the Great Depression, in one of his many books on industrial ethics, Msgr. John A. Ryan wrote two sentences that sum up his views on labor. This is my credo, as well as his:

"Effective labor unions are still by far the most powerful force in society for the protection of the laborer's rights and the improvement of his or her condition. No amount of employer benevolence, no diffusion of a sympathetic attitude on the part of the public, no increase of beneficial legislation, can adequately supply for the lack of organization among the workers themselves."

I have spent my life saying this, in one way or another. I believe it remains true, and I hope the religion-labor dialogue will help us see the relevance of Ryan's words to the problems of today.

Bishop James Rausch and Msgr. George Higgins with United Farm Workers President Cesar Chavez

3

A Union in the Fields

Life in the Country

In 1958 Harvard economist John Kenneth Galbraith captured the mood of the times in the title of his classic work *The Affluent Society*. The book gave rise to more discussion and probably sold more copies than any other serious work on economics published since the Great Depression. One reason for its success may have been Galbraith's engaging literary style. More important, though, seemed the readiness of Americans to believe that we had finally solved the problem of poverty and indeed become a society of affluence.

As may happen when serious books become popular, Galbraith's carefully qualified conclusions were oversimplified to the point of distortion as they were bandied about the cocktail circuit and digested in overly brief reviews in the press. Many people concluded from a cursory reading of the book that poverty in the United States had almost entirely disappeared. At the time, Galbraith himself alluded to this misunderstanding and conceded that the book might have been more realistically titled, "The Quasi-Affluent Society." Galbraith's affluent society, more than he realized, was a society of wealth and poverty, side by side. He pointed to strongholds of poverty, mostly in rural areas. Yet Americans were inclined to ignore poverty in the midst of plenty, Galbraith wrote, "because we share with all societies at all times the capacity for not seeing what we do not wish to see."

Within a few years, Americans would begin to see what they did not wish to see. Many of them would do so through the illumination of the late

Michael Harrington's book, *The Other America,* which drew a stark (and accurate) picture of poverty amid plenty and heralded the so-called war on poverty of the 1960s. As for the happy 1950s, the faces of the poor and powerless were mostly hidden, and among the invisible were migratory agricultural workers. Before the publication of Galbraith's book, their miserable plight was described in a little-noticed Congressional study.

"The migrant and his family are lonely wanderers on the face of our land. They are living testimonials to the poverty and neglect that is possible even in our wealthy and dynamic democracy that prides itself on its protection and concern for the individual," the study said. "Behind the screen of statistics showing migrant labor toiling often for as little as 50 cents an hour and working only 131 days a year, we see families crowded into shelters that are more like coops for animals, with children undernourished and in poor health, two or three years behind in school, with little chance to develop their talents and become fully useful to themselves or their country. This is the ugliest kind of human waste. The plight of the migrant and his family is a charge on the conscience of all of us."

The passing of decades did not remove this charge on the American conscience. Rather recently, as a matter of fact, Americans were still debating whether the migrant laborer, even in theory, had title to some of the plainest rights of self-determination. In the early 1970s, it became clear that many migrants did not have the right to determine who could visit them, and when. In New Jersey, employers claimed the right to decide unilaterally who may or may not have access to the miserable labor camps where the migrants lived. Fortunately the state took steps to correct this intolerable situation.

And then there was the enlightened Commonwealth of Massachusetts. By law, a farm owner, if so inclined (and some were), could prevent his workers from having any visitors whatsoever, the argument being that it was his land and his property and that he and he alone had the right to say who could and could not come on it. In some cases friends and even relatives were barred from labor camps in Massachusetts under the general rule of "property rights." Social workers and even health officials had to "keep out." The director of Family Health Services for the State Department of Public Health reported that a doctor could not get in to see a man with cancer. On another occasion a public health worker and a dentist tried to visit a migrant worker, without success. When they insisted, the owner of the labor camp called the police, who sided with the owner. In response to this and other incidents, Massachusetts passed a law in August of 1971 that gave the migrant "reasonable rights of visitation in his living quarters outside of regular working hours."

Clear across the country, in the Yakima Valley of Washington State, the treatment of migratory workers was even more apalling in some of the labor camps owned and operated by the Del Monte Corporation, one of the largest agricultural combines in the United States. Del Monte officials had barred two local priests and two seminarians from giving religious instruction to Mexican-American children in six of the corporation's nineteen migrant camps. When Bishop Cornelius Powers of Yakima wrote to Del Monte, asking why religious instruction was denied these children, a top official of Del Monte laid it on the line. He said, in effect, that the company feared the priests and seminarians might say good things about the United Farm Workers Organizing Committee. He informed the bishop that Del Monte's local camp manager had the impression that the priests and seminarians "also wanted to enter employee housing in the interest of the labor union," in addition to the interest of religious education.

The same local farm manager stated the company's policy even more bluntly in a conversation with Father Francis Duffy, one of the priests turned away from the camps. When asked by Father Duffy if the farm workers themselves had no say in the matter, the farm manager replied: "No say at all."

There is a word for this. "Peon," which comes to us unchanged in spelling from the Spanish language, has taken on different meanings in different parts of the world. (1) In India, according to *Webster's Collegiate Dictionary*, it means a foot soldier, or a native policeman, or an attendant of one kind or another. (2) In Latin America, it means a landless member of the working class who is forced to serve virtually in bondage or servitude to his creditors. (3) In certain southwestern states of our own country—once part of Mexico—it refers to a person bound to service for owing a debt or a prison convict leased to a labor contractor. The second of these definitions is probably the most common of the three. The migrant farmers living in those labor camps were perhaps not peons in the strict sense of the word. That is to say, they were not held in bondage to their employers and were legally (though not economically) free to quit their jobs and pull up stakes on a moment's notice. On the other hand, it would not be an exaggeration to say that, even at this late date, the farm labor system in some parts of the United States closely resembles peonage. Call it what you will, it's dirty business. And we have not seen the last of it. Repudiated in principle, this form of neo-peonage survives in practice, in too many migrant labor camps around the country. It remains an issue for farm workers and their advocates.

The plight of the America farm laborer was not an accident of free-market economics, a problem that simply awaited the beneficent intervention of government. It was rather by design of public policy. The power and authority of the government were used in such a manner as to uphold a farm labor system based on poverty and destitution both at home and abroad. This policy was enshrined in what became known as the "bracero" program. Actually, we have had two such programs in post-war history, one in the 1940s and another which ran from 1954 to 1964. Under the latter program at its peak, more than a half million "braceros" (farmhands) came to this country in one year alone. They were recruited by the Department of Labor at the expense of the U.S. government.

This particular form of welfare for the well-off made it easy for employers to live outside of the real world of labor supply and demand. Through the largesse of the federal government, the braceros were flown to the doorsteps of the growers, who benefited from a virtually unlimited supply of laborers. They worked hard, scared and cheap. With this pool of destitute workers, growers in the United States could perpetuate the extremely low standards of pay and working conditions for American farm workers. When the growers could not get people to work for next to nothing, they didn't have to pay more to attract workers (as employers in other industries had to do); they only had to call in more "guest workers," courtesy of Uncle Sam.

As it was, the growers did not have to worry themselves with most of the nation's social and labor legislation. In passing these laws, Congress had carved out an exemption for the agriculture industry. The growers could legally ignore taxes for unemployment insurance, insurance rates for workers' compensation, industrial child labor laws, and laws which guaranteed workers the right to organize into unions. All of these legislative reforms passed over the agricultural sector. Most important, because there was no floor on wages for agricultural workers, the grower could recruit workers at wages far below the level necessary to maintain human dignity.

Ironically, the American farm workers were denied even the irreducibly minimal benefits afforded to the Mexican contract workers, under agreements with Mexico. The braceros were at least entitled to (what passed for) decent housing, free transportation, and a minimum hourly wage of fifty cents for a guaranteed number of hours in each contract period. Yet, as a matter of public policy, the United States government denied American migrants even the substandard guarantees provided to the temporary foreign workers.

*   *   *

It was government that gave us the bracero program and a great servant of government who took it away. In the late 1950s, Secretary of Labor James P. Mitchell made political waves by taking on the agriculture bloc. Just before the changing of the presidential guard in 1960, Mitchell identified the commercial farm bloc as the toughest pressure group he had encountered during his eight years in the Cabinet. "The most powerful opposition I have ever seen comes not from Jimmy Hoffa's Teamsters or from Big Steel or from Republican job-seekers, but from big commercial farm groups every time legislation is introduced that would stop the importation of migrant farm workers from foreign countries," he said in a public address.

A few weeks before Mitchell took a swing at the agribusiness lobby, a committee of more than four hundred commercial growers from the Rio Grande Valley in Texas beat him to the punch by calling upon President Dwight Eisenhower, in a formal petition, to put the Secretary in his place. The petition alleged among other things that Mitchell was harassing the commercial growers of the United States for purely political reasons. "We have many, many reasons to believe," the growers told the president, "that Secretary of Labor Mitchell is using the farmers of the southwest for political reasons. Most of the time when we contact an official in Washington for relief of the harassment we are advised that Secretary Mitchell is working desperately for a spot on the Republican ticket for Vice-President." It was a frivolous allegation not taken seriously by anyone with the least bit of political sophistication. The plain fact of the matter was that Mitchell had spent an enormous amount of political capital on the cause of migratory labor.

He couldn't have expected to curry favor with the special interests when, in May 1959, he appointed a three-member commission, including myself, to investigate the bracero program. Fortunately, for the American migrant, their moral champion in government was also politically adroit. At one meeting in his office, with the other appointees present, I was pushing hard on a particular point in the commission's final report, when all of a sudden Mitchell got tough with me. "Wait a minute," he interrupted. "Who do you think you are? Do you think that just because you're a priest you could come in here and dominate this meeting?" Later on, I dropped by his office at the appointed time for a drink. "Thanks a lot, Jim," I said, alluding to the episode earlier in the day. He said, "My God—couldn't you see what was up? I was just playing a little game. Of course I agreed with you." Mitchell was playing the neutral observer, and in the end his performance on this and many other occasions paid off.

Six months after starting its work, the commission submitted a final report to Mitchell. In brief, the panel found that the bracero program—by guaranteeing the growers, at no administrative expense to themselves, a cheap and docile labor force—was having a disastrous effect on American farm workers. We recommended that the program be phased out as rapidly as possible.

When the program met its merciful end in 1964, the growers predicted in dire terms that it would be impossible to recruit an adequate supply of American workers. They said crops would rot on the ground throughout the entire southwest. That was obviously special pleading on their part. They really meant that it was easier and cheaper for them to have the government recruit their workers than to do their own recruiting from the American labor force. In other words, they knew a good thing when they saw it and hated to have it taken away from them. Most of all, they dreaded the prospect of having to offer higher wages and better conditions as the only way of recruiting an adequate number of American workers.

Since then, senators from Eastland of Mississippi to Packwood of Oregon have tried to bring back the braceros, in legislative maneuvers ranging over four presidential administrations, from Nixon to Reagan. (Senator Robert Packwood's proposal in the mid-1970s was far worse than the old bracero program, removing even the minimal conditions of decency afforded to braceros in the past.) The bracero program, however, never recovered from the blow it received from a dedicated public servant in the twilight of his years in office (and of his life, as it would turn out). Mitchell was an extraordinarily decent human being, one of the greatest Secretaries of Labor we have ever had—and a Republican!

The Church Meets Cesar Chavez

We may never have heard of Cesar Chavez if the bracero program and its dreadful system of indentured servitude had remained the norm for farm laborers. At the very least, it would have remained extremely hard to organize American farm workers. With the bracero system in force, they could easily lose their jobs to foreign workers by pressing for better conditions.

Other unions had tried to plow the fields of farm labor in the days before the United Farm Workers Organizing Committee (UFWOC). In 1946, the old American Federation of Labor chartered a union to organize what author Carey McWilliams would later describe as "Factories in the Field" (the title of his 1969 book). Seven years later, on four large plantations in the sugar fields of south Louisiana, the National Farm Workers Union staged its first major strike.

In its simple demand for the right to organize, the union had the support of a militant group of priests in the archdiocese of New Orleans. The owners were bold enough to state, in so many words, that agricultural workers had no right to bargain collectively, eliciting a response from the New Orleans unit of the Catholic Committee of the South. There was only one issue in the strike, the committee said. "That issue, transcending all others, is one on which the Catholic Committee of the South may not remain silent . . . and that issue is the basic moral right of any workers, industrial or agricultural, to organize." (By 1961, Catholic action for farm workers had become a matter of papal directive; Pope John XXIII devoted an entire section of his encyclical *Mater et Magistra* to the need for organization of rural and agricultural workers.)

Yet despite the stirrings of farm labor in south Louisiana and a few other places, the farm workers remained un-organized until they began to organize themselves.

Born to a migrant family near Yuma, Arizona, Cesar Chavez took part in his first strike in 1949, when several thousand cotton pickers (led by the AFL union) walked out of the fields in protest of a deep cut in their wages. Shortly afterward, Chavez crossed paths with a group of priests who ministered to the rural poor. One of those priests, Rev. Donald McDonnell, a long-time activist in the San Francisco archdiocese, went knocking on doors in the San Jose barrio of Sal Si Puedes ("leave if you can"), and one of the doors was Chavez's.

The priest told Chavez about the church's teachings on labor, beginning with Pope Leo XIII. "I would do anything to get Father to tell me more about labor history. I began going to the bracero camps with him to help with the Mass, to the city jail with him to talk to the prisoners, anything to be with him," Chavez recalled in an interview with his biographer, Ronald B. Taylor (*Cesar Chavez and the Farm Workers*, 1975). McDonnell also introduced Chavez to the community organizing techniques of Saul Alinksy, the master activist from Chicago. It was Chavez's genius to translate those techniques into the formation of a union.

In September of 1965, quoting Pope Leo XIII, Chavez convinced farm workers to go out on strike against the grape growers. No one had reason to believe that Chavez would prevail. In fact, when he led his Mexican-American workers out of the fields, there was every reason to fear that he was leading them over an economic cliff. Yet in Holy Week of 1966, Chavez and the farm workers scored their first major victory in the drive to organize California's massive farm labor force. Schenley Industries, Inc., the primary target of the strike, recognized their new union as the sole bargaining agent for its grape pickers. Schenley was the second largest of the thirty-three grape-growing firms that were struck by the National Farm Workers Association, as it was known then. The largest firm, DiGiorgio Corporation, would soon follow.

The question of the hour was: Why did Chavez succeed, where so many other labor leaders before him had failed? "More than anything else," *Time* magazine concluded in its round-up story on the Schenley strike, "this first breakthrough in the bitter fight between growers and workers . . . had been achieved by the massive support given to the strikers by California churches." Chavez himself referred to church backing as "the single most important thing that has helped us."

Maybe so. For my own part, however, I am inclined to think that Dick Meister of the *Herald Tribune* came closer to the truth when he gave the lion's share of the credit to Chavez himself. Chavez, he wrote, "grasped the essential fact that if something was to be done, it would have to be done differently. Carefully, he put together, not a union, but a community organization." Indeed, for three years Chavez gathered the Mexican-Americans in Delano, a little town in the heart of the vineyard area, into a closely knit group. He established a credit union from which his farm workers could borrow the money so often needed to tide them over. His members also found that by banding together, they could pool their resources and buy the things they needed at discount prices. In short, the Delano workers learned what outside union organizers had never been able to teach them. They learned the lesson of solidarity, and they practiced it daily in the affairs of their own association. After three years, they began asking the inevitable question: If unity could bring them cheaper automobile tires, why not better wages and working conditions as well? The strike soon became as inevitable as the question.

I had heard much about Chavez, though most of the news was second-hand, often through whatever press reports I came by in Rome, while attending the Second Vatican Council. Not until the summer of 1967, when I met Chavez and heard him speak in Boston at the convention of the National Catholic Social Action Conference, did I really get the measure of the man. My impressions at the time reflected the general optimism surrounding Chavez and the future of farm workers.

"He is an extraordinarily gifted leader possessed of a happy combination of unbending toughness and calm serenity, organizational shrewdness and prophetic vision, dead seriousness and a saving sense of humor—and of legitimate pride in his own Mexican-American heritage coupled with a remarkable degree of personal humility," I wrote shortly afterward. "It has been a long time since the United States has produced a labor leader of comparable stature. He is a great credit to the movement—which owes more to him for his example of dedicated and courageous leadership than he owes to it—and a tremendous credit also to the Mexican-American community from which he comes and to which he is so deeply devoted."

Yet even amid the hope and cheer, I could not ignore the warning signals down the road. "Cesar Chavez, then, has demonstrated, at least on a small scale, that it is in fact possible, after all these years, to organize farm workers into a viable union and to negotiate collective bargaining agreements with powerful growers in spite of the fact that the workers he represents are not covered under the terms of the National Labor Relations

Act and comparable legislation at the state level," I said in my column. "It is extremely doubtful, however, that he will be able to complete the job of organizing the nation's agricultural workers unless and until their right to organize and bargain collectively is effectively guaranteed by law."

As things turned out, Chavez would find it hard to complete even the job of organizing California's agricultural workers. Just as I spent most of the first half of the 1960s in Rome, so would I, unfortunately, spend most of the first half of the 1970s in California. It was unfortunate in that I and many other church people would have had no business there if the growers had recognized the wisdom and necessity of settling their differences with the farm workers at the collective bargaining table.

In their campaign against unionism, growers found aid and comfort in U.S. labor law. When the National Labor Relations Act was enacted during the New Deal, congressional leaders, under what must have been terrible pressure from influential growers, gave no plausible reason for specifically excluding farm workers from the law's coverage. Even Chairman William Patrick Connery of the House Labor Committee, a progressive leader in Congress during the Great Depression, could come up with nothing better than a lame excuse. "I am in favor of giving agricultural workers every protection, but just now I believe in biting off one mouthful at a time," said the Massachusetts Democrat. "If we can get this bill through and get it working properly, there will be opportunity later . . . to take care of agricultural workers."

That was 1935, and the nation's agricultural workers still haven't been "taken care of." In the 1970s, not even overwhelmingly pro-union votes in secret-ballot elections managed to bring growers to the bargaining table. If those votes were tallied in another industry, the employers would have had no choice but to recognize the union. But workers in the agricultural sector enjoyed no such protection under the nation's labor law. Against the combined force of law and commerce, Chavez enlarged his strategic field. One tactic that he used effectively, and famously and controversially, was the boycott. (Complicating matters, Chavez dropped the effort to bring farm workers under federal labor law; he reversed course when he realized that the 1947 Taft Hartley Act banned "secondary boycotts," one of the tools in his arsenal.)

*   *   *

Chavez turned to the National Conference of Catholic Bishops, asking for its support of the California grape boycott. The bishops could have taken their cue from Msgr. John A. Ryan and his article on labor unions in the original *Catholic Encyclopedia*, published in 1910. The first director of the bishops' social-action department took the position that a boycott is legitimate "when the injustice inflicted by the employer is grave, and when no milder method will be effective. To deny this would be to maintain that the employer has a right to pursue his advantage in an unreasonable way, and immune from reasonable interference. The laborers are endowed with the same right of seeking material benefits on reasonable conditions and by reasonable methods; in this case the boycott is a reasonable method." In my judgment, the California grape boycott provided a case in point. It had one and only one purpose: to persuade the growers, at long last, to recognize their workers' right to organize. Yet the bishops, at least initially, decided on a different course of action.

Before the bishops gathered for their annual conference in 1969, I drafted a statement on the farm labor problem, including a supportive reference to the grape boycott. At the November meeting, two California bishops, now deceased—Bishop Hugh Donohoe of Fresno and Archbishop (later Cardinal) Timothy Manning of Los Angeles—said that the bishops would perform a better service if they put off a statement on the boycott and offered their services in some way as mediators between the farm workers and the growers. The two bishops wanted to try their hand at bringing the parties together.

With some reservations, I withdrew the pro-boycott resolution and hastily arranged for Donohoe to meet with William Kircher, the AFL-CIO's director of organization and the farm workers' best friend in organized labor. Kircher was also a committed Catholic, deeply concerned about the church's role in the dispute. From his private meeting with the Fresno bishop emerged the idea of a committee that would offer to mediate the dispute.

By the time the bishops adjourned their meeting, Cardinal John Dearden of Detroit, then president of the conference, had appointed the Bishops' Ad Hoc Committee on Farm Labor. The committee included Manning and Donohoe, the two Californians who slammed the brakes on the boycott resolution. The other members were Bishop Joseph Donnelly of Hartford, Connecticut; Bishop Humberto Medeiros of Brownsville, Texas, who had worked among Chicano farm workers and later became archbishop of Boston; and Bishop Walter Curtis of Bridgeport, Connecticut, an active member of the bishops' Social Action Committee.

Significantly, the committee chose Donnelly rather than one of the California bishops as chairman. An auxiliary bishop in the Hartford archdiocese, Donnelly had gained renown as a leading "labor priest" and served for many years as chairman of the state mediation board in Connecticut. He asked me to serve as staff advisor to the committee, which became, for all practical purposes, a committee of three—Donnelly, myself, and Msgr.

Roger Mahony, a Fresno priest and future archbishop of Los Angeles who acted as our field secretary in California.

It was Donohoe and Manning, after urging mediation rather than advocacy, who were supposed to lay the groundwork for talks in California. In January, Donnelly asked me to find out what they had done, and I had to report to him, in all honesty, that they had done nothing. "Well, that's all I need to know. I didn't want to move in unless these two California bishops weren't going to do anything," Donnelly told me, and he moved swiftly. Within a week or so, Donnelly called a meeting of the committee in California. And within days of that first session, the committee arranged a meeting between Chavez and the major growers in the San Joaquin Valley. That was the first of a seemingly endless series of meetings with growers up and down the valleys of California, individually and in groups, as well as with Chavez and his people.

In the beginning the reception was hesitant. We had to assure the growers that the committee had no plan or desire to play an adversarial role. We told them that we did not go to California to beat the drums for Cesar Chavez and the farm workers nor to oppose the growers. We offered to help the parties come together around the negotiating table and hammer out contracts. At the same time, we made it clear to the growers that the church could not remain basically neutral.

I, for one, did not go to California as a neutral bystander on the major ground of farm labor dispute—the right to organize and bargain collectively. (It seems to me that no one who speaks for the social tradition of the church can or should claim neutrality on this matter.) Most of all, we stressed that the only way out of the farm labor crisis was for growers and workers to sit down together and negotiate bona fide collective bargaining agreements. The organization of farm workers was only a matter of time, we told the growers. We said they might as well reconcile themselves to dealing with the one union that can legitimately claim to represent their workers, the United Farm Workers Organizing Committee.

Not all of the growers opposed a union in principle. Some of them felt they had been burned in negotiations that broke down the year before. They accused the UFWOC of holding circus-like negotiations, with twenty or thirty union people in the room at the same time. The union, they said, did not negotiate—it made demands. At the same time, growers admitted to us that the grape boycott was hurting them badly. They indicated a willingness to negotiate as long as the bishops' committee sat in on the meetings. The first offer of this kind came from Lionel Steinberg, owner of the largest table-grape farm in the Coachella Valley. In April of 1970, Steinberg signed a contract with Chavez in a widely-publicized ceremony at the chancery of the Los Angeles archdiocese. Soon afterward, other Coachella growers came to the bargaining table, one by one, and agreed to recognize the farm workers.

As things began to settle in Coachella, orchard workers struck in the San Joaquin Valley. There, a big, tough-talking farmer named Hollis Roberts owned a peach, plum and vineyard operation south of Fresno. He and his wife had fled the Dust Bowl during the Depression, so poor that when they reached California, they worked together in the fields, picking cotton and fruit crops. Roberts worked his fields into a farming empire, and when his workers signed up with Cesar Chavez, he became one of the union's fiercest adversaries.

Roberts branded Chavez a communist agent. He called the UFWOC a menace to the free market system. He said he would sooner sell off all he owned than enter into an agreement with the union. Yet the cigar-chomping farmer was also a man of surprises. When the strike began to threaten his crop, he decided to meet with Dolores Huerta, the union's relentless chief negotiator. And just before the contract was signed, Roberts—a Protestant fundamentalist—asked the Catholic bishops to step in and observe the last stages of negotiations.

When we arrived at his sprawling ranch for the final session, I wondered for a second if we were in the right place. The scene was unlike any other during the usually tense negotiations with growers: Chavez and his aides, with their feet up on the ostentatious coffee tables, everyone looking relaxed and having a drink. Roberts was circulating among the guests, and we were curious. What had changed his mind? "Well, I'll tell you, Reverend, I learned I was wrong. I learned that Cesar Chavez is not a communist, that he is a God-fearing, Christian gentleman," Roberts explained. "And besides," he said, after a meaningful pause, "I can't get anyone to pick my goddam peaches and plums."

As years passed and other growers went back on their word, Roberts kept faith with the union. His change of heart provides a lesson in how confrontation may sometimes go hand in hand with the goal of cooperation between workers and employers. To put it simply, sometimes you have to make it hard for the Hollis Roberts' of this world to harvest their peaches and plums. Or their grapes, in the case of the Delano growers, the original target of the grape strike by Mexican and Filipino workers.

In July of 1970, the five year old Delano grape strike ended in an historic settlement with the valley's twenty-six grape growers. In addition to recognizing the union, the growers settled for a pay rate of $1.80 an hour, forty cents more than what the farm workers originally demanded. They also agreed to pay another ten cents an hour into the Robert Kennedy Health and Welfare Fund for farm workers and their families. The Delano settlement, added to the agreements with the Coachella and Arvin valley growers, brought more than three-quarters of the state's table-grape harvest under the collective-bargaining umbrella of the farm workers. It would turn out to have marked the high season of organizing for farm laborers in the United States.

*   *   *

The bishops' ad hoc committee kept talking to growers, farm workers and labor leaders, holding literally hundreds of sessions in the early 1970s. From that point on, however, the settlements became few and far between. Old battles returned and new ones flared on many fronts.

Sad to say, a tiny but boisterous segment of the Catholic clergy took their place among the union's most obsessive critics. One of them, a priest in Milwaukee, published a petulantly anti-Chavez booklet entitled *Battle for the Vineyards*, widely distributed by growers and plugged by conservative politicians on network television programs. The 1969 booklet by Cletus Healy, a Jesuit priest, was drawn from a series of articles in *Twin Circle*, a conservative Catholic newspaper published on the West Coast.

In the interest of full disclosure, I should acknowledge a personal reason to recall this particular tract. In a laudatory introduction to the booklet, then Father Daniel Lyons, founder and editor of *Twin Circle*, wrote that when Healy's articles first appeared in the newspaper they were "sensational because Catholics had been nurtured on the writings of men like Monsignor George Higgins, Social Action Director of the National Catholic Welfare Conference, who has been leading Catholics to believe for the last twenty years that every union operates on the highest principles of justice, represents the vast majority of workers in any industry, and has the good of the workers at heart above all else. This is sometimes not the case."

Truth and modesty compel me to say that the number of Catholics who had been "nurtured on the writings of men like Monsignor George Higgins" was undoubtedly much smaller than Lyons (a former Jesuit) had made it out to be. In any event, whatever their number, I trust that they were shrewd enough to understand that my occasional writings on the subject of labor-management relations were quite beside the point. The issue was the right to organize. On that issue, one might think that Healy and Lyons, whatever their opinion of Cesar Chavez and the farm workers, would have been prepared to admit that collective bargaining between growers and farm workers was legitimate and perhaps even desirable. They were prepared, however, to admit nothing of the kind.

On the contrary, they went to considerable lengths to persuade their readers that unions and collective bargaining in agriculture, and presumably in a number of other industries as well, were something to resist. Furthermore, as Healy wrote, the union-free arrangement in agriculture was completely satisfactory from every point of view and "far closer to the Catholic ideal" than what was being proposed "by people who fancy themselves as champions of 'Catholic social thought.' " In other words, Healy and Lyons opposed not only this or that particular organizing effort in the field of agricultural labor. They positioned themselves against the very idea of trying to organize farm workers under any and all conditions.

Yet Healy's principled opposition to labor unions seemed less odious than his persistent efforts to smear the personal reputations of Chavez and his community-organizing mentor, Saul Alinsky. Even Healy's fellow Wisconsinite, the late Senator Joseph McCarthy, would have blushed to sign his name to the following paragraph:

"From studying the two men (Chavez and Alinsky), it is evident that Alinsky's influence on Cesar Chavez has been considerable. But is it communist? There is more than enough evidence to warrant the question, but most people have fallen short of calling Alinsky a communist. After watching Alinsky's recent performance at Syracuse University, however, the mayor of Syracuse complained that Alinsky's function in their War on Poverty program seemed to be to train agitators and to teach Marxist doctrines of class conflict." Healy went on to say: "I read Alinsky's *Reveille for Radicals*. I saw nothing in the book that would contradict the mayor's analysis. I saw much that would corroborate it—very much. In my opinion, there is much about Chavez's conduct to betray an Alinsky influence." So while not prepared to test the libel laws by saying point-blank that Chavez and Alinsky flew the red flag, Healy was perfectly willing to leave the fuzzy impression with his readers (and television audiences) that they were in fact communists.

(This fixation on Alinsky, by Healy as well as other critics of the farm workers, was a curious and ironic feature of the farm labor dispute. As a matter of fact, Alinsky had tried to dissuade Chavez from turning his community organization of field-workers into a union. Alinsky argued that the community model provided their most effective tool. Chavez broke with Alinsky on this issue and proceeded to organize the first viable union of field workers in American agricultural history. Furthermore, I enjoyed a close friendship with Alinsky for more than twenty years, and—just for the record—I know he was no more Marxist than his close friend and "spiritual mentor," as he once described him—Catholic theologian Jacques Maritain.)

Five years later, Healy published a sequel, *Why Chavez Does Not Deserve Support*, from articles originally in *The Wanderer*, a national conservative Catholic newspaper. With all due respect, I must say that with this publication, Healy went off the deep end. He tried to argue—so help me—that the ultimate goal of Cesar Chavez and the farm workers was to "destroy the grower and to take the territory back for Mexico."

As busy as Healy was, grinding out his tracts on the evils of the UFWOC, he was not the most prolific of the anti-Chavez priests. That distinction belonged to his then fellow Jesuit, Lyons, who probably spread more disinformation about Chavez and the farm workers than anyone else in the fourth estate. Editor of *Twin Circle*, Lyons wrote and commissioned countless attacks on Chavez. In one unbelievably shoddy performance, a correspondent presumably went to see Chavez in the hospital after one of his fasts, and came away with this gem: "I noticed a rosary dangling from above Cesar's head, high on the exercise bar of his hospital bed. It never occurred to me until much later that the location was unusual—much more conspicuous to a visitor than useful to a patient with a bad back. Most Catholic patients I have visited keep their rosary under the pillow." (The point of this exercise in religious sociology, of course, was to impugn Chavez's personal faith and motives.) After leaving *Twin Circle*, Lyons renewed his broadsides against Chavez as a regular columnist for the *National Catholic Register*. In one of them, he accused Chavez of hoodwinking the bishops into endorsing (in 1973) a new grape and lettuce boycott.

There were others.

In the mind of Father Donald Happe, the bishops had broken faith with the Spanish-speaking of America when they lent their support to the UFWOC. He said that Chavez could not speak credibly for any group of Latinos. Who could? The answer, wouldn't you know, was the thirty-fifth president of the United States. Referring to his connections in the White House, whatever they may have been, Happe claimed in the pages of *The Wanderer* to have known "for certain that President Nixon genuinely desired to open up every opportunity for the Spanish-speaking . . . and to assist them in removing traditional obstacles."

This was the same president who went out of his way to let it be known that he was eating grapes during the farm workers' original table grape boycott, whose Pentagon bought tons of grapes in an effort to neutralize the boycott, and whose secretary of agriculture, Earl Butz, publicly urged the American people to eat more lettuce once the boycott had extended to that product. (Later on, Nixon's associates, notably Charles Colson, would play footsie with the Teamsters in a ruthless and disgraceful campaign to destroy the farm workers' union.)

Another priest, a Franciscan from Paterson, N.J., wandered into the lettuce fields of Salinas and Soledad. He took a look around and managed to conclude that the UFWOC's charges of child-labor violations (confirmed by independent studies) were a fabrication. In the fields of his dreams,

Father Joel Munzing revealed in a "confidential" memo sent to all the bishops, "I never saw any worker who appeared underage."

In a certain sense, the frustration of anti-Chavez Catholics was understandable. If you were a Catholic who detested the farm workers, you had to look far and wide for affirmation by any kind of spiritual authority. Pope Paul VI had extended his blessing to the farm workers in a private audience with Chavez. The American bishops' position was a matter of record. Even so, the *National Catholic Register* found an ecclesiastical voice in the bishop of West Texas—the Episcopal bishop, that is, who had resigned from all committees of the Texas Council of Churches in protest of its vote to support the boycott of lettuce and grapes. The *Register* proclaimed the resignation "a ray of sunshine" stealing through "the lowering clouds to assure us that, sundry indications to the contrary, God's in his heaven and all's right, fundamentally, with the world." In fact, the newspaper exulted, the Texas announcement was so comforting that "we lifted our bruised and battered head and broke into cheerful if tuneless song."

I must admit that while I personally know a number of farm workers whose heads were "bruised and battered" in the heat of the California farm labor dispute, I was not aware that the staff of the *Register* had suffered a similar fate. Be that as it may, their joy over the bishop's protest was not completely unalloyed. "Our only regret is that the bishop in this case was not a Roman Catholic," the newspaper ruefully admitted. This seemed to confirm the biblical dictum that, while God is still in his heaven, his inscrutable ways are not always our ways, and, in this particular case, not the ways of the *National Catholic Register*.

The Catholic critics of Chavez and company were at least tempered by the fact that the church's highest authority had blessed the aspirations of the farm workers. The more plentiful secular critics had no such inhibitions. One of the loudest of these, Ralph de Toledano, disseminated many rumors through his book *Little Cesar*, a nasty little diatribe against Chavez, published in cooperation with the so-called National Right to Work Committee.

One rumor, silly in retrospect but maddening at the time, had it that Chavez slipped out from his twenty-five day fast to get a bite to eat. Another outlandish rumor had to do with the bishops' committee. According to one of de Toledano's nameless "informants," Chavez was turning over to the Catholic Church money that the growers were required by contract to contribute to the union's social-welfare program. Chavez was doing this as a kind of under-the-table pay-off to the bishops for favors rendered to the farm workers, according to de Toledano's rumor mill.

*　　　*　　　*

As galling as the Healys and de Toledanos could be, Chavez and the Farm Workers never lost sleep over them. The same, however, could not be said about one large and powerful institution. The International Brotherhood of Teamsters were no strangers to California agriculture, having organized workers in the packing houses and sheds. Yet they had stayed out of the fields—that is, until the farm workers turned the corner in their long fight with the Delano grape growers. On the night of the Delano victory, word came that the Teamsters had signed thirty back-door contracts with lettuce growers in Salinas, covering five thousand fieldworkers. Quickly, the bishops' committee arranged a jurisdictional pact between the two unions. But the agreement fell apart in ten days, setting off a new war in the California vineyards.

April 15, 1973, was, in my mind, one of the darkest and most shameful days in American labor history. On that day, the Teamsters signed "sweetheart" contracts with thirty grape growers who had been under contract for three years with the United Farm Workers (by that point no longer an organizing committee but a full-fledged affiliate of the AFL-CIO). Several months before, the Teamsters had secretly negotiated contracts with one hundred and seventy-five lettuce growers in California. By their own admission, however, the Teamsters had never held a meeting of the farm workers whom they claimed, incredibly, to represent. Obviously, the growers used the Teamsters to avoid having to deal with a legitimate union of farm workers.

Teamster leaders were boorishly honest about their intentions. Fresh out of prison and posturing to recapture the union's presidency, Jimmy Hoffa had predicted that the Teamsters would put Cesar Chavez and the Farm Workers out of business. "We will fight Chavez just like we fight employers—until we win, and we will win," he said in a speech at Stanford University on February 20, 1973. (According to the newspaper reports, Hoffa drew boos and hisses from a crowd of some two hundred students.)

Teamster president Frank Fitzsimmons, an old friend of mine, began making for public consumption the kinds of inflammatory statements that I had heard in our heated personal exchanges. Fitzsimmons said he would never negotiate with the farm workers because Chavez, in his mind, was not a real trade unionist. "I wouldn't even let him be a janitor in a trade union office," he said in an interview with Dick Lyneis, a highly respected labor reporter for the Riverside (California) *Press Enterprise*. "Chavez is leading a cause, not a trade union, and his cause has nothing to do with the welfare of the Mexican-American worker. His cause, his teachings, and his ideals have all been taken from Saul Alinsky and his brand of Marxism." Once again, the spectre of an imaginary Saul haunted the farm labor dispute, although by that point the great Alinsky was no longer with us.

During the UFW's most desperate struggle for its existence, I broke my golden rule of cooperation with organized labor by plunging into a dispute between unions. From the beginning I tapped whatever good will I had in the labor movement, called in all I.O.U.'s, and seized every opportunity to oppose the Teamsters and bid unions to stand behind the farm workers. With the Teamsters, it was strictly open warfare. I made no apologies for this, except perhaps for a half-hearted apology, in passing, while giving what was supposed to be a sermon at the annual mass of the Chicago Building Trades Council.

I started off by telling the congregation that nothing caused me more pain than to get into a quarrel between unions. I also praised the AFL-CIO's Executive Council for having voted, a few days before, to provide a strike fund of $1,600,000 to the farm workers (a fund which, regrettably, would have to be used to fight another union). But I added that I, for one, would not be able to support the labor movement in this case unless the entire movement came down squarely on the side of the farm workers, the most exploited workers in the American labor market. I later released an edited transcript of the sermon in the form of an open letter to the American labor movement, saying in part:

"The argument is being used that some other union with more muscle, more money, more power, more political influence . . . could do more for these people economically than the UFW would be able to do for them. That's a phony argument. Clearly aside from the fact that Chavez's contracts are better than the Teamsters' contracts, no self-respecting trade unionist has ever judged the value of a union purely in economic terms.

"He doesn't want to be handed an increase in wages by a paternalistic employer or a paternalistic union. He wants the right to have a voice in determining his own wages and working conditions. That's what this fight is all about. The farm workers want their own union. They want a union of their own choosing. They have struggled for ten years to get such a union, and it now becomes the responsibility of the entire labor movement to see to it that this, the last of the major unorganized groups in our society, is able to achieve the same kind of rights you people in the rest of the labor movement have had for generations. This is a very important test of the credibility of the labor movement.

"My reason for making this personal plea (for which I apologize, because a sermon is not the proper place ordinarily to do this sort of thing) is to clear the record and let it be known that no one that I know of in the church is in the slightest degree interested in tangling with the Teamsters or any union. On the other hand, we are determined to do everything in our power (even if it means an all-out struggle with another union) to make sure that these poor exploited farm workers get the right to economic self-determination."

The labor movement, from George Meany in Washington to construction workers in Chicago and other unionists around the country, did come through for the farm workers. Yet the UFW did not survive because of support from labor leaders, churches and synagogues, and a generally sympathetic public. Ultimately, for all their money and muscle, the Teamsters were no match for the poverty-stricken but inspired and selfless members and officers of the farm workers.

The author of a *Sunday Times* magazine article, who prematurely announced the "fall" of Chavez in his battle with the Teamsters, might have done well to heed the words of Chavez quoted in his own article (September 15, 1974): "We have been wiped out before. . . . We have been wiped out every day of our lives—by the short hoe, by the work of the day and the exhaustion of the night. We are very experienced in this business of getting wiped out. The Teamsters can't wipe us out. We will win."

In 1976, after a few near-settlements, the Teamster offensive ended. By then, the bishops' committee had stepped out of the picture for the most part. Yet playing a key role in the final agreement was its untiring California field secretary, Roger Mahony. During that year Mahony had become a bishop as well as the first chairman of California's state agriculture labor board. (He served in that position for one year, before moving to Stockton to serve as bishop.) The law that brought the board into existence gave a shot in the arm to the farm workers. The California Agricultural Labor Relations Act required official elections, which the UFW could win, hands-down, rather than the grower-union pacts that had let the Teamsters in through the back door.

It was the first law of its kind anywhere in the United States and the product of a minor miracle worked by former California Governor Jerry Brown. The governor had brought labor and grower representatives together for a series of meetings that he personally chaired. The last session, in May of 1975, was later described by Chavez as "the strangest meeting in the history of California agriculture." Chavez was not there, but Brown connected his phone to loudspeakers in his office and put in a call to the UFW leader, because the growers insisted on knowing whether Chavez would support the compromise law. Chavez agreed to the compromise and promised to abide by its terms. The growers made the same commitment.

Within a year, the growers double-crossed the farm workers. They waged a campaign to weaken the legislation and, for all practical purposes, put the California Agricultural Labor Relations Board out of business. The law and its one-sided administration have hampered the UFW ever since.

The Golden State and Beyond

On a Sunday in August 1988, thousands of people gathered in Delano, California, to take part in a mass marking the end of a long fast by Chavez. The scene conjured up images of an earlier celebration, when Robert F. Kennedy shared communion with Chavez at the end of his fast during the original Delano grape strike. There with Chavez, more than twenty years later, was Kennedy's widow, Ethel, along with three of her children, Kerry, Rory, and Christopher. Yet unlike the time before, the farm workers and their friends had come together less in celebration than in relief. Chavez had undertaken the fast, as he explained from the beginning, to purify his own soul as well as to protest the use of cancer-causing pesticides on table grapes. By the end, an alarmingly weakened Chavez had to be assisted to the mass with his arms draped around the necks of two of his sons, Anthony and Paul. If we were celebrating anything, other than the mass, it was that Chavez had come out of the fast alive.

As I watched from the altar, I thought back to a happier moment, some fifteen years earlier, when Chavez and his wife Helen met with Pope Paul VI at the Vatican. At the time Chavez was touring the continent to drum up support for a European boycott of lettuce and grapes. I was in Rome, with Donnelly, to set up his meeting with the pope. On September 24, 1974, I spent hours on the telephone, frantically trying to track down Chavez in Europe. Finally, late in the afternoon, I got a message to Chavez—who was meeting behind closed doors with Swedish labor leaders—through the U.S. embassy in Stockholm.

For some peculiar reason I never quite grasped, Chavez disliked labor attachés, as a rule. So when the message was handed to him, he crumpled the piece of paper without reading a word of it. Back on the phone, I persuaded the American attaché to make another go at it, and the word was relayed to Chavez. The message: he had to arrive in Rome by 10 A.M. the next morning for an audience with the pope. Chavez was beside himself with excitement and, despite the fact that there were no scheduled flights to Rome, was determined to get there. He managed to arrange a rather complicated connection through London on a Nigerian jet. When he arrived in Rome, Chavez—who expected to be part of an audience of thousands—was stunned to learn that he and his party (including Donnelly and myself) would have a *private* audience with the pope.

After chatting cordially with Cesar and Helen, the pope delivered (in clear English) a brief address of welcome. He praised the UFW leader for his "sustained effort to apply the principles of Christian social teaching" and for working with the American bishops and their Committee on Farm Labor. He closed by extending his prayerful wishes for the success of Chavez's efforts. "In the spirit of our predecessors in the See of Peter," he said, "we renew the full measure of our solicitude for the human and Christian condition of labor and for the genuine good of all those who lend support to this lofty vocation." During the customary exchange of gifts, Chavez presented the pope with the UFW flag. "What does *huelga* mean?" the pope asked, pointing to the word above the black eagle on the red flag. "It means strike," his aide replied, and the pope, in good humor, threw his hands up in the air: as it happened, it was one of those weeks in Rome in which almost everyone seemed to be on strike.

The next day, Chavez was greeted with an extraordinary reception by the Holy See. At the headquarters of the Pontifical Commission on Justice and Peace, leaders of Rome-based international religious orders turned out for a gathering held especially for him. There, one of the most influential men in the Roman curia delivered a remarkable message of support for Chavez and the cause. "We are all, indeed, grateful to Mr. Chavez for the lesson which he brings to our attention. It is a very important lesson: to know how to be conscious of the terrible responsibility that is incumbent on us who bear the name 'Christian.' His entire life is an illustration of this principle," said Archbishop Giovanni Benelli, then the Vatican's under-secretary of state and one of Pope Paul's closest advisors.

A decade and a half later, ending his third and longest fast, Chavez was still promoting his boycott of table grapes. This time, however, fewer people were listening. The fact that the farm workers had a new grape boycott would have come as news to most Americans in the 1980s and 1990s. The reason for this had less to do with any flaws in UFW strategy than with consumer boycotts in general, which have multiplied to a point of diffusing their appeal. In the lobby of the AFL-CIO building in Washington, a visitor can pick up a list of national boycotts endorsed by organized labor; it numbers a few dozen or so at any given time. Apart from when I drop by the AFL-CIO, I never hear of these boycotts, and I would guess that neither do all but an tiny portion of the American public.

I should admit here that I have never been an enthusiast of boycotts, despite my support for a few of the major ones over the years. They tend to have an almost hypnotic effect on the boycotters, appearing far more effective than reality would suggest. This illusion of efficacy seemed to have taken hold during the labor movement's boycott against J.P. Stevens, the union-busting apparel company in the south.

Unions have credited the boycott with eventually forcing a settlement in that bitter dispute in the 1970s. Activists were enthralled by the idea of housewives marching into department stores with a long list of the one hundred and fifty or so Stevens products, investigating labels and brand names and shunning the forbidden underwear, socks and bedsheets. In fact, the Amalgamated Clothing and Textile Workers, which spearheaded the boycott, exerted its greatest influence through the use of union pension funds. The labor movement, in effect, told banks in the southeast: put pressure on Stevens, or we'll pull out our pension funds. This, more than the boycott, drew Stevens to the bargaining table.

On the other hand, the old boycott campaigns of the farm workers proved uniquely effective. This was due not only to the wide popularity of the UFW but to the relative simplicity of the union's boycotts. Table grapes made for an easy target. No one ever went to great inconvenience by having to pass them up at the grocery. In elegant homes from Long Island to Long Beach, stylish friends of farm workers would throw grape-free cocktail parties. The agriculturally correct would invite guests to donate one hundred dollars to "Cesar's cause" and pledge never to indulge in this fruit of the vine. Quite possibly, though, the only grapes they ever consumed were of the kind that ended up in their wine glasses. In other words, it was no great sacrifice and an easy way to exercise the self-styled social conscience.

*   *   *

These days, when people ask me how things are going with the farm workers, I have to tell them I really don't know. I do see Chavez a few times a year, usually after meetings of the Robert F. Kennedy Memorial Fund, a social welfare fund jointly administered by farm workers and growers (which I have chaired from the beginning). Our conversations are fairly general and rarely, if ever, touch on union business. Apparently I am not the only one who feels somewhat out of the UFW's loop. Long-time friends of the movement, whether rightly or wrongly, have remarked that the UFW of today seems distant and removed from those who have helped the union along the way. (If so, the remoteness is perhaps symbolized by the union's out-of-the-way headquarters at La Paz, housed in a former TB sanitarium in the low mountains.) These friends, from a distance, have seen the successive departures of long-standing, dedicated UFW people who have left the organization in apparent policy disagreements with Chavez. The union, as far as I know, never explains the problems and differences. Neither do the departing staffers, who admirably remain loyal to the end.

Generally speaking, from my point of view, the problems have to do with the UFW's failure to organize new workers. At the time of his fast in 1988, newspapers reported on data compiled by the University of California at Davis, which indicated that the union had only thirty-one contracts, far fewer than the one hundred it had a decade earlier. Whatever the exact numbers, all indications are that the UFW's membership has gone down rather than up. Chavez would say that this owes in large part to an unfairly administered farm labor law in California; the union has no other choice, he would argue, but to put off organizing for another day and a better political climate. Over the years, people closer to the scene than I am (including now-Cardinal Mahony) agreed with Chavez's reading of the political situation, up to a point. Yet Chavez, it should be noted, originally organized the farm workers with no farm labor law and no agricultural labor relations board.

There are those in organized labor who look upon Chavez, unflatteringly, as a charismatic leader of a social movement rather than president of a bona fide labor union. In their view, this explains why he has lost ground over the years in the organization of farm workers. The fact is, however, that the farm workers are a labor movement and, like many other labor movements, have fallen on hard times. The question of whether the union is overly identified with a single "charismatic" personality seems beside the point.

Some labor leaders have gone so far as to tell me, usually in whispers, "As much as I dislike the Teamsters, maybe it's too bad they didn't win, because the Teamsters would at least have contracts." I disagree profoundly. A union of farm workers must be just that—an indigenous movement led by farm workers themselves. A Teamster victory would have given us nothing of the kind. I think most people in the labor movement realize this, however they may express their disappointment with the way things have turned out for the UFW.

The criticism by fellow labor leaders partly reflects the distance between farm workers and the rest of organized labor in the United States. To some extent, the distance is cultural in character. To see it, one only has to go to the AFL-CIO convention and observe Chavez, who dresses much like a farm worker, moving about in a sea of double-breasted suits. Not surprisingly, he feels and looks slightly out of place. For this, I must accept a certain share of responsibility, having encouraged Chavez, from the beginning, to work from the inside of the American labor movement. I felt then, as I do now, that organized labor in the United States has much to learn from the creative leadership of Chavez and the example of dedication and solidarity offered by farm workers.

When the UFW received its charter in the AFL-CIO, I told Chavez that it came with a price. "If you want to be in the federation," I told him, "you're going to have to be in the federation. You're going to have to take an active part in the state and regional bodies and go to the conventions." I

have often tried to interest Chavez in getting up at an AFL-CIO convention to address the delegates (which is his due as president of an affiliate
union), preferably on an issue that applies not only to farm workers but to
the entire labor movement. But he shies away, and I do not criticize Chavez
for doing so. Culturally speaking, there is a lot that stands between the farm
worker in California and, say, the steel worker in Pennsylvania.

The perception that Chavez is a lone wolf, working outside the mainstream of organized labor, has not helped him in a movement that puts a lot
of stock in teamwork. Some years ago I spoke to a large gathering of the
International Brotherhood of Operating Engineers, a rather successful
union that was holding its annual convention in Hawaii. "You fellows have
made it," I told them. "Why don't you pitch in and help Cesar?" Afterward, a west coast official of the union came up to me and said, "You're
wasting your breath. We're never going to help that guy, because he plays
his own game. . . . He doesn't play ball."

Ultimately, though, the UFW's troubles have less to do with the per-
ceptions of some labor leaders than with a certain change of political ethos
in our country over the past generation. Those who wonder why Chavez is
not organizing workers as he did in the early 1970s might do well to ask
themselves when they last saw him on the cover of a national magazine.
The plight of farm workers, quite obviously, is not uppermost in the minds
of people today.

At one time Chavez had legions of volunteers across the country, sent
around like troops into battle. College students and other young people, on
a few days' notice, would get their marching orders and move into a city or
town, find their own place to live, and start up a boycott committee. They
would show up at a church and ask: Do you have an empty office? Can you
lend us some typewriters? And they would spend several months there,
before moving on to some other place. I do not know for sure what young
people today are doing with their spare time. I do know, however, that they
are not knocking on doors for the United Farm Workers.

Whatever the reasons for the stall in organizing, the reality is that
Chavez and the farm workers have never really made it out of California.
When Chavez was on the move, I and others had realistic expectations that
he would develop substantial organizations in at least a few states outside of
California, namely Texas, Arizona, and Florida. In addition we had reasonable hopes that Chavez, in due time, would gain footholds in other migrant
states in other parts of the country.

The organization does have a few contracts in Arizona, though mostly
overlapping the ones in California. It also has a single contract in Florida,
with Coca Cola's citrus operation (where the company produces Minute
Maid orange juice). When the UFW was riding high in the early 1970s,

Coke was running its multi-racial advertising campaign about teaching the world to sing "in perfect harmony." It was not a good time for the company to contend with a (threatened) boycott campaign by Mexican-American farm workers, and Coca Cola agreed to recognize the UFW. Elsewhere the UFW has held what it calls "mock conventions" in Texas, in preparation for the day when the union wins contracts in that state.

Yet for the most part, the UFW remains a phenomenon of the Golden State since, after all these years, the farm labor problem in the United States is a vast field, barely touched by the labor movement. Even if the UFW had fifty thousand members (an extremely high estimate, from what I know), it would have just a drop in the bucket considering the multitudes of migrants all across the country, from Massachusetts, New York, New Jersey, and Maryland, to Colorado, Washington state, and Oregon.

Outside of the UFW, a young man named Baldemar Velasquez has been organizing tomato and cucumber pickers in Ohio and Michigan. A protégé of Chavez, Velasquez leads the Toledo-based Farm Labor Organizing Committee. FLOC is probably best known for its boycott campaign against Campbell's Soup Company, during the first half of the 1980s. This time, the question of whether to endorse a farm worker boycott fell into the lap of the National Council of Churches, the federation of liberal Protestant and Eastern Orthodox denominations. Taking its turn, the Council, much like the bishops' conference before, opted for the role of mediator.

The Council was instrumental in the formation of a five-member commission headed by John T. Dunlop, an economics professor at Harvard University and Secretary of Labor during the Ford administration. In 1986, the commission negotiated a settlement to the Campbell's boycott. The dispute ended in a three-way collective bargaining agreement between the workers, Campbell's and the growers who sell their tomatoes and cucumbers to the soup company. Then came an agreement with Heinz USA and Vlasic Inc. (In the course of negotiations, Dunlop's role has been utterly indispensable. Without him, FLOC would have no contracts.) The Dunlop commission, on which I serve, has continued its work, mediating other disputes between FLOC and growers in the region.

Whether in Ohio or California, the work of organizing farm laborers has become tedious and slow. The loss of momentum behind union organizing in the fields has meant a tragic loss of possibilities for the advancement of farm labor in the United States. Consider, for example, what ought to be a fairly simple moral and political question—that of whether farm workers have a right to decent sanitation and drinking water in the fields. At the rather late hour of 1986 (February 5), I and others had to go to Capitol Hill and testify on behalf of such an obvious requirement of human dignity. For fourteen years, advocates of farm labor had pressed for federal guidelines requiring growers to provide drinking water, toilets and other sanitation facilities for workers in the field. The unsanitary conditions bring on a variety of diseases among the fieldworkers.

It was but another instance of the double standard that has placed such a heavy burden on the farm worker in our country. Try to imagine the outcry we would hear if drinking water in a local bank (or in the Congress of the United States) was stored in a barrel and served in a single cup. Try to imagine the outcry if other women were forced, as happens in the fields, to go behind the bushes to relieve themselves. Yet in 1986, the Labor Department, once again, declined to issue a set of federal standards on field sanitation. Finally, a year and one day after the congressional hearing, a federal court in the District of Columbia ordered the government to do just that. (Yet to a large extent, the rules go unenforced.)

My point: if farm workers had a union, they would not have to wait around for the federal government to deem them worthy of toilets and safe drinking water. They would have means to write these and other "benefits" into their collective bargaining contracts. That is, they would enjoy benefits similar to those of the relatively few and fortunate members of the United Farm Workers.

Whatever problems the UFW has had in trying to broaden its base, the fact is that the union has significantly improved the lot of its members. UFW workers are better off than non-union farm workers anywhere else in the country. Their pay rates, though meager by most standards, run well above those of other farm workers. They have benefits such as health insurance (practically unheard of elsewhere in farm labor) and decent working conditions. Furthermore, the union has substantial funds for serving the needs of its members.

As for the future, many people believe that time is on the side of the UFW. They believe this for a simple reason: they have implicit confidence in the decency and good sense and good judgment of the American people. Americans, as one historian of the farm labor movement has written, "are capable of selfishness, prejudice and other human failings. But the value system of the United States stresses the very qualities called for by the farm labor movement: freedom of association, self-determination, fair play. It is always to the advantage of any social movement if, rather than demanding a whole new set of social values, it asks society to live up to those which it already professes."

That is what the farm workers want of American society: to live up to the values it already professes. The fundamental point remains that farm workers have a right to organize into a union of their choosing; no other union and no group of growers should be permitted to interfere with this right. For decades the agriculture industry has been needlessly caught up in the most bitter kind of conflict. For what purpose? To avoid dealing with the UFW—a union that can validly claim to represent the workers who harvest the nation's crops. The time has come for the industry's leaders to begin developing a mature system of labor-management relations. It is rather late in the game for the agriculture industry to face up to its responsibilities and opportunities—but better late than never.

The men and women of the UFW believe that they will eventually reach their goal of recognition by the agriculture industry in the United States. And if or when they do, it will stand as a tribute to the heroic commitment and determination of rank-and-file farm workers, and to the vision of a great and good man, Cesar Chavez.

Archbishop Rembert Weakland and Msgr. George Higgins with Rita Schwartz and John Reilly of the National Association of Catholic School Teachers

4

Practicing What We Preach

While the Church is bound to give witness to justice, she recognizes that anyone who ventures to speak to people about justice must first be just in their eyes.

—Synod of Bishops, 1971

All the moral principles that govern the just operation of any economic endeavor apply to the Church and its agencies and institutions; indeed, the Church should be exemplary.

—National Conference of Catholic Bishops, 1986

Are Catholic Institutions Afraid of the "U" Word?

Pronouncements like these point to a relatively recent development in the tradition of Catholic social teaching. The church has a history of speaking out on social problems and issues of justice and peace in the world. Yet only in more recent times has the church made it clear that these teachings apply as well to the workings of its own institutions. The purpose of this collective self-examination—prompted in large part by the synod's 1971 statement *Justice in the World*—is to make sure that basic human rights are guaranteed within the church itself. "No one," the synod declared, "should be deprived of his ordinary rights because he is associated with the Church in one way or another."

During the Great Depression, one of the more prominent advocates of the ordinary right to organize and bargain collectively was Bishop Bernard Sheil, the outspokenly progressive auxiliary bishop of the archdiocese of Chicago. When I was in seminary, Sheil appeared with John L. Lewis in the stockyards of Chicago, rallying support for the packing house workers. He became known all across the country as a pro-union bishop and seldom failed to live up to his reputation. Yet Sheil also had his own bureaucracy. He ran the Catholic Youth Organization and a few affiliated groups. And when his office workers decided to organize a union, he nearly went berserk. Like so many others, Sheil believed himself a good employer who treated his workers well. He wanted to know: Why do they need to organize *me?*

I would not pretend to know what was on the mind of Archbishop Francis Spellman when his gravediggers walked out of the New York archdiocese's cemeteries in 1949. But I would guess it was more or less the same question asked by Sheil. In this case, the gravediggers had already organized with the blessing of the archbishop. But they also wanted time-and-a-half pay for overtime, and when the cardinal refused, they went out on strike. It grew into a long and bitter strike, the most memorable labor dispute in the history of U.S. church-related institutions. Accounts of it appear in many histories of American Catholicism as well as of the American labor movement.

The Catholic Church of Sheil's and Spellman's day had yet to come to grips with its role as an economic actor, an institution with its own set of responsibilities in the area of labor relations. In 1986 a subsequent generation of American bishops issued a pastoral letter which, among other things, defended the rights of labor not only in the nation's economy but in the church's economic domain. But labor problems, like problems of any other kind, do not miraculously go away with the promulgation of a church document.

In the early 1990s, it was, as Yogi Berra has said, *déjà vu* all over again. There was labor unrest, once again, in the graveyards of the church, but only this time the grounds of quarrel had shifted from New York to the West Coast. There, the archdiocese of Los Angeles became embroiled in a confrontation with the Amalgamated Clothing and Textile Workers Union. The union spearheaded an organizing drive among one hundred and forty gravediggers and groundskeepers (mostly Latino immigrants) in ten cemeteries owned by the archdiocese.

The archdiocese charged that pro-union workers used lies, deception and intimidation to narrowly win an election held at eleven cemeteries of the archdiocese. The union denied the charges and, in turn, accused the archdiocese of union-busting. Whatever the case, the commotion in the graveyards was enough to wake up the dead. The ramifications of it went beyond this relatively small group of cemetery workers. The antagonism triggered a virtual collapse of cooperation between the church and organized labor in the nation's largest Catholic archdiocese.

Much of the abounding irony in this dispute revolved around the figure of Cardinal Roger Mahony. He challenged the union victory on grounds, basically, that organizers used rough tactics to win the election. In the 1970s Mahony gained a well-deserved reputation as a skillful and reliable advocate of California farm workers and their right to organize. Nearly two decades later, he became known among some labor leaders, whether rightly or wrongly, as a foe of unions. The dispute ended in October 1991 with a victory by the archdiocese; in a court-ordered election, the cemetery workers reversed their earlier vote and decided against representation by the Amalgamated union.

In this chapter, I could also point to some remarkable achievements in labor-management relations on the part of Catholic institutions. I could offer examples such as the archdiocese of New York, where Cardinal John O'Connor has been dubbed "the patron saint of hospital workers" for his support of their full union rights in health-care facilities, Catholic or other. In these pages, however, I will keep to the matter of labor *problems* in the church. I will do so because the church does not need to congratulate itself for doing the morally obvious—respecting the dignity of its workers. Rather, the church needs to deal with the problem of Catholic institutions violating—in some cases, grossly violating—the "ordinary rights" of tens of thousands of its rank-and-file employees.

The fact that the church itself has labor problems should come as no surprise. For the most part, even at this late date, church-related institutions have had relatively little experience with unions. When American Catholicism was in its bricks-and-mortar period, raising up schools and hospitals and charities at an astounding pace, the labor movement was busy organizing the industrial workplace. Only in more recent years have unions taken an interest in non-profit institutions, including Catholic ones. Partly for this reason, many Catholic administrators have not yet reconciled themselves to the existence of "outside forces" in their institutions.

Although it may be hard to understand, some Catholic administrators feel a profound sense of guilt when their workers decide to organize. I know from first-hand experience that this can become a matter of deep spiritual crisis for sisters who administer Catholic hospitals. In 1981, at a meeting of Catholic hospital administrators in Milwaukee, I saw one sister-administrator testify to this with tears in her eyes. In her religious community (which administers a number of hospitals) she was responsible for developing sensitive labor-management policies. She took pride in all she had done for her own hospital employees. One day, however, she woke up to find a union organizer at her door. Before long, the union had won an election. And she was crushed. She asked, "What did I do wrong? If we had done something better we could have prevented that, and we must go back and reexamine our consciences."

There was only one non-Catholic administrator at that meeting, and he stood up and said, "Sister, I don't know the spiritual tradition of your community—I'm a Lutheran, I know my tradition. But I must tell you— you cannot carry that kind of a burden. It doesn't mean that you failed. It means the people are doing what comes naturally for people. They're organizing. It's been done from the beginning of time. Certainly from the beginning of industrial time."

In other words, the sister had missed the point, one that resonates in the tradition of Catholic social teaching or, as the case may be, in the advice of Lutherans at Catholic meetings. The point is that people have a natural desire to take part in the constructive work of the whole community—and, in light of this, a natural right to participate in the decisions affecting their lives. For this reason, it is normal for people to enter into organizations for the purpose of collective bargaining. It is not exceptional. It arises out of our very nature as social beings. (Precisely in this context, Pope John Paul II describes unions as "indispensable" in his 1981 encyclical letter *Laborem Exercens*.) That is what the hospital workers, in effect, told the sister-administrator: "Fine, Sister. We're very appreciative but we want to have something to say about our own lives."

*   *   *

What does this mean for the labor policies of church-related institutions? The U.S. bishops spell it out in their 1986 pastoral letter, *Economic Justice for All: Catholic Social Teaching and the American Economy*. In a section on "The Church as Economic Actor," the bishops say:

> All Church institutions must fully recognize the rights of employees to organize and bargain collectively with the institution through whatever association or organization they freely choose. In the light of new creative models of collaboration between labor and management described earlier in this letter, we challenge our church institutions to adopt new fruitful modes of cooperation. Although the church has its own nature and mission that must be respected and fostered, we are pleased that many who are not of our faith, but who share similar hopes and aspirations for the human family, work for us and with us in achieving this vision. In seeking greater justice in wages, we recognize the need to be alert particularly to the continuing discrimination

against women throughout Church and society, especially re-flected in both the inequities of salaries between women and men and in the concentration of women in jobs at the lower end of the wage scale.

In recent years, events in the United States have led some observers to question the church's willingness to honor this right in practice as well as theory. One widely quoted publicist has pronounced the church guilty of hypocrisy because, in his view, "it persists ... in preaching about social justice to others and refusing to practice it itself." This writer was refer-ring specifically to the policy of Catholic institutions concerning the right of workers to organize. Other observers have written that Catholic institu-tions, as a general rule, oppose the unionization of their employees.

It is hard to gauge the accuracy of such statements, since no one knows with certainty how Catholic administrators as a whole feel about unions in their institutions. Nevertheless it would be fair to say that these commen-tators tend to generalize much too freely on the basis of insufficient evi-dence. At the same time, it would be just as fair to say that the right to organize and bargain collectively in Catholic institutions—or the propriety of doing so—has yet to be universally acknowledged. A troubling case in point: those Catholic health care facilities that have waged open warfare with their employees over this issue. Some of the hospitals have gone so far as to hire notorious anti-union consulting firms to prevent their workers from organizing.

On the brighter side, a number of Catholic institutions are facing up to the church's labor problem, realistically and constructively. They seem prepared to negotiate in good faith with a bona fide union if their employ-ees freely choose to organize. At the same time, however, they are nervous about this possibility. They fear, among other things, that unions will create an "adversarial relationship" between labor and management, mak-ing it difficult if not impossible to nurture a gospel-oriented spirit of Christian community in these institutions.

Avery Dulles, S.J., one of America's leading theologians, shares this concern. In his splendid collection of essays *A Church To Believe In* (1982), Dulles at least tentatively questions "the appropriateness of introducing the principles of trade unionism into the Church." He writes that

... in the Church, as the Body of Christ, it is important that all be governed by the law of Christ and that they look out in charity for one another's needs rather than, in self-interest, for their own. The Church is in some respects more like a family than like an industry, for in it love and a personal concern rather than eco-

nomic self-interests are determinative. It is important to preserve
the freedom of individuals and groups to serve even when the
institution may not be in a position to give what in secular areas
might be regarded as proportionate compensation. The patterns
of unionism with which we are familiar from secular life might
tend to erode values of generosity and self-sacrifice. To this extent these patterns may be inappropriate.

It is not entirely clear whether Dulles is referring here to all workers
in church-related institutions or only to priests and "religious," that is,
members of religious orders. I would agree with Dulles when he argues
that it hardly seems fitting for priests or religious to form labor unions—to
organize against their bishops or make use of some alleged right to strike by
ceasing to preach the word or administer the sacraments.

In my memory, the only move along these lines came during the tu-
multuous aftermath of the Second Vatican Council. At the time, Father
William DuBay of the archdiocese of Los Angeles unveiled a plan to organize American priests, who—in all fairness to my brethren—are not one of
the more exploited and downtrodden populations in our country. When he
made the announcement, an enterprising reporter immediately cornered
George Meany and asked the AFL-CIO president if he would grant a
charter to a national union of priests. No doubt with a twinkle in his eye,
Meany referred the matter to Jimmy Hoffa at the International Brotherhood of Teamsters. Meany was merely having a little innocent fun at
Hoffa's expense. But the Teamsters apparently took the idea a bit more
seriously. Shortly afterward, the editor of the *Missouri Teamster* wrote an
article that passionately supported DuBay's proposal and severely casti-
gated any priests who would refuse to go along with it. Yet nothing ever
came of the priestly organizing. The fathers were merely letting off a little
post-conciliar steam.

If Dulles has priests and nuns in mind, then I agree with him. I would
not agree, however, that the same applies to rank-and-file lay employees of
Catholic institutions who organize for the purpose of collective bargaining. Priests and religious are "professionals" who have freely chosen to
serve the church under temporary or permanent vows or at least under the
promise of obedience. A number of lay people, though not under vows or a
promise of obedience, also wish to serve the church for less than they could
earn in some other line of work. They should be commended for their
generosity. The fact is, however, that in large-scale Catholic institutions
with a payroll running into the hundreds and in some cases into the thousands, the majority of the lay employees do not qualify as church "professionals." Moreover, in many cases, they may not even be church members.

They certainly are not hired on the basis of their religious affiliation or commitment. Many of them do not think of themselves (and may not be thought of by their employers) as belonging to a family-style Christian community of the kind described by Dulles.

These are the men and women who mop the floors of our Catholic schools, work in the kitchens of our Catholic hospitals, and perform other tasks in these and other institutions. They have not volunteered to serve the church for "less than proportionate compensation." They are very much like rank-and-file workers in any other large-scale operation. They must punch a time-clock and submit to other personnel policies established—unilaterally as a general rule—by management. Their pay scale is also set by management. Theoretically, of course, they are free either to take it or leave it. But many of them cannot afford to leave it. They have to work to make ends meet. Finally, if the truth must be told, their standard of living, in many cases, is considerably lower than that of church professionals who act out of these values of "generosity and self-sacrifice."

This means, at the very least, that church leaders and administrators of church-related institutions must unequivocally recognize the right of their employees to organize, if the workers so desire, for the purpose of collective bargaining. Any attempts, direct or indirect, to circumvent or interfere with the free exercise of this right will predictably lead to serious trouble. Such interference could divide the Catholic community for many years to come and neutralize the effectiveness of our programs for social justice both at home and abroad. This is simply another way of saying, in the words of the synod of bishops, that "anyone who ventures to speak to people about justice must first be just in their eyes."

Two American Catholic Institutions

Questions about labor relations in the Catholic Church have tended in the direction of Catholic schools and hospitals, major institutions in American Catholicism. For some years those questions were constitutional in nature, boiling down to this: Would federal jurisdiction over labor disputes in church-related institutions violate or inhibit the free exercise of religion? God knows, the church needed to challenge the government in a whole range of matters, such as adequate health care for all Americans and our support for certain unsavory governments abroad. I did not feel, however, that church-related institutions had to confront the government on the question of whether their rank-and-file workers deserved the same protection under federal labor law as other workers. Yet Catholic schools and hospitals did just that, with differing results.

In the late 1970s the nation's highest court took up the question: Are teachers in church-related schools covered by the National Labor Relations Act (NLRA)? Early in 1979 the Supreme Court ruled on this issue. It found "no clear expression of an affirmative intention of Congress" to place Catholic-school teachers within reach of the NLRA. Furthermore, the ruling hinted strongly that even if Congress had intended otherwise, the court might have found the arrangement in violation of the First Amendment's free-exercise clause.

Constitutional issues aside, it is important to understand exactly what the high court did and did not say with regard to the right of teachers in Catholic schools to organize for the purpose of collective bargaining. The court said their right to organize for this purpose finds no protection under the NLRA. It did not question nor negate their right to organize (and, indeed, would have had no authority to do so). Yet the distinction was lost on many observers and commentators at the time of the court's decision. One widely circulated news story, typical of many others, was headlined: "Court Bans Bargaining for Religious Schools."

It was a dubious victory for the church. The court's decision, in effect, tossed a hot potato back into the hands of Catholic school administrators. The ruling did not put an end to labor disputes in these schools. What it did was eliminate one reasonable and effective way of handling those disputes —that is, through the National Labor Relations Board (NLRB). Teachers in Catholic schools could organize and carry on union activities, but they would have to do so without the protection of federal labor law. This pointed up the need for a "Catholic NLRB," some kind of voluntary substitute for the National Labor Relations Board.

The schools needed such an agency in order to handle their labor problems in an orderly manner—to conduct representation elections, for example, and to process charges of unfair labor practices. The alternative, short of willing cooperation by school administrators, was for teachers to go on strike—not a happy result of the court "victory." The National Catholic Educational Association, together with existing Catholic teachers' unions, took a few steps toward creation of such a jurisdictional board. Yet the "Catholic NLRB" never materialized. The church still needs to work up a substitute set of ground-rules for labor relations in its schools. Without it, collective bargaining in Catholic schools will never work effectively.

In the case of Catholic hospitals, the scales of justice have tipped the other way. Congress and the courts, while keeping Catholic schools beyond reach of the NLRB, have placed Catholic hospitals directly within its orbit. The approach has a certain consistency in terms of other church-state rulings.

Basically, courts have found that the distinction between Catholic schools and Catholic hospitals makes a constitutional difference. The legal reasoning, whether credible or not, is that Catholic schools have a primarily religious purpose—education in the context of the Catholic faith; health care, on the other hand, is a primarily secular activity. (Perhaps it did not occur to our judges and policy makers that the ministry of Catholic health care, too, is provided in the context of Catholic faith.) In view of this distinction, Catholic hospitals can receive government aid, while tax breaks for parents of parochial school children supposedly violate the Constitution. By this same reasoning, the collective-bargaining laws can apply to workers in Catholic hospitals but not to those in Catholic schools.

In 1974 Congress amended the NLRA to cover non-profit hospitals, including church-related ones. In this stroke of law, Congress did Catholic hospitals what I regard as an enormous favor. The amendment gave Catholic hospitals a much-needed set of procedures for labor relations. Yet many Catholic administrators (like their counterparts in other non-profit hospitals) did not think of it as a favor.

In Red Bluff, California, St. Elizabeth Community Hospital went to the regional NLRB to get its workers excluded from coverage by federal labor law. The hospital took the position that the NLRB's jurisdiction over church-related hospitals infringes upon the free exercise of religion. The regional board, however, rejected this contention. Undaunted, the sisters of St. Elizabeth took the issue to a federal appeals court, which upheld the ruling by the regional board. In its decision, the court said "there is no evidence that union activities will interfere with the religious practices of the Sisters of Mercy, since the tenets of the Catholic Church are not inconsistent with unionization or collective bargaining." The court could have added, but didn't, that Catholic social teaching strongly supports unionization and collective bargaining. It did, however, make the narrower legal point—that "Catholic doctrine does not counsel St. Elizabeth's to commit unfair labor practices or to refuse to bargain with a labor union."

Mercifully, the court spared the church the embarrassment of ruling otherwise—that labor unions do conflict with the exercise of Catholic doctrine. The hospital elected wisely not to test the issue before the Supreme Court, and church-state law in regard to Catholic hospitals has settled along these lines. Nonetheless, it was sad to see a Catholic institution resort to legalistic arguments to thwart the rights of its workers.

*   *   *

With the legal issues more or less settled, how have Catholic schools and hospitals responded to the challenge of labor relations?

At the time of the Supreme Court's school decision, an authorized spokesman for the U.S. Catholic Conference said that the agency "was and remains committed to the right of employees of Church-related institutions to organize and bargain collectively." He said the court's ruling "does nothing to change that." Two years earlier, a report issued by the conference's Subcommittee on Teacher Organizations went even further in its conclusions. Referring to the principles of Catholic social teaching, the panel encouraged teachers in Catholic schools to "examine the possibility or even necessity of collective bargaining." It further affirmed the right of these employees to determine which labor organization will represent them in the bargaining process.

Yet the U.S. Catholic Conference does not dictate the policies of Catholic schools. These are set by school administrators. There is reason to believe that the majority of Catholic school administrators are prepared to put the bishops' principles into practice, if and when the occasion of organizing arises. Some have long since done so in their respective jurisdictions, and others are in the process of doing so. I am afraid, however, that a small minority of administrators will go down fighting and adopt a legalistic approach toward unionism and collective bargaining—which, in the case of Catholic schools, means they have no legal obligation to honor the right to organize.

In the wider Catholic community there is a similar range of feelings toward collective bargaining in the schools. Some Catholic commentators have argued that "church people," faced with the problem of assuring justice and dignity to those who teach in Catholic schools, could make a big mistake by opting for solutions developed in the public school system— namely, the union solution. They frequently make the point that unions are not the "only way" to meet the legitimate economic needs of school teachers. Theoretically speaking, there is something to be said for this point of view, but as a practical matter it is somewhat irrelevant. The question is not whether "church people" see unions in Catholic schools as a good idea or whether other ways exist to meet the ordinary rights of teachers. The question is: Are "church people" prepared to support the right of teachers to form unions, if and when these teachers choose to do so?

Other Catholic opinion leaders have suggested that with unions in Catholic schools will come ideas and values that contradict or even undermine the faith. This was the gist of a back-to-school editorial published in 1988 by the *National Catholic Register* (which, since its Cesar Chavez-bashing days, has taken moderately progressive views on most economic issues). The editorial started right off with a bang: "As the new school year begins, let's shout from the housetops what's usually whispered only in the most intimate gatherings: Unions are undesirable in Catholic schools, both for the teachers themselves and for the system they serve."

I will set aside the question of whether or not unions serve the interests of "the teachers themselves," trusting that the teachers know this better than I do. The remarks about the system are what concern me here. The *Register* said, for example, that "some associations of Catholic school teachers are dominated or manipulated by public educational lobbies with secular goals. Many administrators have had difficulty correcting instructors who fail to represent Catholic teaching or values—precisely because of union agitation."

The fact is that the overwhelming majority of unionized teachers in Catholic schools belong to unions which are not "dominated or manipulated" by public school unions. To the contrary, these Catholic unions strongly disagree with their public counterparts on a number of crucial issues affecting the integrity and well-being of the Catholic school system. (Indeed, the few Catholic teachers' unions that originally affiliated with the American Federation of Teachers have since broken off ties to the union; this came in protest of the federation's stand against tuition tax credits for parents of children who attend parochial schools.) To suggest that the teachers who belong to these unions and their elected representatives pose a threat to the system is to do them a grave injustice.

I know many officers of Catholic teachers' unions. They are exemplary Catholics in their personal and professional lives. They fully understand that their organizations must take serious account of those elements—doctrinal, financial, etc.—which make church-related schools significantly different from public schools. But these differences should not be exaggerated and certainly should not be used as an argument against the organization of teachers' unions in Catholic schools. I would go further and say that strong teachers' unions, given a willingness on the part of school administrators to cooperate with them in good faith, can make a valuable contribution to the betterment of the entire Catholic school system. To my personal knowledge the officers of these unions are willing and anxious to do just that.

Catholic school administrators may not be eager to see unions in their schools. They may have honest questions about whether an "adversarial" relationship with a union will disrupt the school community. Yet, with notable (and notorious) exceptions, they do seem prepared to live with unions, if and when they have to make a decision. Experience has suggested, however, that a sizeable number of Catholic hospitals may see things differently.

In a sense, much more rides on the question of labor relations in

Catholic hospitals. With their huge staffs of professional and service employees, Catholic hospitals are far and away the largest institutional employers in the church. Not surprisingly, Catholic health care has thus furnished the setting of some of the most unpleasant encounters between labor and church-related institutions. A few years ago, a pamphlet distributed by the Catholic Health Association alluded to this problem. It said that the issue of employee rights "causes consternation" in certain circles of the association, which represents more than eight hundred and fifty hospitals and other health-care facilities in the United States.

"Many administrators believe that Catholic Church teaching in regard to the rights of workers to form labor unions . . . favors unions unfairly," wrote the pamphlet's author, Dominican Father Kevin D. O'Rourke. He was referring, in particular, to a 1981 pastoral letter of the U.S. bishops on health and health care. In it, the bishops made a moderate and temperately-worded appeal for "the full recognition of the rights of employees to organize and bargain collectively . . . through whatever association or organization they freely choose . . . without unjust pressure from their employers or from already existing labor organizations."

This pamphlet, disseminated among hospital administrators, seemed to throw its weight behind opponents of unionization. It argued that if administrators decide that unions would prove "destructive or detrimental to the good of working people," they should feel perfectly free to "discourage" the unionization of employees, within the letter and spirit of the law. In what ways should they feel free to "discourage" organizing? Some administrators have employed the services of anti-union management consulting firms to prevent workers from organizing or to help decertify an existing union. Some have run afoul of the law in doing so.

While making no mention of union-busting, the pamphlet did say that Catholic hospitals should feel free to use management consulting firms that stay on the right side of the law. Those who criticize Catholic health-care facilities for employing these firms, furthermore, "are usually far removed from the scene of controversy, know nothing about the details of the situation and manifest more enthusiasm than prejudice." Whether or not these critics are familiar with the details of hospital administration, of course, has little or nothing to do with the matter at hand: Should Catholic hospitals hire management consulting firms that specialize in breaking unions? This publication had the effect of encouraging more anti-union administrators to retain the services of more anti-union firms (the tactics of which are counter-productive in the long run, causing conflict and antagonism in the workplace). In doing so, the pamphlet did its clients a disservice by advising that they may legitimately and in line with Catholic social teaching engage in systematic union-busting so long as they obey the technicalities of the law.

Some Catholic hospital administrators, not feeling the need to hire professional union busters, have seemed quite willing to take a crack at it themselves. By way of example, let me point to the case of one Catholic hospital in a northeastern city. During this writing, I came across a series of outrageously anti-union bulletins issued by the chief executive officer of the hospital, administered by the Sisters of Mercy. Over the years, I had seen more than my share of anti-union letters and memos, but few more offensive than these. Their immediate purpose was to persuade nurses in the hospital not to join a local of the Communications Workers of America (CWA), which wanted to organize the hospital's professional employees. But the hospital fired its shots in all directions.

In one of her letters, the sister disarmingly conceded that "in the old days" unions helped their members. In fact, she went so far as to admit that some years ago, "the reputation of the Communications Workers was very good. The originators of the union volunteered their time and received no pay. I believe, at one time, they were genuinely concerned about their people." Not so today, sister hastened to add, and then proceeded to smear the union's reputation with no holds barred. In one bulletin, CWA's organizers were painted as "rabble-rousers." Moreover, unions (presumably all unions) "promote hostility so that they can continue to justify their existence." They also engage in "strong-arm, violent, and intimidating strike tactics." Unions, including CWA, were described pejoratively as "big business," their officers and organizers paid excessive salaries at the expense of the rank-and-file. "Don't forget about union dues," one of the bulletins advised. "The more you make, the more they take, just like the IRS."

It was interesting to note that the hospital's official letterhead carries at the bottom of the page this motto: "Compassion, Hospitality, Commitment to Excellence." I have no doubt that, subjectively, the administrators of the hospital had committed themselves to this laudable goal. Moreover, I could sympathize with their desire to foster an atmosphere of unity and harmony among their employees. I respected their stated willingness to dialogue with nurses about wages and working conditions. The sister-administrator even seemed willing to admit that at some point the need would arise for a professional organization in the hospital, but not one that would lump their professional employees "together with truck drivers." (Giving sister the benefit of the doubt, I assumed this was not meant to be as snobbish and offensive as it seemed in bold print.)

In any event, the trouble was that the hospital, for all of its good intentions, was unwilling to see its professional employees decide for themselves which form of organization they wished to represent them. The administrators of the hospital obviously had a right to their opinion that the institution would be better off without a union like CWA, but the almost venomous tone of their anti-CWA rhetoric was entirely unacceptable. CWA is a responsible union with a good track record of labor-management cooperation. It deserved better than to be smeared irresponsibly as a power-hungry, strike-happy organization led by self-serving, money-hungry union bosses. The hospital knew perfectly well, of course, that many of its own dedicated nurses strongly supported CWA. These nurses had reason to feel insulted when told in an anti-union bulletin that the hospital "would be better off without them." The nurses were urged to leave the hospital and go to work for one already covered by a CWA contract.

When it came time for the election, in 1990, the union lost by a few votes. Yet the hospital's tactics ultimately backfired.

Within a year, the nurses started another drive, and the hospital cranked up its anti-union machine to launch a full-frontal attack on the national CWA organization. Before the election, the hospital circulated copies of a handbill titled, "How Does the Union Spend Money?" It pulled seven items out of the CWA's national budget, including what it related as $750,000 for "purchase of Israel bonds." In bold letters at the bottom of the flyer were the words, "Would you want *your* money spent this way?" I find it hard to imagine that the hospital would have ominously called attention to the "purchase of Polish Solidarity bonds," in a city with a major presence of ethnic Poles. The ethnic and religious overtones of the bulletin alarmed many people involved in the union drive. Some of them wanted to bring Jewish organizations into the argument.

I rarely get into local disputes of this kind. But I did this time, partly because I felt it should remain a Catholic matter. On the eve of the election, I sent a letter to CWA president Morton Bahr, who, with my authorization, released it publicly. Referring to the bulletin, I said: "Its indiscriminate catch-all attack on CWA's financial integrity is bad enough, but its poorly concealed attempt to undermine the union by irresponsibly stirring up prejudice against the State of Israel is much worse. In my opinion, it smacks of anti-semitism. I have been observing the labor scene at close range for almost fifty years. In all that time I have seldom if ever seen anything quite so reprehensible." The next day, undoubtedly as a backlash against two years of anti-union propaganda, the nurses voted overwhelmingly in favor of representation by the CWA.

Instead of continuing to challenge the union, the hospital embraced the decision of its nurses. (As a result of the flare-up, I had a long and amicable meeting with the sister-administrators. While admitting to some mistakes, the sisters said that they never intended to stir up feelings against Jews or any other group and were shocked and deeply hurt by the charges of anti-semitism.) At this writing, both union and hospital had pledged to negotiate in good faith and work constructively for the betterment of the hospital.

The campaign of resistance by this hospital was not an isolated incident. I get phone calls nearly every month from union leaders wondering what to do about a Catholic hospital that has hired a firm to destroy their union. Nonetheless I am willing to make a wild prediction. Even with the best of Catholic health care, I may not live to see it come true, but I do believe that no matter how much the administrators resist, no matter how well they treat their employees, unions will not stay out of Catholic hospitals. The main reason for this was articulated by the hospital workers, referred to earlier, in their response to the tearful sister who wondered where she had gone wrong: "Fine, Sister, we're very appreciative but we want to have something to say about our lives." I am not saying that all Catholic hospitals will be organized ten or twenty years from now. But the trend will move in that direction.

Resolving the Church's Labor Problem

Fear that the Catholic Church may be honoring the rights of labor with one hand while thwarting them with the other has caused considerable unease within certain quarters of the Catholic community. Many have raised their voices to insist that the church do something about this problem. By "the church," they more often than not mean the bishops, who bear the brunt of these complaints. The situation, however, is more complicated than this may suggest.

For one thing, the simple response of blaming the bishops fails to take into account the structures of ownership and control of church-related institutions. It overlooks the fact that the largest of these institutions operate outside of their direct control. This is true of Catholic hospitals, the major institutional employers in the church. Relatively few Catholic hospitals are affiliated with dioceses (and therefore bishops), and even when they are, real control may rest with independent boards of lay people drawn from the wider community. These boards do not always see eye to eye with bishops on matters of labor relations, as I observed during a visit to Lourdes Hospital in Paducah, Kentucky.

In 1989 Bishop John J. McRaith of Owensboro (the diocese that includes Paducah in western Kentucky) asked me to sit in on a meeting of the board. The hospital's non-professional staff had voted overwhelmingly in favor of representation by a local of the International Association of

Machinists. In contract negotiations, the union was holding out for a "union shop," in which all employees in the bargaining unit would have to pay union dues. (Federal labor law requires that a union represent all workers in a bargaining unit, members and non-members alike.) The board, however, opposed the union shop, and it seemed that the workers might strike over the issue.

At the board meeting, I argued that the hospital ought to settle for a union shop. Yet as the meeting progressed, it became clear that board members were not unduly impressed with the fact that I had gone there as the invited guest of the bishop. The sentiment was, "Sorry, we're happy to have you here, but this is the way we're going to do it." The board stuck to its position and the Machinists' local settled without a union shop.

Within two years, the already strained labor relations at Lourdes took a sharp turn for the worse. Ownership of the hospital had shifted from the Owensboro diocese to the Mercy Health System, part of the Sisters of Mercy. And after repeated efforts by the hospital to weaken or abolish the union, more than two hundred workers walked off their jobs a few weeks before Christmas of 1991.

In a matter of hours the hospital's lay administrators did something which, to my knowledge, no other Catholic hospital had ever done. It hired permanent (as opposed to temporary) replacement workers, in effect firing the strikers. Meanwhile, in Washington, D.C., the U.S. Catholic Conference was pushing legislation that would ban the relatively recent practice of permanently replacing strikers. (At this writing, union and hospital negotiators remained at a stand-off.)

The vast majority of Catholic hospitals are affiliated not with dioceses but with religious communities of sisters. In some instances the nuns have lost effective control over these hospitals. This was the situation of a small Catholic health-care facility in Norfolk, Virginia, which takes care of retarded children in a poor, solidly black neighborhood. At one time, sisters formed the heart and soul of this institution. Over the years, however, the hospital had fewer and fewer sisters, and those who remained were there more or less as employees. The hospital was controlled by a board made up of lawyers and bankers and other influential people—in a "right-to-work" state with restrictive labor legislation.

Some years ago, the hospital's workers—nearly all of whom are black women—decided to organize against great odds and managed to pull off a victory in the union election. But the board refused to deal with the union and negotiate a contract, as required by law. Instead, the board dragged the argument into the courts, at great expense to the institution. Meanwhile, over a period of two years, Bishop Walter Sullivan of Richmond patiently tried to settle the problem and get the board to recognize the union. His patience, however, ran out at a board meeting in which the directors threatened to go all the way to the Supreme Court to block the union. (The hospital planned to argue the case on church-state grounds.) At that point Sullivan gave them what amounted to an ultimatum. He said that if they went ahead with the legal battle, he would be forced to go public and declare that the institution no longer operates as a ministry of the Catholic Church.

At Sullivan's request, I met at great length with one of the board members, a prominent lawyer in Norfolk. I asked him, "What's the problem? Is it financial? Are you afraid this union's going to break the hospital?" He said, "Oh, it has nothing to do with finances. There's no way they can affect our budget. They'll get the minimum wage and that's about all." I asked, "Then what's the problem?" He said, "We don't believe in unions. And we're not going to have them." (This struggle had a somewhat murky ending; as I understand, the workers did not get their union but they did get better working conditions.)

The sisters had no control over this terrible situation. More often than not, however, hospitals affiliated with religious communities are administered principally by the sisters themselves (even when a board has legal ownership of the hospital). In one case, a Catholic retirement home in a Detroit suburb squared off against a local of the Service Employees International Union (SEIU), which represented the workers there. Basically, the hospital refused to negotiate a contract with the union, which in turn had threatened a strike. When the archbishop learned of the events, he called me up and asked if I could fly out there and represent him in the dispute. Like any other bishop, Edmund Szoka had no desire to pick up the newspaper one morning and read about a strike in a Catholic health-care facility.

Instead of dealing with the union themselves, the sisters had hired a management-consulting firm to do the job. It seemed clear to me that the consultant had no intention of settling with the union. "What's the problem?" I asked him. "I can't do business with the local negotiator for the SEIU. He's hopeless," the consultant explained. I told him, "Well that's no problem. Where's your telephone?" And I called Gerry Shea, a Catholic layman who heads the SEIU's hospital unit. The next morning Shea was in Michigan, ready to negotiate, but the consultant kept dragging his feet. That was when Szoka made his move. He called up the sister-administrator and said, "Listen, you can hire anyone you want. It's your hospital. But there's not going to be any union-busting in this diocese. I want you to meet with the SEIU negotiator tonight, and I want you to stay there until this is settled." They settled around midnight. The next day, Shea and I flew back to Washington.

*   *   *

In this case, the bishop was willing to intervene and able to make a difference. That is not always the case—nor should it be. Religious orders and their institutions are legitimate zones of autonomy in the church. Their control over Catholic hospitals, furthermore, gives them a leading role to play in resolving the church's labor problem. This is simply a matter of arithmetic. Where the bishop of a medium-sized diocese may have (at most) a couple of hundred people working for him, the administrator of a medium-sized hospital normally has a couple of thousand. In Springfield, Illinois, where my parents came from, the second largest employer is the Catholic hospital. Not far from there, in Peoria, the Catholic hospital is the third largest employer. St. Vincent's Hospital may not rank among the largest employers in New York City, but its workforce of approximately four thousand dwarfs that of most Catholic institutions. In short, Catholic health care is no cottage industry. For this reason, any solution to labor problems in the church will require a special effort on the part of religious orders.

I have made this point on several occasions in talks before groups of sisters: "You're asking for leadership in the church. Well, you've got the leadership in the hospital field, and you're not doing much with it. Here's a chance for you to really step forward and show us how to do something better." At a meeting in Pittsburgh, during the question-and-answer period, one sister came out swinging at the bishops. She made comments to the effect that "the church" ought to open up its (mythical) Fort Knox and bestow all its riches upon the poor. I said, "I'd be glad to discuss the matter all evening, Sister, but before we get to that, there's another point. I don't know what religious community you belong to, but I'd be willing to bet you have some hospitals. I see sisters picketing all the time, whether it's against the California growers, J.P. Stevens or the Pentagon. But I seldom if ever see them doing anything about labor conditions in their own hospitals." In my experience, they do not like to hear this.

Sisters are not the only ones who have taken a free ride in the debate over labor relations in the church. So have the Catholic laity. I have frequently heard (legitimate) complaints about the meager standards of pay and benefits for the dedicated men and women who teach in Catholic schools. But seldom do I hear anyone make the connection between this and the evidently meager standards of giving by Catholic parishioners.

Unlike Catholic hospitals, which get federal money, the schools rely on the financial support of Catholics; the schools survive on the collection basket as well as on tuition payments. Yet as Father Andrew Greeley's studies have indicated, Catholics have a habit of dropping relatively little of their disposable income into the collection plate—relative, that is, to other religious groups. This is despite the fact that Catholics, according to Greeley's studies, constitute the most affluent Gentile group in the United States. For my part, I can name parishes all over the country in which families have three or four cars, send their children to Europe in the summer, and go to Aspen in the winter—but they don't want to pay teachers in parochial schools a reasonable salary.

Without a stronger financial commitment on the part of the laity, it will remain extremely hard if not impossible to boost the salaries of our teachers. The most labor-minded bishops in the Catholic Church have found themselves at a loss to figure out how to accomplish this, given present financial conditions. Cardinal O'Connor of New York has said publicly that he keeps asking himself whether the church has a right to run these institutions if it cannot pay a decent wage. (As a matter of fact, at this writing he had announced plans to close down at least several schools in the archdiocese.)

Some years ago at a meeting sponsored by the National Catholic Educational Association, school administrators drove home the point about diminishing resources. Speaking to the group, I made my standard pitch for recognition of labor rights in church-related institutions. The most vocal response came from people who work in the inner city: "You're going to price us out of one of the most important things the Catholic Church does. There's no way we can pay the same salaries as the public schools, and these kids in the ghettos need Catholic schools more than anyone else in the country."

This hardly means that the church should give up trying to assure the minimum economic rights of teachers and other employees. It does mean, however, that the problem will not simply be solved by "the bishops." As they said in their pastoral letter on the economy, providing adequate salaries to church employees is the responsibility of the entire Catholic community. "We bishops commit ourselves to the principle that those who serve the church—laity, clergy, and religious—should receive a sufficient livelihood and the social benefits provided by responsible employers in our nation," the letter says. "These obligations, however, cannot be met without the increased contributions of all of the members of the church."

Unions, too, have to accept certain responsibilities. For one thing, they have to take a closer look at the real financial picture of the church. They have to realize there is no Fort Knox in the Catholic Church. In fact, most of the major dioceses, including my own in Chicago, have fallen on hard economic times. Some of them teeter along the edges of insolvency. They have plunged into the open financial market, borrowing from commercial banks and paying high interest rates. This will require understanding on the part of organized labor as to what they may reasonably expect from church institutions.

Furthermore, as I have told union leaders, dealing with hospitals and other church-related institutions is not the same as dealing with major corporations. By their own design, corporations exist in large part to maximize profits. Catholic hospitals, on the other hand, exist to perform the works of mercy. Unions should always keep in mind that these institutions are, after all, religious. Unions need to appreciate the sensitive nature of certain tactics, particularly strikes, in the context of a ministry such as health care. The nature of the institution calls for a somewhat more tactful approach than when taking on, say, a textile mill in South Carolina. I am probably saying no more than any good unionist would know intuitively— that organizing a religious institution requires a finer touch. The point is worth underlining nonetheless.

Union leaders also would be well advised to refrain from moral posturing when it comes to labor relations in the church. Recently one labor leader was reciting the sins of the church in this regard, when I finally had to interrupt, "Don't get so high and mighty and pious about this. You know very well that a number of unions have caused trouble to their workers when they've tried to organize in their union bureaucracies." This is true. Religious institutions are not the only ones in the non-profit sector that at times take an ominous view of "outside forces" moving into their organization. Unions, too, are known to resist organizing when they become the target.

One well-known labor leader tells of when he took a job in the research department of a major union's international headquarters. As a good trade unionist, the first thing he did, once he got settled in, was join the union that represented the workers there. This did not sit well with the union president, who told the new recruit, "Hey, what's the matter with you? You joined the union. Don't you know I take care of my research people on the side?" It is, in a sense, a very human response: Don't I take care of you? Catholic administrators have so often asked the same question when faced with workers who decide to organize.

*   *   *

Once church-related institutions reach a point of sound labor relations (as many already have), they may discover new opportunities for carrying out the church's social mission. Consider, for example, one of the more alarming social problems of our time—the many millions of people who have little or no health insurance. Among unions, the Service Employees International Union has led the way in tackling the issues of health care policy. I know that Gerry Shea has an agenda that goes beyond collective bargaining between the union and Catholic hospitals. In a letter to the chairman of the board of the Catholic Health Association, he said that as a representative of the nation's largest union of health-care employees, "I have watched with mounting concern the recent roll-back of support in our country for a comprehensive health care system. Rampant inflation, financial squeezes, service cuts and the new proposal for drastic experimentation will sorely test the strength of our health care delivery system in the near future. I feel that all of our citizens will suffer but the poor most of all. I believe it is important that organizations such as ours . . . which have a genuine interest in and a long-standing commitment to quality health care, maintain a dialogue on the important challenges before us."

That letter was written in 1982, just before the young labor leader took charge of the SEIU's hospital unit. Generally speaking, Catholic hospitals have yet to take him up on the offer—perhaps because they would find it hard to "maintain a dialogue" while opposing the right of unions to exist in their institutions. (Needless to say, no real cooperation can exist if one side aims to destroy the other.) Yet as far as I know, the offer still stands, and it seems only a matter of time until Catholic hospitals and unions sit down and work together for the good of patients and the good of the health care system.

No doubt there are those who will honestly wonder if unions and collective bargaining are compatible with the spirit of sacrifice that marks a genuine Christian community. They will question whether the principles of labor in the secular realm should apply as well to those who "serve the church." I would ask that they carefully consider their use of the all-encompassing word "church" in this context. Large-scale Catholic hospitals and educational institutions are church-related, to be sure, but they are not synonymous with "the church." Many of their workers, as I have said, do not think of themselves as working for the church as such.

This means that Catholic institutions—hiring hundreds or even thousands of workers, Catholic and non-Catholic alike, who have not volunteered to serve the church at a personal sacrifice—should be prepared to bargain collectively if their employees choose to organize for this purpose. Collective bargaining may not be the best conceivable way of handling labor-management relationships, whether in secular or church-related institutions. But as Churchill is so often quoted as having said of political democracy, collective bargaining is better than any other system of labor-management relations yet devised. No one has come up with a more equitable way of resolving differences which are bound to crop up between labor and management in any large-scale operation.

As for genuine Christian communities, I am all in favor of them. I sympathize with those administrators who seek to nurture a spirit of community in church-related institutions. But a Christian community which fails to respect the dignity of its own employees is a contradiction of terms—or, in any event, will be perceived as such by its disaffected workers. This is not to say that workers must belong to a union in order to have a sense of their own dignity. It is to say, however, that their right to organize must be respected. Wherever the free exercise of this right is thwarted or obstructed, there can be no such thing as a genuine Christian community.

United Auto Workers President Walter Reuther

AFL-CIO President George Meany

5

Labor Leaders

The Dedicated and the Decadent

A number of commentators—usually leaning toward the left—have come up with a rather simplistic explanation for the present crisis of organized labor: the decadent leaders of the labor movement. In their view, the crisis stems largely from an attitude of complacency and lack of missionary zip and zeal on the part of labor's top leadership. The critics like to set off labor leaders of today against their predecessors of the distant past. In the old days, labor leaders were more dedicated, zealous, and self-sacrificing, we are told; now they have gone soft.

The parable of the prodigal labor leader is preached from the pulpits of many a self-styled progressive journal, religious as well as secular. The commentaries in these publications tend toward the moralistic side. Witness the lead story in the *National Catholic Reporter*'s 1990 Labor Day issue. "Labor's real problem: It's not a moral force," was the headline, with the subhead, "Venal leaders don't worry about workers." The heading was faithful to the tone of the article by former *New York Times* labor correspondent William Serrin.

Undoubtedly, of all the wayward union-leader stories, some are bound to be true. Like any other group of people, labor leaders are a mixed bunch. Some are better than others, just as some pastors are better than others and some editors of progressive journals are better than others.

A while back I read a newspaper story about the decadence of labor leaders that told of David McDonald, former president of the steelworkers. McDonald fancied himself as a man-about-town. He was a familiar face at

New York's trendiest night spots and went around with actors and musicians. In stark contrast is the union's current president, Lynn Williams. The son of a Protestant clergyman from Canada, Williams leads a simple lifestyle and exudes moral vigor in his labor work. The article I read judged McDonald on his moral qualities, which to some would illustrate the problem of venal labor leaders who fail to provide a moral force in the movement. By contrast, his successor may seem to exhibit the moral qualities needed to restore labor to its earlier position of strength.

Yet to me, the relevant point is that under McDonald the union had twice as many members as it has today. The moral of the story: in searching out reasons for labor's decline, one must look beyond the moral character and inspiration of its leaders. One must look to, for example, historic shifts in the economy, like the kinds that have displaced so many steelworkers.

As hard as it may be for moralists to admit, there is no easy connection between moral commitment and labor achievement. This bears out in the lives of not only contemporary labor leaders but the great ones of the past as well.

It would be hard to call up two figures in labor history with such differing human qualities as John L. Lewis and William Green. Lewis was the bombastic leader of the United Mine Workers who led the charge of industrial unionism during the 1930s. Green, a mine worker and member of Lewis' union, was the soft-spoken president of the American Federation of Labor during the 1940s.

A devout Baptist who taught Sunday school, Green's commitment to the labor movement had deep roots in the Protestant "Social Gospel" movement. Lewis' commitment was rooted, at least to some extent, in a lust for power. Green was kind and humble, Lewis blustering and sarcastic. Green drew inspiration from the Social Gospel vision of perfect harmony between workers and employers. Lewis preferred confrontation as a rule; he would call a strike at the drop of a hat. Green was a great believer in labor unity and wanted to make the movement respectable. Lewis cared little about labor unity or respectability, and yet he did accomplish the great feat of uniting the industrial unions.

As one could imagine, the mines were not big enough for two national labor leaders of such different moral bearings. As UMW president, Lewis stripped Green of his union membership, which left the AFL leader in a vulnerable position: membership in a bona fide union was, understandably, a minimum requirement of election to the AFL presidency. Yet in short order Green regained his status of union member in good standing. A fiddler, Green found a home in the American Federation of Musicians, keeping his position of leadership in the American labor movement.

The point I want to illustrate has to do with effectiveness. Green had the depth of moral commitment prescribed by many who have analyzed the condition of labor today. The only problem is that, compared to Lewis, he was ineffectual. Although personally sympathetic to the organization of industrial workers, Green offered weak leadership to their cause in the top ranks of the AFL (wedded, as it was, to skilled workers in the crafts). Furthermore, he never fully grasped the significance of rank-and-file militancy at the time. By temperament, Green distrusted militancy and had an implicit trust in the ultimate good will of employers, as did many others with Social Gospel leanings. In a sense, Green's moral bearing may have diminished his effectiveness as a labor leader. It may have served to hold him back as a force in the organization of industrial workers.

In the 1930s, the question of moment was not whether to stir up militancy among the rank and file. The militancy had already come to a boiling point. And the opportunistic Lewis (though a registered Republican who backed Wendell Willkie in the 1940 presidential election) ran with it. He translated rank-and-file discontent into collective bargaining contracts for workers.

*   *   *

In many ways, Philip Murray combined the better qualities of Green and Lewis, those of moral inspiration and hard-headed unionism. Interestingly, however, the accusers of labor leadership today rarely find a place for Murray in the halls of union fame. In fact, many of them count Murray among the "bad guys."

The Scottish-born Murray grew up in an isolated mining patch of western Pennsylvania. When still a boy, he took his pick and lantern and went to work in the mines. With a fifth grade education, Murray climbed rapidly up the ladder of union leadership. He went from vice president of Lewis' United Mine Workers to president of the United Steelworkers of America to, finally, president of the Congress of Industrial Organizations. (He succeeded Lewis as CIO leader in 1940.) A brilliant orator, and blessed with gifts of strong leadership, Murray presided over the CIO during a period of industrial organizing that brought the labor movement to its power peak in the 1950s.

Although a pragmatist, Murray saw beyond the bread-and-butter unionism of organizing and collective bargaining. He was an articulate and forceful advocate of the Industry Council Plan (ICP), actually less a plan than a concept of innovative labor relations. The idea called for a system of labor-management cooperation that would give workers, through their unions, real influence in business and economic planning—or co-management, as it is sometimes called. In pushing the plan, Murray drew inspiration from Catholic social teaching, at least as filtered through the ranks of the Catholic social action movement in the United States. The movement supported the ICP as a practical application of Pope Pius XI's encyclical *Quadragesimo Anno* which called for a structured program of labor-management cooperation. A devout Catholic, Murray was influenced, directly or indirectly, by the encyclical teachings, although the details of this influence were probably exaggerated by social-minded Catholics and even sometimes by Murray himself.

He could calmly resist tremendous pressures from industry and government in economic affairs, and yet was completely at the mercy of his friends and associates whenever they needed a favor or help with a personal problem. He was an uncommonly decent and humble human being, one of the least pompous and pretentious public figures I have ever known. In his later years, Murray enjoyed taking the children of his younger associates to the movies and was always as respectful toward clerical workers in his office as he was toward the high and mighty. He was a simple, practical Catholic who would no sooner think of missing mass on Sunday than flying to the moon.

I came to appreciate these qualities in Murray when I met him for the first time in 1940 during one of his frequent trips to Washington. As a graduate student of labor economics at the Catholic University of America, I managed, through the good offices of a mutual friend, to be invited to Murray's apartment for an evening's conversation—or so I had expected —on labor-management relations. We never got around to the subject. The only formal education I received that evening was an undergraduate course in poker. Mrs. Murray ended up with all the chips. It was characteristic of Murray that he was embarrassed at my having lost a couple of dollars and referred to his embarrassment whenever we happened to meet in his remaining years, which were too few. I last had the pleasure of talking to Murray ten days before his death in 1952. I called at his office in Pittsburgh, without an appointment, merely to say hello. I remained, unreasonably, for more than an hour, during which time Murray shared his concerns about the personal problems of mutual friends of ours.

In recent years the figure of Philip Murray has not received the best of press from those who dwell in labor's so-called Golden Age. Murray is often counted among the "conservative" labor leaders because of his anti-communism. Yet like the whole question of labor's anti-communism, the question of Murray's is somewhat cloudy. As a matter of fact, at one point Murray aroused considerable controversy by refusing to expel communists from CIO leadership posts. His reluctance to move against communists came out of concern for labor unity. Yet Murray, like other leaders, did eventually go after the communists, and there are those who believe he did so because of his Catholic influences. There may be some truth in this. But when Murray took on the communists, at his side, as part of his inner circle, were not Catholic activists but a few union officials including my dear and departed friend, Arthur Goldberg, who was Jewish. (Later on, after Murray's death, Goldberg drew up the legal briefs that reunited the AFL and CIO.)

In the organs of so-called progressive opinion, Murray's advocacy of the Industry Council Plan is frequently ignored or figured against him. The reasons for this are not altogether clear to me, although the whole idea of labor-management cooperation, Murray's passion, finds hostile reception in many quarters of the left. And with good reason, in certain cases. Industry leaders have tended to define labor-management cooperation more in terms of concessions by labor than as any real system of co-determination.

Yet the critiques of Murray's cooperative view cry out for historical context. In its day, Murray's plan was regarded as truly progressive. Industry leaders did not oppose the ICP because it promised to give them too much power; they opposed the ICP because they believed it would challenge their total control over business policy-making. For years after the ICP faded from the public agenda, industry leaders would sound alarms over the most remote signs of the plan's revival. In 1958, for example, the U.S. Chamber of Commerce warned in its publication *The Nation's Business* that the plan was "sneaking up on us" in the form of "piecemeal demands" by allegedly "imaginative" labor leaders. With Murray gone, the article trained its fire on the president of the United Auto Workers.

"If Only Walter Were Alive ..."

When recalling labor's intrepid past, the leftward critics of labor's present frequently invoke the memory and legend of Walter Reuther. In the United Auto Workers, the union that he led for a generation, until a 1970 plane crash that cut short his life, Reuther has become the symbol of a dissident movement. Leaders of the movement call on the UAW leadership to end all programs of labor-management cooperation and otherwise urge a more confrontational posture toward industry. An irony of this crusade is that the UAW ranks among the nation's most progressive labor unions.

"If only Walter Reuther were alive," the critics are sometimes heard to say, proceeding with any number of claims—"we would have a more militant union," "the union wouldn't make any concessions," "the workers would get better settlements in contract negotiations," and the like. For all we know, some of the if-Walter-were-alive-today claims may well be true. (Other claims, though, seem a little ridiculous. For instance, in 1987, when the AFL-CIO decided to welcome the long-expelled Teamsters back into the federation, a writer for *The New Republic* declared that if Reuther were alive, he would never have stood for this realignment with a tainted union. The writer either didn't know or forgot that Reuther once joined with the Teamsters in an ill-fated alliance—more of which later.)

Walter Reuther was a daring and imaginative labor leader, one of the great figures in the history of organized labor in the United States. Few in the history of that tradition have served the American labor movement more faithfully, unselfishly, and with greater effectiveness. Yet the UAW insurgents have tended to place the image of Walter Reuther on a pedestal, without anchoring it to the realities of his life and times.

Born on Labor Day 1907 into a family of Lutheran socialists, Reuther was a tool-and-die maker who left his home in Wheeling, West Virginia, for the Michigan industrial center. He was down-to-earth and practical, a highly skilled craftsman whose home was furnished with cabinets and decorated with splendid wood carvings made with his own hands. As UAW president, Reuther tried to move beyond bread-and-butter unionism, setting his sights on a system of profound union participation in company decision-making. The vision was of labor and business cooperating not just for themselves and their own interests, but for the good of all. For this, Reuther was distrusted and, to a large extent, feared by industry. (He was severely wounded by an unknown assailant in 1948, as was his brother Victor a year later.) With Reuther in search of new and different forms of cooperation, industry leaders never knew what he might do next.

In August of 1957, what Reuther did next was propose a two-way anti-inflation proposal in a widely publicized letter to the presidents of Ford, General Motors and Chrysler. He called for an average cut of one hundred dollars in the price of 1958 cars, in return for which, he pledged, the UAW would shape its 1958 contract demands according to the resulting financial position of the companies. Reuther's proposal, amid widespread concern over what passed for high inflation in those days, was summarily dismissed by the Big Three auto companies as a publicity stunt. Yet the UAW leader was eminently serious. His letter to the Big Three offers a glimpse of Reuther's philosophy of labor-management cooperation for the common good.

> Much is being said about the growing problem of inflation but unfortunately little is being done. We can all agree that in our free society, free labor and free management, in addition to having privileges, share joint responsibilities. One of these joint responsibilities is to find a way to raise collective bargaining above the level of a struggle between competing economic pressure

groups. We in the UAW believe that collective bargaining, to be sound and socially responsible, must serve the public need. In practical terms, this means that free labor must shape its economic demands and free management must determine its pricing policies so that they will not only protect and advance the interest of workers and stockholders but will also protect and advance the interest of all American consumers. This joint responsibility to the whole of our society and to the well-being of the whole nation transcends in importance the more narrow responsibilities that labor and management have to their respective groups.

Pressing the point, Reuther told the Big Three: "Neither stockholders nor workers . . . have a right to insist on levels of income through inflationary prices that deny to other citizens their full and proper equity in the national product. . . . Unless free labor and free management voluntarily take effective steps to halt it, and soon, the inflationary spiral will be stopped either by the onset of recession or by the intervention of government acting on behalf of a justifiably aroused people."

The foregoing excerpts from Reuther's letter can be boiled down to one basic principle: labor and management must subordinate their particular interests to the common good, not only because this is the right thing to do in itself, but also because it is the price of freedom. The same philosophy undergirded another set of proposals issued shortly afterward by Reuther. Among the UAW's 1958 collective bargaining proposals was the establishment in every major corporation in the industry of joint labor-management committees to address the issues of a shorter work week and the impact of automation and technological advance.

These were not revolutionary, or even new, demands. Indeed, they would have put into practice the principles enunciated earlier by Pope Pius XI and repeated by the pope's more conservative successor, Pope Pius XII. Around the same time, Pius XII was repeatedly insisting on the necessity of a joint labor-management approach to the problem of automation. "Recent instances show that the risk of mass unemployment as a result of the sudden modernization of factories is not illusory. A judicious participation of workers in the effort of expansion," the pope said, would not only help workers avoid this danger but would also "bring about a progressive and profound transformation of the present condition of the working class."

Yet the similarities between Reuther's proposals and the Roman pontiff's principles did not shield the UAW leader from charges of subversion. It was Reuther's 1958 collective bargaining program that brought on the U.S. Chamber of Commerce's warning, referred to earlier, that the Industry Council Plan was "sneaking up on us" in the form of piecemeal demands by imaginative labor leaders. The article said Reuther and others were seeking "business control." (Actually Reuther made no secret of the fact that he still believed in the ICP, which by then had slipped into the background of public debate. Reuther appreciated the fact that the ICP had to develop gradually and through voluntary agreements between labor and management. He opposed the idea of doing so by government fiat, believing that such a move would pose the danger of statism.) During the 1950s, scores of letters arrived in my mailbox—I stopped counting at around one hundred or more—branding Reuther a communist. One batch of letters followed almost immediately upon my appointment by Reuther to the UAW's Public Review Board (more of which in the following chapter). Many of the letters were anonymous, most of them rather venemous.

*   *   *

Walter Reuther was one of the truly progressive labor leaders, well deserving of his image as among the boldest of them. Yet some elements of this picture do not fit the image held up by latter-day Reutherites. The fact that Reuther championed the ICP is frequently and conveniently overlooked by many who attack labor leaders of today in his name. In their demands for a more adversarial stance toward industry, certain reformers typically scoff at the idea of labor-management cooperation—which, ironically, was one of Reuther's passions as a labor leader. Beyond this, although a man of high ideals, Reuther was also a pragmatist. His rhetoric was usually more radical than his actions.

For one thing, Walter Reuther was—and there is no disagreement among historians on this point—a formidable enemy of labor's communist wing. Some historians say he carried his anti-communism to the point of red-baiting within his own union. In his rise to leadership in the UAW Reuther fiercely opposed communists in the union's ranks and, after becoming president, purged them from leadership positions. In doing so Reuther was glad to have the support of the Catholic social action movement, particularly the Detroit chapter of the Association of Catholic Trade Unionists. I remember Reuther becoming upset when his brother Victor publicly scolded George Meany and the AFL-CIO for accepting money from the Central Intelligence Agency for labor work overseas. Reuther was irritated because the UAW, too, had taken CIA money.

A progressive unionist of firm integrity, Reuther nonetheless formed an alliance with the conservative and tainted International Brotherhood of Teamsters. It was an odd alliance—between the UAW, one of the nation's most respected unions, and the Teamsters, one of the most checkered. The coalition grew out of Reuther's rivalry with George Meany. Reuther stood against Meany's brand of unionism. He looked upon Meany as a staid, old-style labor leader, more a bureaucrat than social-movement leader.

More to the point, Reuther desperately wanted Meany's job at the AFL-CIO. But Meany, a smart man despite the ludicrous image of him, in some quarters, as a bumbling neanderthal, frustrated Reuther's every move. Reuther would complain about the AFL-CIO holding its Executive Council meetings in the posh surroundings of Bal Harbour, Florida. He believed that the annual meeting site projected the wrong image for an organization of working people. So one year, when the criticism began to sting a little, Meany announced that the conventioneers would travel to Puerto Rico instead. They held the meeting in a hotel on one of the island's most fashionable avenues, but Meany could say that the AFL-CIO was gathering among the poor people of Puerto Rico.

In 1968, after making little headway into the AFL-CIO, Reuther decided to bolt the federation. He joined with the Teamsters in a breakaway federation of American labor unions. Reuther believed that the unions formerly affiliated with the old Congress of Industrial Organizations (which he led between 1952 and 1958) would follow him into a new federation. But not a single one did, aside from the Teamsters, which had already been kicked out of the AFL-CIO on charges of corruption. Once again, Reuther underestimated Meany, who kept his federation intact. (It wasn't until 1981 that the UAW returned to the AFL-CIO.)

The quixotic alliance with the Teamsters revealed a certain weakness in Reuther, the mirror image of his strengths of moral leadership in the labor movement. A private man, Reuther had some of the qualities of an ascetic. He opposed alcohol—I never saw him take a drink—and during AFL-CIO conventions was rumored to squeeze out his own fresh orange juice in his hotel room, while other union leaders gathered over sausages and eggs in the dining room. In short, Reuther was never one of the boys, as it were. Like his brother Victor—and unlike his late and more gregarious brother Roy—Reuther never won any popularity contests in the AFL-CIO. He could not or would not work the political machinery of the federation. As a result, Reuther proved less effective in pushing his programs in the wider labor movement. He eventually found himself before an altar with the Teamsters, at a wedding he really didn't want.

The realities of Reuther's time, and how they have changed since, are perhaps most telling. They suggest a response to those who would use him to hammer away at the reputations of today's labor leaders. It is hard to believe that Reuther, faced with a different set of circumstances, would use the same tactics as he did back then. Reuther led the UAW during the good times, when the economy ran strong and unions enjoyed the fruits of generous settlements with management. The years following his death in

1970 ushered in a new industrial era, marked by the globalization of markets—e.g. transfer of industry to low-wage regions and lagging competitiveness of U.S. industry. In the years since Reuther, American labor—and the auto industry in particular—faced a moment of decision when the Chrysler Corporation came to the brink of insolvency. Under Douglas Fraser, the UAW made concessions to help keep the company afloat and worked with Chrysler in securing federal loan guarantees for the company. I do not believe Walter Reuther would have wanted to see Chrysler go belly up. I believe he would have done what Fraser did.

George Meany and the Intelligentsia

The UAW dissidents have at least one point, and an important one, in their favor—they are by and large real unionists, not armchair activists who yell out calls from the sidelines. For the most part, the loudest complaints have come from the latter group, disaffected liberal intellectuals who snobbishly patronize the labor movement. They seem to take delight in ridiculing labor's elected representatives as a bunch of simpletons who haven't had a new idea in years and hardly know enough to come in out of the rain. In recent times, perhaps no labor leader has come in for more of this treatment than George Meany.

Marking Labor Day 1974, *The Nation* repeated its tiresome characterization of Meany as a reactionary clod, a kind of neanderthal man who stood in the way of progress in the labor movement. In another one of its temper tantrums, two years before Meany died in 1979, *The Nation* called Meany a "vain old panjandrum" (pretentious official) and his associates a bunch of "aging golfers." (The editorial lambasted Meany's opposition to granting a visa to leaders of the Soviet Union's state-controlled unions.)

Interestingly, during the same week *The Nation*'s editorial appeared, Meany delivered the strongest speech I had ever heard in support of Cesar Chavez and the United Farm Workers of America. Meany's critics might have been surprised to learn that Chavez was exuberantly happy about the speech and, in several conversations with me, was unstinting in his praise of Meany's vigorous leadership in the farm labor cause. Needless to add, Chavez knew very well—even if Meany's critics were unwilling to admit it—that Meany's support of the UFW was worth considerably more than that of any of the UFW's supporters in the ranks of the intelligentsia, and may have well been the decisive factor in bringing about a victory for Chavez's union in its struggle for survival.

Both as a labor leader and as a human being, Meany was always more complex than the public images of him. To the public he was the gruff, cigar-smoking labor leader, and yet these qualities, to me, always seemed the opposite side of his shyness in private. A plumber by trade, who never finished high school, Meany had a thorough and detailed knowledge of the labor movement and what could only be called a freak memory that amazed people wherever he went. A deeply religious man who sent his children to Catholic schools, Meany was instinctively diffident about parading his religious faith.

Unlike another Catholic labor leader, Philip Murray, Meany never sat comfortably in the surroundings of clergy—that is, when it came to union business; he was a personal friend of his own pastor in Washington. Murray, on the other hand, enjoyed the company of clergy and cultivated close personal and professional ties with Msgr. Charles Owen Rice, who led the Catholic Radical Alliance in Pittsburgh. (Murray was amused, I think, by the rambunctiousness of the Pittsburgh labor priest.) Meany was of another generation of Catholic leaders, perhaps more assimilated into the mainstream and certainly less open to any overt attempts at influence by clergy of their own faith.

My mentor, the Rev. Raymond McGowan, learned this the hard way. Once, McGowan complained to a priest-friend about a certain decision made by the old American Federation of Labor in regard to its dealings with the Christian labor federations of Europe. This priest happened to be Meany's pastor. "Go talk to Meany. He's Catholic," the pastor advised, poorly. When he met with Meany at AFL headquarters, McGowan told him, in so many words, "You can't do this." Meany bristled: "Who are you to tell me what to do?" It was one of McGowan's few tactical errors in his many years of dealings with labor and management.

Meany, though, was not adverse to the more reasonable approaches of clergy, including one in the late 1970s. At the time, the AFL-CIO pulled out of the International Labor Organization (ILO) over political and administrative differences with the United Nations agency. This move by Meany and his colleagues disturbed the Vatican, which has a long tradition of support for the ILO as well as other international organizations. The church has stood with the ILO from the beginning, despite the fact that the agency started up at a time of tension between religion and labor in Europe. Since its founding in 1919 as part of the old League of Nations, the ILO has always had a priest on staff, a succession of French Jesuits and one American. (They have served as liaisons to the religious world.) And two popes —Paul VI and John Paul II—have visited the ILO's headquarters in Geneva. When Archbishop Jean Jadot, the papal delegate to the United States, asked me about the AFL-CIO's decision, I suggested that he invite Meany over to the Vatican delegation to talk over the matter.

At the apostolic delegation (now better known as the Vatican embassy or "nunciature"), they gave Meany the red carpet treatment. Typically, when people of position visit the nunciature on Massachusetts Avenue in Washington, they and their party are treated to a formal lunch with the archbishop. When the papal nuncio stands up, that means it is time for the final blessing, and out the door they go. On the occasion of Meany's visit, he and the Belgian Jadot met privately for twenty minutes or so. Then came the formal lunch. From there the parties retired to the parlor, where Vatican aids poured the brandy and handed out cigars.

To start off the conversation, I asked Meany if he could remember the first time he attended an ILO conference. Meany, who had a memory like an elephant, served up all the details. Then he threw the question back to me. "Do you remember the first time *you* went to an ILO meeting, Father?" I said tentatively, "Oh, I'm not sure, I'd have to check . . ." I didn't have to. Meany reminded me of the place, time and circumstances (including the hotel where I stayed) of the 1949 ILO meeting in Geneva.

As for the matter at hand, Meany had come to present the AFL-CIO's position, which he did courteously and without contention. He told the archbishop that the federation was unhappy with what it viewed as the ILO's bloated bureaucracy, its exceptionally critical resolutions against Israel, and its deference toward the Soviet Union. Archbishop Jadot, for his part, was there to listen; his job was to file a report with the Holy See, which did not alter its position of support for the ILO.

As the ILO dispute may suggest, Meany was unapologetically anti-communist. In contrast to his religious faith, which he kept private, Meany wore his patriotism on his sleeve, and unashamedly so. This provided the case against him by his leftward critics. While I, too, did not always agree with the AFL-CIO's international policies (the ILO matter being a case in point), I felt nonetheless that the critics had badly misunderstood the quality of Meany's patriotism. Mainly because they thought he was too anti-communist, they wrote him off, sometimes rather disdainfully so, as a myopic and narrow-minded chauvinist. They were wrong about that—completely wrong, in my view.

In leading labor's crusade against communism, as well as other forms of authoritarianism, Meany did not defend the so-called American way of life as such, however devoted he was to his own country. In his mind, he was defending human rights and, more specifically, trade union rights: the freedom of workers to organize into autonomous unions of their own choice. In his 1979 Labor Day Statement, the last of twenty-five such statements he had written as president of the AFL-CIO, Meany succinctly stated his position as follows: "One cannot have a trade union or a democratic election" without freedom of speech, association and assembly. "Without a democratic election, whereby the people choose and remove their rulers, there is no method of securing human rights against the state.

No democracy without human rights, no human rights without democracy, and no trade union rights without either. That is our belief; that is our creed."

*   *   *

Of course, the ridicule of labor leaders has come not only from disaffected liberals. Peter Drucker, the management guru, blames the decline of organized labor primarily on what he terms "the steady deterioration in the quality of union leaders." (He also cites the "sharp decline in the public's attitudes toward unions.") This explanation of labor woes, whether coming from right or left, strikes me as superficial. I would go further and agree with an observation made years ago by John T. Dunlop and Derek C. Bok in their 1970 book *Labor and the American Community*. "There are dangers in assuming too quickly that the faults of unions lie mainly with their leaders," the authors write. "If the assumption proves inadequate or incorrect, not only will a great disservice be done to many union officials but society may also go badly astray in trying to construct a viable labor policy." (This seems, at least to some extent, to have come true in the years since Bok and Dunlop issued the warning.)

This is not to say that the labor movement is without its faults and imperfections. Like all our major institutions, including the church, the labor movement is beset by a crisis of identity and credibility which only the painful process of self-criticism and internal renewal can resolve. I am confident that the movement will undertake this process on its own. It needs all the help it can get from people outside the movement, but it can do without the self-congratulatory advice of self-styled progressives who, in many cases, lack the courage and staying power to deal with the grubby reality of labor problems today. Instead, these critics prefer to take a romantic flight into some distant past or future, which allows them to escape —with all the honors of war—from the day-to-day drudgery of real life.

Most labor leaders are not disposed to take these ivory tower types as seriously as they take themselves. In 1982, at the annual convention of the Industrial Relations Research Association, Lane Kirkland said with tongue firmly in cheek that he was "fascinated by the glib speculations" of some of labor's more opinionated critics in the ranks of the intelligentsia, but hastened to add that he rarely found them useful in his own line of work. The stock lamentations about the dearth of "new ideas" in the labor movement, he pointed out, are seldom, if ever, joined with any sign that their authors have any stirring or creative ideas of their own. "To those critics," he concluded, "I can only respond with a plea, in the manner of Dickens' characters: "If you have any intelligence, please put me in possession of it."

Fortunately, American labor leaders have not sat around waiting for any special deliveries of wisdom from the intelligentsia. In many respects, they face tougher challenges than ever. For all the resistance to unions in the early days, the heralded leaders of labor's past, the Reuthers and the Lewises, came on the scene at a time of sweeping change in labor-management relations. Today, however, retrenchment is the order of the day in the labor field. And given what they have to work with, some union presidents have proved *more* innovative and resourceful than any of their predecessors.

John Sweeney, president of the Service Employees International Union, is one of the new labor pioneers. Under his leadership the SEIU has set the pace in the movement for national health insurance and in the organization of hospital workers. Thousands of custodial workers have entered the ranks of organized labor through the SEIU's national campaign, "Justice for Janitors." The union has also opened up new trails in its drives to organize maids and other domestic workers—a hidden and easily exploited work force that practically no one, in labor's past, ever believed could be organized.

Msgr. Higgins and striking Corn Mill workers in Clinton, Iowa, in February, 1980

6

State of the Unions:
Part I

Admittedly, a State of Crisis

During the late 1980s there appeared a dozen or more scholarly books on the state of the unions and future of the American labor movement. They are among the least cheerful books I have read in recent years on this or any other subject. The authors, with few exceptions, conclude—some more regretfully than others—that the American labor movement is in a state of crisis and that its future is, at best, problematical. A few suggest that the crisis may be terminal.

As one may expect, AFL-CIO president Lane Kirkland, a guest contributor to one of the volumes, disagrees with the doomsayers. He points out that labor's obituary has been prematurely written many times during the past century. "It seems," he says, with a wry turn of phrase, "that we are forever perishing so that others may be forever publishing" books, articles, and monographs about labor's imminent demise.

I should immediately confess that, increasingly as time goes on, I feel below the task of understanding, let alone critiquing, much of what emerges from the hallowed groves of academia. I say this for the simple reason that so much of academic economics, including labor economics, is written today in a foreign language which, alas, I have never mastered—the arcane language of higher calculus. In this connection, I take comfort from a letter that Sar Levitan, director of the Center for Policy Studies at George Washington University, fired off to the *Journal of Human Resources*, canceling his subscription. Levitan's letter reads in part: "Should you decide that there is something to be gained by reaching the public outside the immediate select fraternity (and sorority) of numerologists, even including some policy makers and practitioners, you may want to consider emulating the practice of the old 'ponies.' When the teaching of Greek was still in fashion, enterprising publishers printed the Greek version together with an English translation on opposite pages."

Jonathan Rauch, writing in the *National Journal* (September 23, 1989), offers a few examples of this dense and almost impenetrable prose. One is enough to suggest that the return of opposite-page translations, as recommended by Levitan, may not be such a bad idea. Rauch quotes from an article whose author wanted to say that the family situation of poor young people affects whether they stay in school and that when outside jobs are available these people are more likely to drop out. The writer put it this way: "Schooling outcomes for poverty population youths are conditioned by the household structure they experience while growing up. When exogenously determined employment opportunity is added to this equation, it exerts a significantly positive effect on dropout."

As Rauch laments, that was one of the more readable passages, a summary passage, mind you, and not a technical section. The technical parts are much worse. Rauch cautions his readers that if they crack the covers of many an economics journal these days, they had better be prepared for page after page of "The model is a discrete-time, finite-equation, discounted utility maximization model where individuals make labor force participation decisions in an environment with uncertain job offers and layoffs."

It would be an unseemly and obviously self-serving rationalization for an illiterate amateur like myself to cover up his own inadequacies by lampooning the prose of the numerologists. This is not my intention here. I am simply pleading, like a drowning man, for the infusion of a little more oxygen into academic prose. As Rauch has correctly observed, computers and equations have proved to be powerful tools, "but they have tended to push out two other values: contact with the common sense world of everyday observation, and the ability to communicate with the public."

Be that as it may, one writer who has no problem communicating with the public is Peter Drucker, often called the father of the modern science of management. In *The New Realities*, Drucker writes that the labor union "rose with the industrial worker; it was in fact the industrial workers' own institution. It is falling with the industrial worker. Can it survive at all?" The labor union, Drucker continues, "might be judged this century's most successful institution. In 1900 it was outlawed in most countries or barely tolerated. In 1920 it had become respectable. By the end of World War II, twenty-five years later, it had become dominant. Now the labor movement is in tatters and disarray, apparently in irreversible decline."

Drucker could conceivably be right, but, frankly, I doubt it. This is not to say, of course, that all is well with trade unionism and collective bargaining in the United States. To the contrary, both are admittedly in a state of crisis. There is virtually unanimous agreement on that score among both theorists and practitioners.

In a sense, the crisis of organized labor, and the literature it has spawned, are as old as the movement itself. In his 1985 presidential address before the Industrial Relations Association, the late Everett Kassalow noted that the wave of attention to the plight of labor continues a tradition of long standing in the scholarly and popular press. "Why this endless fascination with the plight of American trade unions?" he asked. His answer was that it "reflects the almost continuously precarious position of unions in American society. Despite occasional periods of growth, it does appear that U.S. unionism has never been fully institutionalized in American life," he argues. "Unlike the case of Western Europe, the bulk of U.S. employers have never accepted that permanent, institutional role of unions, especially in their own companies."

That said, the labor movement appears to have entered a new and dangerous phase in its tradition of crisis. As a matter of fact, "the decline of organized labor" in the United States has become a cliché of American political discourse. And while the labor movement has reason to send word that reports of its demise are greatly exaggerated, the cliché is grounded in sobering realities of contemporary unionism. Some of these realities, in vastly oversimplified form, are as follows:

—The unionized segment of the workforce—much of it concentrated in smokestack industries—has been shrinking for three decades.

—Union victory returns in elections supervised by the National Labor Relations Board have declined significantly.

—Attempts to "decertify," or abolish, existing unions are succeeding more often.

—In recent years, concession bargaining—often in exchange for increased job security—has been the rule and not the exception, in certain industries.

—Public opinion of organized labor and labor leaders has plummeted over the years (although, at this writing, the labor movement had begun to score higher approval ratings in opinion polls).

No one needs to pick up any of the scholarly tomes to have a general sense of all this. If your memory stretches back a few decades, you know that unions have seen better days. Over the past forty years or so, I have made it my business to attend many of the major union conventions. (I go strictly as an observer, to learn whatever I can about the trade union situation.) At one time, the press tables at these conventions were crowded with first-rate reporters from newspapers all across the country. Labor was one of the plum assignments on a daily newspaper and labor writers had reputations as well-informed specialists in their field. Today, by contrast, members of the fourth estate are few and far between in the corridors of union conventions. And although I keep up with labor reporting, I would be hard pressed to name more than a few experienced labor writers still on the beat.

*   *   *

While many have seen the signs of labor's crisis, few have come to any agreement about its underlying causes or what to do about it. Experts and commentators have offered an array of explanations. Some have no doubt that the woes of labor stem from the movement's (supposedly) adversarial ways. Others say with equal certainty that labor's fortunes will continue to sag as long as it remains timid and complacent. As already discussed, a number of critics, on both the "right" and the "left," point to the supposed deterioration of the intellectual and moral quality of labor leaders. Indeed, of the making of articles and books about the alleged decadence of the American labor movement and its leaders there is seemingly no end. I might add that there is a dreary sameness about many of these jeremiads. By and large, their diagnosis of what is wrong with the labor movement tends to be superficial and simplistic.

Yet while the authors differ in their diagnoses and prescriptions, they almost unanimously agree on one thing—namely, that employer opposition is a major cause of labor's decline since the 1960s. The consensus is summarized by a single passage from one of the volumes, *The Transformation of American Industrial Relations*, by Thomas A. Kochan, Harry C. Katz, and Robert B. McKersie (1986):

> An understanding of the transformation that has taken place in industrial relations since 1960 must start with an understanding of the deep-seated resistance toward unions that historically has been embedded in the belief system of U.S. managers. It is through the lens of this value system that managerial decision makers weigh their options for responding to cues from the external environment. Unfortunately, many researchers in industrial relations and the behavioral sciences have been slow or unwilling to acknowledge the existence and the power of this managerial belief system.

One respected figure in labor relations explains how managers have put this belief system into practice. Addressing the 1984 industrial relations convention, Wayne Horvitz said that "management has resisted, first, the existence and, secondly, the expansion of unions and therefore of the collective bargaining process as an institution for joint decision making. . . . The inability or unwillingness to recognize and accept unions has been a hallmark of (U.S. industrial) history," said Horvitz, an experienced arbitrator and former director of the Federal Mediation and Conciliation Service. "The intensity of opposition has varied over time, but even in the most genial of times, it is just below the surface of good will and accommodation. And today the evidence is clear that the cycle is repeating."

Horvitz finds this disturbing. "The uniqueness of America," he told his colleagues, "lies in the vitality of its free institutions. Among these, a free labor movement and a free enterprise economy are essential to the achievement of social and political stability and economic prosperity for all. It is destructive to society and to business and to organized labor if in our legitimate adversarial roles we question the right of our institutions to exist and perform their legitimate functions."

I would only add that, in my judgment, researchers have been even slower to explain why American employers are and always have been more aggressively and more ideologically anti-union than their counterparts in other industrialized countries. Why this American exceptionalism? Why, for example, is Canada different from the United States in this regard?

Seymour Martin Lipset, in a comparative study of Canada and the United States, holds that a large part of the answer lies in the ways in which the conditions of the Canadian and U.S. labor movements are mediated by differing national values. "Contemporary America," Lipset contends, "is the outcome of processes which began with an egalitarian, individualistic revolution. The United States remained through the nineteenth and early twentieth centuries the extreme example of a classically liberal or Lockean society which rejected the assumptions of the alliance of throne and altar, of ascriptive elitism, of statism, of *noblesse oblige*, and of communitarianism. This tradition was reinforced by America's religious commitment to the individualist 'non-conformist' Protestant sects."

Canada, by contrast, "dominated by a Tory counterrevolutionary ethos, developed a more communitarian orientation. The two major Canadian national groups sought to defend their values and culture by reacting against classically liberal revolutions. English-speaking Canada exists because she opposed the Declaration of Independence; French-speaking Canada, largely under the leadership of Catholic clerics, sought to isolate herself from the anti-clerical democratic values of the French Revolution."

Lipset—writing in his 1986 book *Unions in Transition: Entering the Second Century*—notes in conclusion that "the greater strength of the Canadian unions is linked to a more union-friendly legal environment, more cooperative politicians, less hostile employers, but, more important than these, to the greater propensity of workers to join than in the United States."

Not everyone agrees with this theory. Kochan, Katz and McKersie, in a review symposium on their book, doubt that a "declining acceptance of unions and an American culture of individualism are the underlying explanations for the union decline in the United States. Although we do think there is something to the argument of American historical exceptionalism," they write in the April 1988 *Industrial and Labor Relations Review*, "we do not believe that argument fully accounts for the differences unions recently have had in the United States. . . . Nor are we convinced that American and Canadian values and cultures are so different."

I am not qualified to referee this dispute, but I am pleased that the argument is taking place. For I am convinced that, whatever the differences or similarities between Canada and the United States, Lipset's argument serves to highlight the fact that the prevailing American ethos of individualism, even among many workers, is a major reason for the weakness of U.S. organized labor. The problem goes deeper than employer opposition to unions. In my judgment, it grows out of our traditional philosophy of individualism.

Union-Busting—and the Law

Anyone with even a casual knowledge of American social history will know that union-busting is not a new phenomenon. During the late nineteenth century and the first four decades of the twentieth century, the use of this tactic all too often involved physical violence, industrial espionage, the infiltration of unions by hired thugs or detectives, etc. In our day, union-busting has taken a more sophisticated turn. Violence is out for the most part, and hired thugs have given way to consultants in three-piece suits who have mastered the fine art of breaking or decertifying unions while staying, barely, within the letter of the law. The 1980s was a boom period for professional union-busters. In the 1970s there were only a handful of management consulting firms that specialize in breaking unions. A decade later the figure ran well into the hundreds.

Though usually at work behind the scenes, these firms increasingly parade their aggressive anti-union propaganda in the open. Unfortunately a number of colleges and universities have been known to march along with the spectacle, promoting what is euphemistically referred to as a "union-free environment." Together with the consultants, universities have offered training programs for employer representatives to show how to exploit the fears of workers and convert those fears into a rejection of collective bargaining.

Many of these programs proudly announce that union-busting is the main order of business when it comes to industrial labor relations. For example, one brochure bearing the imprint of a well-known college is entitled "Management in a Union-Free Environment: A Unique One-Day Labor Relations Program." There is nothing "unique" about this union-busting program. It is typical of countless other seminars and training groups held throughout the United States.

The purpose of these programs, as one union official has stated in congressional testimony, is "the denial of democracy in the workplace. The bottom line is unchallenged management rights." The university brochure puts it bluntly: "Without unions, there are no restrictive work rules, no strong union officials, no time wasted in processing union grievances and arbitrations, no time lost in contract negotiations, strikes, or other non-productive activities."

Some of the union-busters are prepared, if necessary, to resort to what may charitably be called sleazy tactics. One influential management consultant, speaking in what he obviously thought was an off-the-record forum, advised his clients to hire as few black workers as possible because, in his words, "Blacks tend to be more prone to unionization than whites. . . . If you can keep them at a minimum, you are better off." According to newspaper accounts, he said he felt the same way about native Americans and Puerto Ricans.

I am not suggesting that all management consulting firms are ready to sink as low as this. However, the record will show that far too many of them, while staying within the letter of the law and eschewing racist tactics, have only one objective—to prevent workers from organizing for the purpose of collective bargaining. I find this impossible to reconcile with the basic principles of social ethics, Catholic or other, and long established federal labor policy.

By comparison with such adversarial or confrontational tactics on the part of management consulting firms, the labor movement's philosophy of labor-management relations is, by and large, surprisingly conciliatory. Think about it. Have you ever heard of a union that hired a corporation-busting consulting firm for the purpose of preventing stockholders from exercising their right to invest their savings in a given company? Such a move on the part of organized labor would be universally assailed as an immoral act against nature and society. Why is it, then, that the use of union-busting tactics—aimed at preventing workers from exercising their free-association rights—is widely seen as a respectable profession? Why this double standard?

*   *   *

In 1990, one of the estimated ten thousand "professional" union busters decided to step forward and expose in frightening detail the dirty tricks of the trade. His is a true conversion. He left his so-called profession because of the deep sense of guilt he felt at having done serious harm not only to people's working lives but to their personal lives as well. In his own words, he "just couldn't deal with it anymore." Over a period of twenty years, he played a leadership role in more than three hundred anti-union drives in many parts of the country. Most of his clients were health care institutions. Today he educates labor and government on "the tragedy and the terrorism that is the reality and substance of union-busting."

In a typical union-busting campaign, he testifies in a notarized, sworn affidavit, the name of the game is control—establishing absolute, hour-by-hour control over all aspects of the business that relate to employee relations. As a first step, the chief executive or operating officer hands over supervision to the anti-union consultants for the duration of the campaign. The supervisors, who quickly become hostage to the union-busters, must provide the consultants with as much personal information as requested on each worker—the more damaging the better. The consultants, with the full cooperation of their supervisory conscripts, then begin a systematic and relentless one-on-one effort to wear the employees down, until they say "Union No" in a representation election.

The tactics are reprehensible. Union-busters try to dig up dirt on the credit rating of individual workers, their sexual preferences, the strength or weakness of their family life, their substance abuse problems—in short, on "every vulnerability of every individual worker." What they cannot pull from confidential files, they squeeze out of supervisors and fellow workers in star-chamber interviews.

The consultants force supervisors to violate friendships, for example, by calling in personal loans and other favors. If the consultants know that a pro-union employee has had some kind of embarrassing personal problem, they will go after him on that, using the information either to win the employee over to their side or to attack his credibility with fellow workers. The writer of the affidavit says that the consultants would even circulate a false reputation-wrecking rumor about a pro-union employee and then have the employee's supervisor reinforce that one-on-one, throughout the facility.

The list of dirty—and illegal—tricks goes on and on. "We would plant company property in an employee's car and then have it discovered by supervisors, or plant drugs in an employee's locker, or call the employee's spouse and suggest that they (sic) were not at a union meeting, but having an extramarital affair, or start rumors about flattened tires, broken windows, and 'union vandalism.' " Moreover, he says, the consultants "had to divide to conquer." They would study the demographics early in the campaign and, if necessary, would pit black against white, or old vs. young, or educated vs. uneducated. All this, he says, was standard procedure.

Pity the poor supervisors who are conscripted by their bosses to carry out the consultant's instructions down to the last detail. The writer says that a majority of the supervisors, in his campaigns, did not want to do what they were instructed to do. They were unwilling accomplices, fearful of losing their own jobs.

I know from experience that this account will bring forth cries of anguish and anger from representatives of certain management consulting firms. They will argue that the union-busting tactics described above are extremely rare exceptions in the trade. The writer of the affidavit strongly disagrees. He says that tricks of the kind he has testified to under oath are the rule rather than the exception. Not a union-buster in the country, he says, cannot lay claim to breaking the law regularly. I hope he is wrong about that, but, in any event, even if only a relative few of the nation's management consultants conduct their business in this fashion, that's still too many. It's time for their peers in the trade to blow the whistle on them with the hope of driving them out of business.

*   *   *

There ought to be a law. And as a matter of principle, there is.

In 1935 Congress passed the nation's first comprehensive labor law, the National Labor Relations Act (also known as the Wagner Act, after its Senate sponsor). The NLRA had a clear and simple goal, as expressed in the preamble: "It is . . . the policy of the United States . . . to encourage the practice and procedure of collective bargaining . . . by protecting the exercise of workers of full freedom of association, self-organization, and designation of representatives of their own choosing, for the purpose of negotiating the terms and conditions of their employment or other mutual aid or protection."

When the act was before Congress, the late Msgr. John A. Ryan, the first director of the Catholic bishops' Social Action Department, joined with those urging its adoption. Years later, in reviewing the highlights of a long and distinguished career in the field of social reform, Ryan said in his autobiography that the NLRA was "probably the most just, beneficent, and far-reaching piece of labor legislation ever enacted in the United States." Frank W. McCulloch and Tim Bornstein, authors of one of the better books about the history of the NLRA and its administration, went even further when they described it as "perhaps the finest social invention of the twentieth century. It has softened the sharp, often brutal edges of the industrial revolution and enriched political democracy by extending opportunities of self-determination to the daily lives of millions of Americans on the job."

In more recent years, however, this social invention of the twentieth century has too often been turned on its head and against workers. The procedures of the National Labor Relations Board have seriously hampered the right of workers to organize and, to an intolerable degree, nullified the basic purpose and objective of the original NLRA. Needless delays in scheduling union representation elections and in processing complaints of unfair labor practices are among the procedural problems that have made life easier for union busters. Even the business-oriented weekly *Barron's* conceded that delaying tactics by employers had thwarted the NLRA's purpose.

Where an employer challenges a union election, "it is generally postponed for an average of two-and-a-half months for hearings, and for an average of ten months if the employer's case is heard by the board itself. And the longer the delay, the more organizing momentum is lost, and the weaker the union's showing invariably proves. Moreover," *Barron's* said, "if a worker involved in the organizing drive or with union sympathies is fired and successfully challenges his dismissal as an unfair labor practice, it is likely to take about two years before the courts finally order his reinstatement with back pay, even if his complaint is upheld by NLRB."

That was the story of the great NLRA as told in 1977. Since then, by all accounts, employers have felt even freer to fire pro-union workers. Studies have shown that in any union drive, a critical mass of workers are likely to be fired or threatened with loss of their jobs. And even if they win reinstatement in two or three years, there is nothing—besides an anemic labor law—to stop the employer from firing them again. Seldom, if ever, do these illegally fired workers win back pay. As Thomas Geoghegan, a Chicago labor lawyer, explains in his superb 1991 book *Which Side Are You On? Trying To Be for Labor When It's Flat on Its Back:* "Maybe, after three years of litigation, the employer would lose, and have to pay a few thousand bucks, if that much: a cheap price, though, for keeping out the union."

In the 1970s, unions started pushing a labor-law reform measure to make the NLRB work more efficiently, quickly and equitably. A rather mild proposal, the bill triggered a political holy war waged by the conservative wing of the business community. In Congress, one of the Ayatollahs in this jihad was Orrin Hatch of Utah, leader of the Senate's Republican opposition. He called the bill a "monstrosity . . . the type of thing that will help bring this country down if anything will." He said the bill "would not do much for the employee, but it would do a great deal to centralize power in the hands of those who are already very powerful," meaning "big labor union leaders." The senator was describing a figment of his imagination, not the bill before the Senate.

Nevertheless, propaganda and scare tactics—manufactured in large part by the U.S. Chamber of Commerce and the National Association of Manufacturers—won the day. In 1978, the Labor Law Reform Bill was turned aside by a one-vote margin.

*   *   *

One of the rights guaranteed by the neglected NLRA was the right to strike without fear of reprisal. In 1938, three years after passage of the act, the Supreme Court issued a strange decision with respect to workers who go on strike. The ruling is known as *NLRB v. Mackay Radio and Telegraph Company*. First, the Supreme Court said that strikers had every right to their jobs when they returned to work after the strike was settled. But then the court also ruled that employers had the right to keep their business going during a strike. If their only recourse was to hire permanent replacements for the strikers, that was all right, too—and thus the court negated the strikers' right to their jobs when the strike ended.

In the United States of the 1930s and 1940s and up through the 1970s, few employers chose to exploit the court's ruling. But the floodgates opened when President Ronald Reagan fired 12,000 striking air traffic controllers in 1981. The PATCO strike was in the public sector, and thus not covered by the NLRB or the Mackay decision, but nevertheless the corporate world took the signal. Employers realized that they could use this weapon to break unions and collective bargaining (which was not the purpose of the justices who wrote the 1938 decision).

During the 1980s, more and more corporate managers used the Mackay decision to fire their strikers and replace them permanently with strikebreakers. As an added incentive, managers could wait twelve months and then petition for an NLRB election to decertify the union. Since the strikebreakers could vote—and the strikers could not—the results were predictable.

Such was the fate of twenty-four hundred workers, mostly Hispanic, who worked in the mines and smelters of the Phelps-Dodge Company in four Arizona towns—Clifton, Douglas, Ajo and Morenci. In 1983 these workers had reason to believe that they had won a small share of the American dream. Most of them were long-time members of the United Steelworkers or one of twelve other unions, and over the years they had achieved a living wage and a measure of job security. Unlike thousands of other Hispanic workers in the southwest, through their unions the Phelps-Dodge workers had working conditions that enabled them to live decent lives and raise their families in some comfort.

Six months later the dream turned into a nightmare. The Phelps-Dodge management, demanding severe concessions in negotiations for a new contract, refused to budge, and the workers felt they had no recourse but to strike. Almost immediately it became apparent why Phelps-Dodge had been so unyielding in negotiations. The company tapped the large pool of unemployed Hispanic workers in the southwest and brought on permanent replacements for the strikers. With the help of the Arizona National Guard, Phelps-Dodge resumed full production. More than two thousand workers suddenly found that a legitimate strike had cost them their jobs. Twelve months later, after an election in which only the strikebreakers could vote, it also cost them their unions—permanently.

The workers at Phelps-Dodge were not the only ones who learned the hard way that the right to strike in the United States amounts to little more than a right to quit. In Tennessee, thirteen hundred workers on strike at Magic Chef lost their jobs permanently; at three plants of the International Paper Company, the same fate befell twenty-three hundred members of the United Paperworkers Union; and at Eastern Airlines, nine thousand machinists lost their jobs forever when they tried to resist the efforts of Frank Lorenzo, the airline chairman, to force their conditions down to non-union levels.

America is virtually the only industrialized country, along with South Africa, that permits this abuse. Firing strikers in most European countries is either banned outright, or is a practice which does not exist. Only in South Africa do workers face the prospect of losing their jobs permanently when they go on strike, and South Africa is not a country with which the U.S. normally likes to be compared. As a South African labor leader asked at the end of a visit here in 1989, "In my country when we strike we are fired. In your country you are permanently replaced. Tell me, what is the difference?"

The ruling that invented the distinction between being fired and being permanently replaced covers the largest category of strikes—the "economic strike," resulting from disagreements over such issues as wages and benefits. Not all strikes, however, are of this kind. Some strikes are judged by the National Labor Relations Board to have resulted from an unfair labor practice on the part of the employer, such as unilaterally changing working conditions. In these cases employers can only hire temporary replacements. There is a big difference here. When replacement workers are *temporary*, strikers retain the right to return to their jobs after a settlement is reached. (This has been the historic practice in the United States and throughout the free world.) When replacements are *permanent*, it represents a major stumbling block to settlements, for in an economic strike, when the economic issues are settled, then union and management have to decide what to do with two sets of workers—strikers and strikebreakers. The secondary problem usually becomes harder to resolve than the economic differences that set off the strike in the first place.

Employers know the consequences of hiring permanent replacement workers. Most who do so are not motivated solely by the need to keep their businesses operating, but by a desire to get rid of the union and its collective bargaining rights along with their union work force. The desire is apparently so strong among some employers that increasing numbers of them have tried to provoke strikes by making incredible demands. In some instances, after going on strike, unions have agreed to all of management's demands and made unconditional offers to return to work, only to be rebuffed by management. Then come the permanent replacements, frequently recruited ahead of time, and, later on, the decertification vote.

The exploitation of the Mackay decision by employers has implications for the future of collective bargaining. The basic strategy of collective bargaining is to avoid creating big winners or big losers; it is a time-tested and supremely democratic way of settling differences between employer and employees through compromise. When collective bargaining reaches an impasse—which it seldom does—the workers' only resort is to strike. The theoretical justification of the strike is to put equal pressure both on the workers, who are without income, and on the company, which is without production. When settlement is achieved—again, presumably, without any big winners or losers—the workers are entitled to regain their jobs.

Permanently replacing strikers upsets the entire balance between the bargainers. During the collective bargaining process itself, workers who fear that they may be replaced if they strike are not likely to bargain forcefully or effectively. The mere threat to replace strikers gives the employer a strong advantage in the collective bargaining process. And the strike itself becomes an almost useless weapon if workers are immediately replaced. In short, instead of negotiations between equals, the collective bargaining process becomes a weapon that employers may manipulate to their own ends, which may include destroying collective bargaining and the union itself.

Beyond collective bargaining, the erosion of the right to strike has implications for all of us, and indeed for democracy itself. Although not listed in the Bill of Rights, the right to withhold one's labor is as essential in a democratic society as the rights we celebrate in the first ten amendments to the Constitution. If we had any doubts about the importance of the right to strike in a democratic society, the experience of Poland during the past decade should serve as a useful lesson. Members of the Polish Solidarity union can testify that their nation may have lingered under authoritarian rule if not for the willingness of the rank and file to put down their tools and leave their factories.

In the United States, after a decade of hammering by employers, the labor movement struck back with a campaign to recapture the right of workers to withhold their labor without penalty. Bills were introduced in both the House and the Senate to overturn the unintended result of the Mackay case and guarantee the free exercise of the right to strike. Despite the automatic opposition of the Bush administration and some elements of business, labor gathered considerable support in Congress. The unions also reached out to their traditional allies among religious, civil rights and civic groups, appealing for help in what promised to be a long-term struggle.

Meantime, the religious community was already facing the wrenching consequences of permanent replacement, for workers, their families, and their communities. In communities such as Jay, Maine, Clifton, Arizona, and Cleveland, Tennessee, the permanent replacement of strikers had resulted in divided communities and families, with strikers and strike-breakers sometimes in the same family or living on the same street. When labor called, scores of national religious leaders endorsed the right of workers to strike, free of fear, in the knowledge that this right is important not only for workers but for the community as a whole.

*   *   *

The assault on the right to strike is but one illustration of how the people who break America's unions have often been aided, however unwittingly, by the people who make (and interpret) America's laws. Nearly a decade after the Mackay decision, it was Congress' turn to take action that would, in due time, have the effect of chilling the right to organize. In 1947 Congress passed the Labor-Management Relations Act, better known as the Taft-Hartley Act. In so doing, the lawmakers came up with an unusual constitutional device. Previously, federal labor law (the NLRA specifically) had superseded all state laws where interstate commerce was concerned. However, in passing Taft-Hartley, Congress gave the states concurrent jurisdiction, *provided only that the state laws were more restrictive than the federal law*. Within two decades, at least nineteen states (mostly in the south) accepted the legislative invitation by enacting so-called "right-to-work" laws.

Strictly defined, right-to-work laws make it illegal for a company to require that its workers pay dues to a union as a condition of getting or keeping a job. (The requirement, of course, results from collective bargaining agreements, not the initiative of employers.) Even without these laws, the "closed shop"—which requires full membership in a recognized union as a pre-condition of employment—is prohibited by the 1947 federal act. The state laws, however, go further and ban the "union shop," an arrangement in which all workers must pay fees to the union, regardless of whether they individually choose to be regular members. (These "agency fees" are for the various representation services—collective bargaining, processing of grievances, and so forth—that unions are compelled by law to provide to all workers in a given bargaining unit, union members and non-members alike.)

In the argument over right-to-work laws, the first thing to get straight is that these laws have nothing to do with the right to work. That is, the very term is a verbal deception, a play on words used to cloak the real purpose of the laws, which is to enforce further restrictions upon union activity. Such laws do not provide jobs for workers; they merely prevent workers from building strong and stable unions. (In 1954, the Supreme Court of Idaho took judicial notice of this fact by refusing to permit such a deceptive title on a ballot initiative to be proposed to the voters.) Further, the pressure for such legislation did not arise from workers seeking their "rights." The measures, rather, were uniformly backed by employers' organizations and related groups, which continue to apply the pressure that keeps these laws on the books. In some cases, the laws came about as part of an economic program by underdeveloped states seeking to attract industry by the lure of a docile and low-paid labor force.

A favorite argument of the right-to-work lobby revolves around the concept of states' rights. They argue that states should have the right to regulate labor problems according to their own desires, and that federal standards should not be imposed upon them. Frankly, the argument is less than honest. Under present conditions, the right to regulate labor unions has not been returned to the states. What is conceded is the limited power to enact union-security regulations *more stringent* than those in the federal law. But a state may not constitutionally enact regulations more favorable to the union movement.

The essential right-to-work argument is partly political, partly ethical. It holds that compulsory unionism runs counter to the American tradition of freedom and individual rights. The slogan of freedom and liberty is superficially attractive, but in reality it falls even on its own terms. Right-to-work laws, while giving minorities of workers the so-called right to opt completely out of unions that have won representation, do not grant workers the right to opt "into" unions that have lost elections. That is, workers who vote "Union Yes" in a losing election have no right to bargain collectively; in such cases, the union that lost its bid for recognition has no legal authority to represent any of the workers.

Aside from this, the argument about individual choice does raise serious questions. Even if an overwhelming majority of workers want a union shop, do they have the right to demand that the minority step into line with this decision? Since the right to work is the right to life itself, may conditions be imposed upon this right?

The answer to both these questions, from my standpoint, is a straight yes. People are more than individuals; they are members of society. Such is their nature. For this reason, the rules necessary for harmonious social living may be binding, not merely optional. So, as members of civil society, we must obey laws, pay taxes, and fulfill our duties as citizens. As members of the family society, we have rights and duties, whether we be parents or children. Likewise, the common good of industrial society may demand that individuals conform to rules laid down for the good of all.

Medical societies and bar associations generally have rights to lay down binding rules for their professions. Teachers accept many obligations as conditions of employment. In business, few if any workers enjoy an unconditional "right to work." The employer imposes rules concerning safety, performance of work, health and hygiene, and miscellaneous matters such as smoking and appearance. In some cases, less now than in the past, employees are required to buy and use company products. Many employees have obligations tied to their pension or health plans. These and other conditions of employment express the principle that the common good of the professional or plant community must prevail. In these matters, the right to impose conditions of employment is rarely questioned, even if the wisdom of particular conditions may be debatable.

Similarly, an employer and a union should have the right to agree, in collective bargaining, that union security—the requirement that workers assume some financial obligation to the union—would aid the industrial relationship. In agreeing to union security (when not prevented from doing so by right-to-work laws), the parties set out a norm of conduct for the common good of their industrial community. When a worker takes a job in that place, he or she is no longer a detached individual; the worker becomes a member of the community and comes under its rules and norms. The alternative to such a system of ordered freedom is chaos and exaggerated individualism in the workplace.

*   *   *

The decimation of labor in right-to-work states, along with all the obstacles elsewhere, has led some to argue that organized labor should no longer play by the rules of the game. A growing number of people in and out of the labor movement believe unions ought to bypass the National Labor Relations Act and its cumbersome procedures. In other words, they ought to be prepared to go it alone. Msgr. Charles Owen Rice, a militant Catholic social activist for more than fifty years, put it this way in *The Pittsburgh Catholic:* "Unions should seriously consider becoming meaner and leaner, and preparing for another type of strategy and tactic. The wildcat strike and the sitdown strike should be legitimized; we may have to go back to some of the tactics and strategy of the Knights of Labor and the Wobblies. If the movement remains tame, shall we expect the return of the yellow-dog contract?"

The yellow-dog contracts were drawn up by employers and handed to individual workers, who could either sign or quit. On the basis of these so-called contracts, courts issued injunctions against union organizing drives during the early labor struggles. Although I doubt the clock will ever be turned back quite that far, Rice's question carries a warning to organized labor. And anti-union employers, for their part, would be well-advised to consider whether they really want a "meaner and leaner" labor movement.

Msgr. George Higgins introducing Solidarity leader Lech Walesa at a labor union rally in Washington, D.C.

7

State of the Unions: Part II

A Response to Critics, Left and Right

"LABOR LEADERS ARE FAT CATS, JUST LIKE MANAGEMENT"

I would refer anyone who believes this to *Business Week*, the leading popular business magazine. Once a year the magazine publishes a chart listing the salaries and bonuses of top corporate executives; a similar chart listing the salaries of top U.S. labor leaders follows in a subsequent issue. Year after year these charts show that the income of business executives is astronomically higher than that of labor leaders.

The last time I checked, Chrysler president Lee Iacocca was raking in millions a year. The president of the union that Iacocca deals with was making roughly $100,000, a comfortable living, to be sure, but not enough to land United Auto Workers president Owen Bieber in Iacocca's neighborhood.

In the game of wealth and privilege, labor leaders do not even play in the same league as their corporate counterparts. When George Meany was at the top of organized labor in the United States, I would on occasion visit his home in Bethesda, Maryland. It was a nice, comfortable place, with every modern household convenience. But it was like thousands of other homes in his Washington suburb. (And the same goes for the Kirkland residence in Washington.) I do not know where the CEOs of major companies went home at night. But I doubt it was to Meany's neighborhood or anyone like it. Those same CEOs, in all likelihood, have corporate jets ready to take off at any time. Yet outside of the Teamsters and perhaps one or two other international unions, I have never heard of "union jets."

Still, labor leaders have found themselves on the defensive because of their supposedly high living. Not until the 1990s did the same questions arise in regard to the astronomical salaries of upper-level corporate managers. In its reporting, much of the news media seemed to operate on a double standard: one for business leaders and a more stringent one for labor leaders. In other words, they seemed to think that a business executive was entitled to make as much as the traffic will bear, while a labor leader, as a representative of the working class, had to place voluntary limits on income and standard of living.

I go along with this argument, but only halfway. I agree that labor leaders ought to place reasonable limits on their income. This is merely another way of saying that trade-union leadership is a vocation that calls for personal dedication and self-sacrifice. The media does a service to the labor movement by keeping this ideal alive. It will be a sorry day for the labor movement if its leaders ever get the idea that they are entitled to live in the lap of luxury at the expense of the rank and file.

On the other hand, certain media outlets have done a disservice to both labor and management by failing to point out that business leaders should also place reasonable limits on their standards of living. To say that the president of a big union ought to be satisfied with a salary of, say, $50,000 to $75,000 but the president of a corporation with which he bargains is justified in asking for ten or twenty times that amount is flattering to labor but insulting to business. It suggests that the only incentive of the business person is materialistic.

It is, ironically, the self-appointed friends of the business executive who would reduce him or her to a purely economic unit, devoid of ideals and motivated solely by pecuniary incentives. I like to think they are made of better stuff than that. And, in fact, most executives of my acquaintance are reasonably dedicated individuals, as are a majority of the labor leaders I have met.

"HIGH UNION WAGES HAVE DRIVEN EMPLOYERS OUT OF BUSINESS"

Put another way, labor's unrealistic demands have caused American companies to price themselves out of a market. In effect, according to this argument, labor has killed the industrial goose that lays the golden eggs. The labor movement had better be more "responsible"—i.e. more moderate—in its wage demands.

Except perhaps in a few isolated cases, I do not know of a serious economist who subscribes to the notion that labor unions priced themselves and their companies out of business. The general consensus among the experts is that it wasn't the high price of labor that made Japan take over the leadership of selling cars in this country but the slowness of our industry to adapt to market needs. General Motors unveiled a recent line of Saturn cars without a General Motors logo on them, reportedly because company officials wanted Saturns to look like Japanese cars. I consider that an unhealthy situation.

It is true, nonetheless, that dirt-cheap labor in poor countries can price itself "into" the market. For example, I looked at my raincoat recently and realized it was made in Hong Kong. I do not know exactly what the current monthly wage is for a worker in Hong Kong, but it used to be about one-tenth of an American worker's wage. Yet that did not lower the price of the coat when it came to the stores in Washington. So companies stand to gain enormous profits by going with non-unionized, foreign workers.

Another force behind business decline has been the quick resort to mergers, leveraged buy-outs, and other financial activities that have nothing to do with production. I heard the president of U.S. Steel Corporation say in a videotape: "We're not in the business of making steel. We're in the business of making money." So the company bought into Mobil Oil and other concerns that had nothing to do with steel. As a result, the steel heartland of Pennsylvania has all but disappeared, and America's steel industry is lying on its back.

Yet the impression remains that "high union wages" did in American industry. The complaints persist at a time when the wages of workers have eroded and executive compensation has skyrocketed. (Some union leaders refer to the stratospheric salaries of corporate chiefs as the "annual executive pig-out.") Numerous studies have shown that most of the people today work more hours for less real pay and fewer benefits than in the past. Most families find that they need two wage-earners to maintain the standard of living they once enjoyed with a single paycheck. And even then, too many families, especially the younger ones, can barely keep up. In short, regular working families have received a shrinking portion of the American pie.

Unfortunately, some economists have shown more interest in producing new rationalizations for this decline of living standards than in grappling with causes of the problem.

"Let's talk about the difference in living standards rather than wages," the chief economist of a major U.S. corporation said during the roaring 1980s in a *New York Times* interview. The article dealt with efforts by American companies to bring American wages more in line with third world pay rates. Our economist said, "What in the Bible says we should have a better standard of living than others? We have to give back a bit of it."

The gentleman seemed to imply that this is what the Bible requires of U.S. workers. That is biblical fundamentalism reduced to absurdity. In any event, American workers do not need to be admonished to tighten their belts. Middle income workers already have been forced to give back more than a bit. Government statistics show that average earnings fell by more than 14 percent between 1973 and 1986 in inflation-adjusted dollars. And that trend has continued.

Compare this to figures on executive compensation, which reached a dubious milestone in 1988. In that year, according to *Business Week*, chief executives took home, for the first time, an average of two million dollars in total compensation. In 1988 the CEO record $2,025,285 was ninety-two times the average factory worker's $21,725, seventy-two times a teacher's $22,008, and forty-four times an engineer's $45,680. The disparities have only widened in the years since.

That is only part of the story. The report by *Business Week* (in its May 1989 issue) said corporate chiefs not only set new records on the pay scale, with some earning forty million dollars in salary, bonuses and stock options. It also estimated a new high in golden parachutes, with some executives pulling down more than forty million dollars on retirement.

Not surprisingly, executive salaries have in recent years come under the scrutiny of not only labor leaders but, in some cases, aggrieved stockholders. Public attention to corporate self-dealing reached a high point in early 1992 when President George Bush made his famous and disastrous trip to Japan, bringing with him an entourage of million-dollar auto executives. And with this pressure, some corporate officials themselves have begun to realize that disproportionately high executive salaries and fringe benefits give industry a bad name.

The dramatic upsurge in executive compensation must be particularly galling to American workers who have exercised restraint in recent wage demands and, in many cases, given back benefits gained in earlier negotiations. They have done so with the understanding that other groups were prepared to make proportionate sacrifices to help end recessions during the early 1980s and early 1990s. Things have not worked out that way. UAW President Owen Bieber was right on target when he observed at the end of the 1980s, "On the one hand (executives) say that intense foreign competition requires sacrifices, restraint, and discipline. Yet then they turn around and demonstrate none of those qualities by awarding themselves more compensation for a year's effort than could be spent in several lifetimes."

American workers take it for granted that there will always be a sizeable difference between their income and that of top executives. They accept this as a fact of life and don't spend too much time fretting over it. But they will fight back at the bargaining table if they suspect industry is taking advantage of them. And what else are they supposed to think when they learn that while their wages have fallen, executive pay has steadily and dramatically risen?

"Will Unions Ever Again Be Useful Organs of Society?" asked the title of a magazine article by Peter Drucker, intellectual guru of U.S. management for almost half a century. His answer: a qualified no. Drucker thinks that by the year 2010 unions will represent only five percent of the world's work force—unless they accept a non-adversarial relationship and work with management on productivity, quality and whatever else is needed to keep the enterprise competitive.

Drucker's call for less adversarial, more cooperative labor-management relations is not without merit. However, a more realistic treatment can be found in the U.S. bishops' 1986 pastoral letter on Catholic social teaching and the American economy. "Workers," it says, "rightly reject calls for less adversarial relationships when they are a smokescreen for demands that labor make all the concessions. For a partnership to be genuine, it must be a two-way street, with creative initiative and a willingness to cooperate on all sides."

The American bishops do not oppose labor-management partnership. In fact, the letter's critical reference to appeals for less adversarial relations comes in a section titled "A New American Experiment: Partnership for the Public Good," which heartily endorses industrial cooperation. Clearly, however, the two-way street on which the bishops insist has yet to materialize in the United States. Labor has been steadily losing ground and forced to make most of the concessions in collective bargaining.

Thomas R. Donahue, secretary-treasurer of the AFL-CIO and a former assistant secretary of labor, has put his finger on the real problem in labor-management relations. Speaking at Harvard University in 1985, Donahue said: "While it may seem appropriate for academics and journalists to lecture the trade union movement on the need to abandon a confrontational approach, our very real problem is finding employers, public or private, who wish to deal cooperatively with us."

In other words, what is needed is a less adversarial posture by management. Donahue went on to say that only in a relative handful of organized workplaces, unfortunately, has an enlightened management accepted labor's desire to move from conflict to cooperation. Seldom has management accepted labor as a real partner in the process. "The overwhelming majority of employers," he said, "resist any employee efforts to organize or at

least any spreading of the union to currently unrepresented units." Donahue argues here as much in sorrow as in anger, for he is convinced that
without new forms of labor-management-government cooperation it will
be impossible for the United States to deal successfully with the issues of
growth, international trade, employment and training, investment policies,
wage trends, inflation, etc.

All this suggests an important question: How can we have labor-
management cooperation without a strong labor movement? In my judgment, we cannot. Real cooperation means that both sides have roughly
equal power and authority. Otherwise, one side makes all the sacrifices.
That same side also has little or no opportunity to participate in the enterprise and thus contribute to the public good. As the bishops' letter says,
"Partnerships between labor and management are possible only when both
groups possess real freedom and power to influence decisions. This means
that unions ought to continue to play an important role in moving toward
greater economic participation within firms and industries."

Without strong and effective unions representing the workers, cooperation by labor easily degenerates into the cooperation of a "company
union," rubber-stamping the management program. It becomes a facade. At
best, cooperation—when only one side has real authority—reverts to a
form of paternalism.

It is idle, if not fatuous, to talk theoretically about new forms of
labor-management cooperation unless and until a consensus is reached that
effective unions are not only legitimate but, as the pastoral letter says
(echoing the words of Pope John Paul II), truly indispensable. As I have
already noted, in my judgment no such consensus exists. Indeed there is
reason to believe that we may be moving further and further away from
such a consensus.

"UNIONS ARE JUST ANOTHER SPECIAL-INTEREST GROUP"

Especially in a culture that places high value on individualism, institutions are bound to "look out for their own." And unions, in seeking out
new members, have been known to appeal to workers on the basis of their
economic self-interests. Like it or not, this often carries greater weight
than an appeal to social responsibility and the common good.

That said, however, anyone who thinks unions are no more than a
special-interest lobby should take a look at the AFL-CIO's legislative program. In 1991 the major policy concerns included national health insurance, the minimum wage, housing, and social security, all of which do not
primarily affect union members; they concern all workers. (The agenda, of
course, also included specifically union goals, particularly a ban on the

practice of firing, or "permanently replacing," workers who go out on strike.)

The special-interest argument comes not only from labor's conservative critics but from segments of the left. The complaint mixes in with criticism that organized labor has become much more an institution and much less a movement. So-called progressive spokesmen say they want to "put the movement back in labor." And to put it back, the labor movement will have to, among other things, defend the interests of all workers, not just dues-paying unionists.

These critics seem to believe that the labor movement performed this role much better in its "Golden Age" than it does today. As a matter of fact, labor's self-styled progressive critics had the same beef with the movement in the early decades of this century. And the argument, in many respects, was more on target in those days than now.

"Pure and simple unionism" was the slogan that captured labor's traditional philosophy. It meant that the movement should stick to the business of organizing workers and administering contracts, and steer clear of legislative matters. In the early days of the movement, the hands-off approach to public policy was understandable. Nearly all of labor's experiences with government had proved negative; labor had no experience of legislation that actually helped workers as opposed to thwarting their basic rights. But then, in the mid-1930s, things changed with the passage of laws that greatly benefited the labor movement.

At least for me, the whole matter of "pure and simple unionism"—also known as voluntarism—seemed interesting enough to write a doctoral dissertation on the subject. This is how I described the traditional view in 1944:

> Voluntarism, then, takes the position that capitalism is so strongly entrenched that the workers ought not to attempt to replace it. It is wiser for them to accept capitalism and to organize within the system to protect and advance their interests, relying on their economic strength by functioning primarily through their unions. They can expect little from the government. The only desirable legislation for the workers is that which offers protection to their labor market by restriction on immigration, and which restrains government agencies, such as the courts and the police, from encroaching upon or hampering such union activities as strikes, picketing and boycotts. The workers ought not to demand more positive legislation from the government; the unions are the agency upon which the workers must rely for positive gains.

For this view, the labor movement came in for heavy criticism from liberals and progressives. Referring to criticism of the American Federation of Labor, during the dark labor times of the 1920s, I further said: "It became fashionable during this period for dissidents to lay blame for all of the Federation's failures directly at the door of [Samuel] Gompers and his philosophy of voluntarism." Whether or not valid, the criticism signaled a change of course in the labor movement. As I wrote at the time, "There has been a distinct change since the great depression in the traditional attitude of labor as represented by the A.F. of L., toward social and labor legislation."

I reach back to past arguments in order to shed some light on the present. Even the casual observer of organized labor would recognize that these accounts of voluntarism do not describe the labor movement of today. Organized labor advocates national policies that touch the masses of working people, whether or not they belong to unions. (All this is not to suggest that pure and simple unionism was merely a special interest. Where would the United States and its mass-market economy be if not for the decent wages and benefits achieved through collective bargaining?)

Workers who earn the minimum wage can bet their last $4.25 it was labor that got the law on the books. At the same time, the meager hourly standard points up the limitations of social legislation. A family does not live on the minimum wage. At best, it simply survives. Unionism, pure and simple, would certainly help workers get better pay and benefits.

Ironically, labor is getting hit on the head from the left at a time when right-wing forces are mounting a fierce campaign against labor's right to engage in social advocacy. Anti-union groups have managed to get courts —including the highest in the land—to curtail labor's right to use union dues to lobby on behalf of worker concerns. At least theoretically, workers in union shops can opt out of all or part of their dues if they differ with the union's legislative agenda. That amounts to legal enforcement of pure and simple unionism—except that the architects of the campaign have less interest in unions, pure and simple, than in unions, dead and gone.

"UNIONS SHOULD STAY OUT OF POLITICS"

The campaign against labor activism has raised a set of questions: Do unions have a right to engage in political action? If so, to what extent and in what manner? Is it always wise for unions to get involved in politics?

My answer to the first question is yes. Constitutionally and ethically, unions have the same right to engage in political action as any other economic, professional, educational or cultural organization. While American unions have generally disavowed efforts to form their own political party, they are nonetheless in politics to stay—on a selective, non-partisan basis. They seek not only to protect their own interests but also to support measures which, in their judgment, promote the national welfare and advance the cause of international peace.

The second question—regarding the extent and manner of union political activism—is more difficult. Normally unions should act independently and neither control nor be controlled by any particular party. When unions are too closely linked with a party, as Pope John Paul II has pointed out, "they easily lose contact with their specific role, which is to secure the just rights of workers. . . . Instead they become an instrument used for other purposes."

One of the more sweeping proposals appeared in a textbook for Catholic high schools, *The Common Good—Christian Democracy and American National Problems,* by the late Dr. Thomas P. Neill, who taught history for many years at St. Louis University. According to Neill, unions "have no right to attempt to sway their members in support of public policies that do not affect union interests."

Who defines "union interests"? Can they be limited to wages, hours, Social Security, taxation and the like, or do they not extend, for example, to education, foreign aid, the United Nations and other issues involving national welfare and international peace? If the advocacy of labor unions is restricted to narrowly defined "union interests," will the same kind of limitation be placed on employers' organizations and on educational, legal and medical associations? I certainly hope not. Granted, all these organizations can overextend themselves or take their political activities too seriously. But that's no justification for denying their right to "sway their members in support of public policies" that go beyond their narrow interests.

At the same time, a union or any other organization can at times try to cover too much political ground. Probably all of them could use a little more self-restraint; too much political involvement may antagonize their own constituents. Most Americans would like to know what their union, employers' organization or professional association has to say about political issues and candidates. But Americans are not particularly class conscious. They have many other loyalties besides their particular economic or professional organization, and look to many other sources for political ideas and guidance. A union which tried to monopolize their political thinking would be making a serious mistake.

In recent years, some people in the labor movement have seemed eager to make that mistake. In 1989, I received a letter from a rank-and-file union member complaining bitterly that her local has misused her dues money to aggressively support abortion on demand. After her initial correspondence,

I obtained a copy of an article published in the local union's official newspaper. The article, signed by one of the local's top officials, referred contemptuously to pro-lifers as "frauds and bullies." It further described pro-lifers as anti-union and part of "a concerted effort by the reactionary right to push working people down."

At the time, I said in my Catholic press column that the equation of pro-life with anti-union "reflects an appalling lack of common sense and of sensitivity to the conscientious convictions of pro-life union members and of many pro-labor people outside the trade union movement. As one who has spent his entire lifetime publicly and forcefully supporting the movement through thick and thin, I take it as a personal insult. I might add that at a time when the trade union movement is beset with so many other problems, it needs this divisive and insulting propaganda like it needs a hole in the head."

I thought the article in the union newspaper would prove a one-shot aberration by a fanatical and unrepresentative lone ranger in the labor movement. I was wrong. At the November 1989 biennial convention of the AFL-CIO, several unions submitted pro-choice resolutions. Instead of taking action at the meeting, the federation decided to appoint an eighteen member panel of top trade union officers to hammer out a consensus on the issue. For a while it seemed that the AFL-CIO might plunge itself into the abortion wars. Yet in July 1990, the federation's thirty-five member executive council, meeting in Chicago, voted overwhelmingly to remain neutral on the issue.

The federation's neutrality, however, does not stop individual unions from adopting pro-choice stands, and several of them have already done so. Furthermore, the AFL-CIO is likely at some point to take up the issue again. So abortion remains a live issue in the labor movement. For this reason I think it worthwhile to recount the arguments I made during the debate of 1990. I was one of two witnesses invited to testify before the eighteen-member study panel, which later recommended neutrality. Informally addressing the panel, I made the following points:

> I am here this afternoon at the committee's invitation, not at my own request or on my own initiative. This is by way of emphasizing at the outset that I have too much respect for trade union democracy to get involved, except by invitation, in the internal procedures of the federation and would never have presumed to ask for an opportunity to meet with your committee. In this connection, I would only add that I have scrupulously refrained from discussing the committee's agenda with any of the committee members and, in fact, until very recently I didn't even know

who would be serving on the committee. In short, it is not my style to lobby the federation in an effort to influence its internal policy decisions. I have, to be sure, made two public statements on the issue. It will be the burden of my presentation this afternoon to explain why I felt it appropriate to do so.

A recent news story in *The Washington Post* about today's committee meeting was inadvertently misleading. It said, in effect, that I would be speaking today for the anti-abortion forces. Not so. I have not come here this afternoon to talk about, much less debate, the abortion issue as such. I know perfectly well that there are clear-cut differences of opinion in our pluralistic society on both the ethical and public policy aspects of this divisive and volatile issue. Like every other literate and concerned citizen I have my own personal opinion about both aspects of the issue, but I respect the opinion of those who see the issue, in all its complexity, differently than I do. There are many forums in which men and women of good will can dialogue, with civility, about their differing opinions, but I do not intend to initiate such a dialogue in this committee meeting.

I do not appear before the committee as an instructed representative or spokesperson for any official or any agency of my own church. I am here on my own, speaking in my own name. On this point, I would like to add very emphatically that, in my judgment, some elements in the media and some of the more doctrinaire partisans in the abortion controversy have badly distorted the record by simplistically stereotyping the abortion issue as an exclusively Catholic issue. As one who has followed this debate very closely for many years, I think that's sheer nonsense. The plain fact of the matter is that the controversy over both the ethical and public policy aspects of the issue cuts across all denominational lines. In other words, the debate is being carried on, pro and con, by people of all religious faiths and by many, again pro and con, who claim no religious affiliation. To cite but one example, Nat Hentoff of *The Village Voice* falls into the latter category. Hentoff, a good friend of mine, who is strongly anti-abortion, describes himself as an atheist. So it goes.

The basic point I wish to make is that, in my judgment, based on nearly fifty years of close association with the labor movement in all parts of the country, it would be a serious mistake, for pragmatic reasons, for the federation to take an official position, one way or the other, on the abortion issue. When I say one way or the other, I mean to emphasize that if, hypothetically, the several resolutions that you are considering were pro-life rather than pro-choice resolutions, so-called, I would still argue that the federation, for the same pragmatic reasons, should remain neutral on the issue.

I take this position as one who has been passionately committed to labor's cause. For nearly five decades I have worked almost full-time to promote labor's legitimate goals, letting the chips fall where they may. I am unabashedly proud of my record in this regard. I have spent my entire lifetime supporting labor's cause because, as I said a few weeks ago at the reception which the Executive Council hosted on the occasion of my Golden Jubilee [fiftieth anniversary of priestly ordination], I am firmly committed to the proposition that effective labor unions are still by far the most powerful force in society for the protection of the laborer's rights and the improvement of his or her condition. . . . It is precisely because I am so firmly committed to this proposition—always have been and always will be—and because I am so profoundly concerned about the declining strength of the labor movement, that I feel very strongly that the federation should, for the good of the movement, maintain its traditional neutrality on those issues on which its members, as a matter of conscience, are deeply divided.

With specific reference to the current abortion controversy, I am absolutely certain in my own mind that if the federation were to deviate from its long-standing policy of neutrality by adopting either a so-called pro-life or so-called pro-choice position—or even if it were to fudge the issue—it would seriously disrupt the unity and solidarity of the movement. This would come at a time when the movement needs the fullest possible measure of internal unity and solidarity if it hopes to survive and prosper in today's hostile anti-union environment. The U.S. labor movement has from day one been a "neutral" movement in the best sense of the word—a movement in which men and women of differing ideologies and religious ethical convictions have been able to unite around basic labor issues and to work together in solidarity. No other trade union movement in the world can match its record in this regard.

It is obvious, of course, that this kind of trade union solidarity demands a certain price. It demands that all of the movement's officers and members agree on basic trade union issues and agree to disagree, and to go their separate ways in non-trade union forums of their own choice, on volatile and highly divisive issues in the area of personal morality. Solidarity demands that they refrain from forcing their own personal views on such matters into the movement's official agenda.

"UNIONS ARE FRAUGHT WITH CORRUPTION AND RACKETEERING"

Union corruption has been disgracefully distorted. I do not know of any institution, including the Catholic Church, which is free of corruption. As I write, prominent Wall Street investors are in jail on felony convictions; several members of the U.S. Congress are under investigation for unethical and possibly criminal conduct. Yet outside of former Teamster leaders, it would be hard to name any national union figures in trouble with the law.

In 1957 George Meany did something extraordinary. He expelled the Teamsters, the nation's largest union, from the AFL-CIO. And with the Teamsters went a large share of the federation's per capita income. I was there, at the AFL-CIO convention, when Meany dropped the hammer on the Teamsters. It was a dramatic event. Meany moved against the Teamsters on ethical grounds, and bad press followed the union for more than three decades, deservedly to some extent, but not entirely so.

Even the Teamsters (who were let back into the federation in 1987) did not deserve the image of mob-infiltrated unionism at all levels. There were always some good, clean Teamster locals, not to mention a lively dissident movement—Teamsters for Union Democracy—that scored a few election victories in the 1980s. These Teamsters were victims of corruption, not perpetrators. And in December 1991, the victims turned into victors. Ron Carey, head of a United Parcel Service local in New York, along with his slate of sixteen other Teamster dissidents, swept government-supervised elections for the union's top offices. The elections have made the Teamsters one of the most democratic unions in organized labor.

The racketeers have yet to be completely purged from organized labor, but their days are numbered. In fact, unions today rank among the most democratic institutions in society, more democratic than most, including churches, to say nothing of corporations. Today the big problem in organized labor is not something the labor movement is doing—e.g. corruption—but what it's not doing, or is not able to do. Labor is not organizing workers who want and need to be unionized.

I would not want to close this discussion without a few words about an experiment in union democracy launched in 1957, under the courageous leadership of Walter Reuther.

At the time, union leaders were troubled. The Senate's McClellan

Committee had revealed the alarming inroads that racketeers had made in some segments of the labor movement. The AFL-CIO was attempting to clean up its own house lest responsible union leaders be tarred with the image created by less-responsible elements in the movement. Anti-labor forces were making speeches up and down the country, gloating at the division in labor's ranks.

Today it strikes me as remarkable that out of this crisis arose one of the most innovative vehicles for the enhancement of union democracy— the United Auto Workers Public Review Board, a seven-member independent agency which acts as a kind of internal supreme court. It passes final and binding judgment on all charges brought before the agency on appeal by UAW members alleging violations of the union's constitution and by-laws.

Walter Reuther and the UAW could have reacted defensively to the fear and tensions of the time, closing ranks against real and imagined enemies. Instead, the UAW's 1957 convention chose to open up the union through creation of the review board, offering members an avenue of appeal totally independent of the union's leadership.

Initially, some members of the union and of the press took a jaundiced view of this experiment in union democracy. Some thought that the board would serve as a "patsy" for the international union or as a public relations tool. Others feared that the board would encroach upon the legitimate autonomy of the union.

I predicted in my 1957 speech to the convention that such fears would prove unfounded. More than thirty years later, at the 1989 UAW convention in Anaheim, California, I was able, in my report as chairman of the Public Review Board, to give mostly good news to the two thousand delegates. This is what I told them:

> In the board's thirty-odd years of existence, we have enjoyed the union's complete cooperation. It has never refused us access to information we thought relevant to the resolution of an issue. Similarly, it has never refused to reopen records on cases we felt needed a second look. On other occasions, we have felt it necessary to draw the union's attention to situations reflecting basic injustices done to members which were beyond the board's power to correct since employment rights were at stake. In a number of cases, with help of the international, remedies have been effected.
>
> The union has never tried to pack the board with people who it felt could be expected to act in a manner favorable to its objectives. We have enjoyed complete freedom to propose can-

didates to fill vacancies that have occurred. The fears expressed about the board in 1957 have not materialized nor, as yet, have all the hopes. It takes more than a year, on the average, for a UAW member to process his or her case from the first step through the final appeal either to the Board or the Constitutional Convention. This is too long, though steps are already being taken to reduce the length of time to four months, from start to finish.

Unfortunately, the institution of self-discipline by and large has not found favor with other major labor organizations. As a consequence, members of all unions are becoming increasingly inclined to resort to outside institutions for the redress of their grievances. With this inevitably comes greater federal control over labor unions and hence a loss or diminution of legitimate trade union autonomy.

Obviously, the UAW's public review board has little or no control over this problem. The failure of other unions to adopt a similar program, however, does affect the UAW. The law being made in the courts today is often being made with respect to the worst possible situations. Unfortunately, this law applies with equal force to all unions, democratic or not. Thus we find courts increasingly willing to take matters out of the hands of internal union procedures without even minimal exhaustion of voluntary remedies. This is doubly unfortunate since it increases the burden of our already overburdened courts.

Interestingly, the vast majority of the hundreds of cases we have heard did not involve charges of corruption or unethical conduct. In most cases, all the worker wants is that his union represent him diligently in a given dispute with management. In other words, the root of the grievance is with the employer as well as the union. To me, this points up the need for unions. Employees want and need effective representation.

Relevance and Rebirth

Several years ago I stayed in a hotel in Disneyland for a two-week conference. Anyone who knows anything about Disneyland hotels knows that the rooms are almost always booked, and so the owners make lots of money. I got to know some of the hotel workers, including the woman who cleaned my room. I asked her how long she had worked there. "Twenty years," she said. I asked if she would mind telling me how much she earned. "Minimum wage," was her reply.

I am often asked: Why are unions needed in this day and age? People should not ask me. They should ask the maid at Disneyland and other low-wage workers. If her situation was like that of other minimum-wage workers, she probably had no health insurance, in addition to no living wage. Health insurance, which originated at the bargaining table, represents one of organized labor's great contributions to the American worker. Without this coverage, people can run up bills for health care that would otherwise land them in the poorhouse. And yet, millions of non-union workers have no health insurance; as a result, more than thirty million Americans are not covered and several times as many are under-insured.

Wages and benefits are not the only reasons why many people feel the need and desire to say "Union Yes." A few years ago, in Washington, D.C., hotel workers and management were in accord on bread-and-butter issues and close to settlement. But there was one hitch. The workers, whose first names appeared on hotel uniforms, wanted to see their full names on the uniforms. Management balked at this, saying "Maria" or "Clarence" or whatever name was good enough. Yet for the workers, it was a matter of simple dignity. "What are we? The house slaves?" the mostly black and Hispanic work force wanted to know. The contract negotiations almost broke down. But in due time, the members of the Hotel and Restaurant workers' union got their wish; they celebrated victory in a downtown African-American church. Without a union, it is almost unthinkable that they would have been granted this simple request.

Those who want to know if unions are still needed should talk to hospital workers, many of whom find themselves at the bottom of the wage scale. In New York City, they do not call Cardinal John O'Connor "the patron saint of hospital workers" because of his saintliness. They do so because of his unflagging support of their full union rights in Catholic and other health care institutions.

At the end of a 1990 labor dispute, the hospital association in New York City, including the Catholic hospitals, announced that workers who had gone on strike would not get their jobs back. In effect, the hospitals were going to fire the strikers. O'Connor, however, stepped in and ordered Catholic hospitals to break ranks with the association. "There will be no firing of strikers in this archdiocese," was his message. He told the church-related institutions to negotiate a separate agreement. They did, and by doing so put pressure on other New York hospitals to follow suit.

Those who ask why unions are needed should talk to black workers. In recent years they have moved into organized labor at a rate faster than any other group in the American work force, and recent pollings suggest that the rest of them would do the same if they had half a chance—that is, if not for the many obstacles to unionization. Admittedly, though, the labor movement has not always extended a warm welcome to black Americans.

Like other institutions, organized labor has been guilty of racism; at times in the past, labor excluded blacks from positions of leadership and failed to defend their interests at the bargaining table and in the councils of government. Yet even during the worst of times, leaders of black America —A. Philip Randolph, Martin Luther King Jr., and Bayard Rustin, to name a few—never wrote off the labor movement. In fact, they looked to the labor movement to raise the living standards of poor and working-class blacks.

Rustin, who organized the famous 1963 march on Washington, was pilloried by some of his opponents for this line of argument. He once called organized labor "the only significant social force which (can) be depended upon to press the safeguarding of the social and economic rights achieved (by blacks) through protest and struggle."

Even Robert F. Kennedy, a mainstream liberal politician, disagreed with Rustin. Kennedy is reported to have said just a few weeks before his assassination that "we have to write off the unions and the South now and replace them with blacks, blue-collar whites and the kids." He made this statement during the Indiana primary in an interview with his longtime friend and political confidant, Jack Newfield of *The Village Voice*. After winning that primary, Kennedy said in another interview with Newfield that he had a chance, "just a chance, to organize a new coalition of blacks and working-class white people, against the union and party establishments." I said then that Rustin, in calling for a labor-civil rights coalition, was right and that Kennedy, in writing off the labor movement, was wrong. I still think so.

During those years, as I said in the National Catholic Welfare Conference's 1964 Labor Day statement, organized labor was "on the spot" in the arena of racial justice. Since then, race relations in the labor movement have dramatically improved. Problems remain. Yet, generally speaking, organized labor comes in for less criticism from African-Americans than do other major institutions, such as business, education, mass media and, notably, the churches. When I go to trade union gatherings, I see more black and brown faces than I ever do at other meetings, including those held by liberal church groups.

Today the problem of blacks and organized labor is not labor's treatment of black unionists. The problem is that low-wage blacks, who need the protection of unions, are not getting it. As vulnerable workers, they face enormous obstacles when they try to organize and bargain collectively. They have to contend with labor laws that often hurt more than help workers and with frequent threats of retaliation by employers. (Sadly, in some cases, certain employers feel especially free to thwart the collective-bargaining rights of African-American workers.) In short, not enough black workers are being organized. That is the race problem in the American labor movement.

*   *   *

A strong labor movement is also needed to defend the rights of labor in other countries. The help given by the American labor movement to the Polish labor union Solidarity was indispensable, though unheralded. By and large, Solidarity did not get its help from Washington but from labor unions in the U.S. and Europe.

This seemed obvious every time I attended a Solidarity gathering in Poland. The most celebrated guests at these gatherings were not foreign political leaders, or clerics, for that matter, but members of the American labor movement. In the inner circle of Solidarity, the most popular name was Lane Kirkland, not Ronald Reagan or George Bush. Kirkland and other U.S. labor leaders were there when Solidarity needed them, channeling effective aid to the Poles during the dark hours of repression. And let us not forget that Solidarity, aided materially and morally by U.S. labor, started the chain of events that led eventually to the collapse of communism in eastern Europe and the Soviet Union.

In the years since, some observers have found it hard to accept the fact that regular working people—in Poland and other countries—brought about the triumph of Solidarity. They have searched for another explanation and, at least to their satisfaction, found one in Carl Bernstein's celebrated article, "Holy Alliance," published by *Time* magazine in February 1992. The article alleged in great detail that President Ronald Reagan and Pope John Paul II "conspired" in a "secret alliance" to thwart communism in Poland by aiding the Polish trade union movement. No outside observer —and least of all this one—can say whether or not or to what extent Bernstein's story was verifiably accurate. The Vatican flatly denied the report, although Bernstein quoted Cardinal Agostino Casaroli as noting "a real coincidence of interests between the U.S. and the Vatican" on the issue of Solidarity. A coincidence of interests, however, hardly adds up to a conspiratorial "secret alliance."

In the flurry of debate that followed, hardly anyone seemed to notice what appeared to me as one of the more interesting points about the *Time* cover story. Whether fully accurate or not in every detail, the article put the lie to those who charged in the 1980s that the Catholic Church, in its own self-serving interests, had abandoned Solidarity or at least had tried to slow it down. Ironically, some of those critics were themselves by no means fully supportive of Solidarity. That goes for a segment of the European peace movement during the early and middle 1980s. So, whatever else may be said about Bernstein's story, it did, at the very least, clear the record on this score.

In any event, the people who know best—the leaders of Solidarity—constantly refer to the crucial role played by U.S. labor representatives in their triumph over totalitarianism. It goes without saying that if the American labor movement continues to lose ground, it will become less and less effective in helping oppressed workers in other countries to follow Solidarity's history-making lead. Will the American labor movement be able to help the workers of China, for instance, when their time comes? Will it be able to help the developing nations of east Asia to achieve political and economic democracy? How ironic it would be if, ten or twenty years from now, labor movements that have thrown off the yoke of communist domination were to end up stronger and more influential than the American labor movement, which has done so much to help them win their struggle for freedom.

Even in a perfect world, unions would have a vital role for reasons much larger than the struggle for a living wage and decent working conditions. In recent years, many have begun to recognize the need for new forms of labor-management relations. Call it co-determination, co-management, or partnership: by any name, it means greater employee participation in the making of industrial policies. How will we create these new forms if employees have no representation? Without strong organizations behind them, how will workers have a voice?

Those who dismiss the need for representation would seem to take us back to an old form of individualism. "We're 220 million individuals. We don't need structures," is the attitude. Others, including myself, start from the premise that it is natural to organize. Human beings do not organize merely for the sake of putting bread on the table, although this is not a bad reason for doing so. People organize because of their nature as social beings. Employers can do nice things for their workers and lawmakers can pass kind and gentle laws. But only strong and independent organizations can give employees a genuine say in their economic lives. Like the hotel workers in Washington, D.C., workers of all kinds do not want to be treated like the house slaves; they want their dignity.

Let me state the argument in the more technical language of natural-law social ethics. Incredibly, at this late date, the argument comes off as counter-cultural in the United States.

In modern life, the structure of society is such that the individual must ordinarily act through organized groups to secure his or her rights. So great is the power of the civil state, and the size and might of industry, that the unorganized worker is left without an effective voice in matters of vital concern. Only through the existence of buffer groups, close enough to the individual to hear his or her plea, but powerful enough to be recognized by governmental and economic societies, can we hope to safeguard the ordinary worker from the tyranny of entrenched power. Workers cannot normally achieve their rights by acting merely as individuals. They may lack the ability, experience, knowledge and power to bring their case effectively to the employer. Even when employers are conscientious and anxious to be fair, the sheer size of much of modern industry makes individual dealings impossible. With the utmost of good will on both sides, it is still necessary to have formal and organized methods of handling grievances, rights, and claims. Such a procedure is effective only when the machinery of appeal is distinct from the employer and his or her representatives.

This representative and coordinating function of unions takes on new meaning at a time when the fundamental issue facing the U.S. economy is how to balance our human values with the economy's need for flexibility in a globally competitive market. In the current economic environment, American industry and labor are struggling with the problem of lagging competitiveness, particularly in our manufacturing base. They are formulating strategies for becoming more profitable and competitive in an increasingly complex world economy. Our responsibility and challenge is to accomplish this task without sacrificing our hard-won human rights gains in the workplace. Among those: equal employment opportunity, safe and decent working conditions, adequate wages, security in both employment and retirement, and the opportunity to improve one's standard of living.

In other words, people need and want to organize. Every professional group has an organization. Doctors have the American Medical Association. Lawyers have the American Bar Association. Business executives have any organization they want. No one would ever dream of trying to stop doctors, lawyers, and business executives from organizing. But in this country, resistance to the organization of workers happens all the time.

*   *   *

In 1989, a general strike at Eastern Airlines invited a new round of analysis of labor's future. The strike was marked by a revived spirit of trade union solidarity. Did the unity and strength shown by the labor movement signal, as some observers said, "a comeback of organized labor"? Or was the strike, as others argued, just a "last hurrah" by the labor movement?

Among those seeing a last hurrah was Bruce Fein, who wrote in a *Washington Times* column that U.S. labor unions were moribund and "fading into the sunset." Fein is a Washington-based commentator who specializes in legal issues and has appeared on national TV talk shows. "The years of private-sector unions," he wrote, "have dawned. Like Gen. Douglas

MacArthur's old soldiers, old union men like Lane Kirkland will experience no dramatic death, but simply fade away." Fein looks too young to remember the Great Depression of the early 1930s. But before calling in a coroner to certify the death of the American labor movement, he might want to read the many premature obituaries of the labor movement published at the height of the Depression.

"American trade unionism is slowly being limited in influence by changes which destroy the basis on which it is erected. . . . I see no reason to believe that American trade unionism . . . will become in the next decade a more potent social influence," the American Economic Association was told by its president in 1932. To the chagrin of such critics, millions of workers marched into the ranks of organized labor during the following years, and the labor movement's funeral had to be postponed indefinitely. By the end of the decade, almost forty percent of eligible workers were organized. The labor movement emerged stronger than ever.

I am no more a prophet than is Fein or any of the other happy messengers of labor's doom. But I think history is on my side when I predict that the labor movement will be going strong long after Fein and I have faded into the sunset. It is at least possible that an historical replay will happen in our own generation—probably less dramatically or, if you will, more incrementally than in the mid-1930s—if we can summon the will to enact a kind of and degree of labor law reform more radical than the pallid type of reform which narrowly failed enactment in the 1970s.

With or without the support of law, the labor movement is moving ahead. In the case of the United Mine Workers, the labor movement and the law clashed head-on. It happened during the 1989–1990 strike against the Pittston coal company in southwestern Virginia. For many months the miners seemed, on a superficial reading of their situation, to be waging a battle against hopeless odds. They must have felt abandoned and forgotten. Media coverage of the strike was sparse and intermittent. In fact, one survey showed that the news media gave considerably more coverage to a miners' strike going on at the same time in the Soviet Union than they gave to the Pittston strike here at home.

In addition, the miners, who adhered strictly to a policy of non-violent civil disobedience, were harassed by the state police. The union and its officers were hit with ridiculously high fines for minor acts of civil disobedience. (A judge levied $60 million in fines for "obstructing traffic" and other minor infractions.) In view of all this, it appeared to many observers that the strike was doomed and might well prove the last gasp of the United Mine Workers and, to change the metaphor, one more nail in the coffin of the American labor movement.

The doomsayers had it all wrong. They failed to reckon with the fact that the miners, historically, have been known for their solidarity and their dogged staying power against all odds. They failed to take serious account of the fact that the strikers enjoyed widespread support from many other unions and from an effective, inter-denominational network of religious organizations.

Far from a last gasp of the United Mine Workers, the Pittston strike gave a shot in the arm to labor across-the-board. It may represent what one commentator (writing in the *Wall Street Journal,* of all places) has described as "the embryonic stirrings of a rebirth of the labor movement."

In Sheridan, Wyoming, more than halfway across the country from southwestern Virginia, another two hundred and fifty UMW members had been on strike for more than two years. In February 1990, as the Pittston strikers celebrated victory, I was privileged to take part in a solidarity rally in support of the beleaguered strikers in Sheridan. It was an uplifting experience. The mood of the strikers and their families was buoyant and optimistic. They made clear their determination to stay the course for as long as it took to get a settlement. And the UMW, with the Pittston settlement about to be ratified, was able to concentrate more of its resources on the Sheridan dispute. Other unions and church-related organizations from across the country also joined hands in a spirit of solidarity as they did in the case of the Pittston strike. A year after my trip to Sheridan, word came that the miners had finally prevailed in their struggle.

Both in southwestern Virginia and in Sheridan, the miners went on strike very reluctantly and as a last resort. As the record clearly shows, it was their only alternative. I emphasize this point in order to counter the lingering impression among many Americans that U.S. unions are "strike happy." In my opinion, nothing could be further from the truth. Does anyone seriously think the miners enjoyed being out of work—for nine months in Virginia and three years in Wyoming? They deserved praise rather than condemnation for their willingness—and the willingness of their spouses and families—to make this sacrifice for the good of the cause.

I say "for the good of the cause" because the miners struggled not only for their own rights but for the rights of their fellow workers and for the betterment of our national economy. This point—the connection between labor struggle and the common good—was underlined in the 1989 Labor Day Statement of the United States Catholic Conference:

> A strong trade union movement, with widespread collective bargaining, can strengthen all of society. We need to examine how government policies encourage or discourage employers from campaigns to dismantle established unions, unilaterally rescind health and retirement benefits or restructure so as to block or-

ganizing efforts. . . . The value of democratic labor unions to a free society must be recognized at home as well as abroad.

After rejoicing in the gains that workers had made in eastern Europe, the Labor Day Statement hastened to add: "In the United States, ironically, workers are measurably worse off than they were ten years ago. Structural changes in the economy, increased reliance on imports, union-breaking efforts and a growing shift to lower-paid and part-time employment have left millions of Americans without the protection of unions. For many, this has meant lower living standards, no health benefits and less security for their family."

If the stirrings of labor are real, workers in the not-so-distant future may be measurably better off than they are today. Nonetheless the obstacles facing labor will not go away by themselves. Like other institutions in crisis, the movement needs to look at its problems in a fresh and open way. In a sense, labor needs a Vatican II. In the 1960s, faced with its own crisis, the Catholic Church underwent a four-year process of self-examination through the Second Vatican Council. The church looked at what needed to be changed in order to move into the modern world. Like the church, the American labor movement has to look at what needs to be changed in order to move into a new world of workplace realities.

Needless to say, the labor movement cannot rest on its laurels. It cannot turn away from the new world and put all its energy into protecting the gains of dues-paying union members. It has to reach out to those who need help the most—the masses of unorganized Americans. If labor and its friends fail to do this, we will strike a sour note with the public. We will not be taken seriously.

I am happy to say that the labor movement has already begun to throw open the windows of a new industrial era. Part of what they see is a growing population of low-paid service workers, ably represented by the Service Employees International Union. One of the most progressive unions in the country, the SEIU has tackled the problem with a long-term organizing campaign among the nation's estimated one million custodial workers who clean and maintain the office buildings of our cities. Called "Justice for Janitors," the campaign is aimed at a largely female, largely minority work force. A major goal is winning health insurance for workers and their families.

"Justice for Janitors" challenges the comfortable assumptions of many of America's well-to-do. During the 1980s, newspapers regularly touted the miracle of America's service sector pumping new money and new jobs into our communities. But the success in this "new economy" was troublingly one-dimensional. The people at the top—executives, attorneys, financiers, etc.—did very well indeed. But the people at the bottom who make the money machine run usually did quite poorly. Those are the janitors, clerical workers, computer operators, and myriad of people who staff today's information industries and form the backbone of a lucrative sector of our economy.

*   *   *

I cannot prove it and may not live to see it, but somehow or other I am convinced that the United States cannot much longer remain immune to the virus of freedom that is so dramatically and unexpectedly sweeping the globe. The full rights of labor, reclaimed by formerly totalitarian societies, will eventually find their way back to the United States. In this connection I take comfort in the thought that in 1932, when the fortunes of organized labor had sunk to a much lower level than today, the experts and pundits completely missed the signs of the times. The signs of our own times may well point to labor's renewal.

We shall see about that. But of this much I am certain—that George P. Shultz spoke the truth when he told the National Planning Association in 1991 that "free societies and free trade unions go together." Those words —in a speech that lamented the decline of organized labor—came from a man who has held the top cabinet posts in several Republican administrations, including Ronald Reagan's State Department. Ray Marshall, like Shultz, a former secretary of labor, has elaborated on this message: "We should be particularly concerned about the weakening of labor organizations since the 1960s, because we are not likely to have a free and democratic society without a free a democratic labor movement. Trying to have economic democracy without unions is like trying to have political democracy without political parties."

Will we keep on trying?

Msgr. Higgins returns from Gdansk with a Solidarity flag for AFL-CIO President Lane Kirkland and Secretary-Treasurer Thomas Donahue

8

On the Condition of Catholic Social Teaching and Action

My Rerum Novarum *Speech*

The year 1991 marked the one hundredth anniversary of Pope Leo XIII's ground-breaking encyclical letter *Rerum Novarum* ("New Things"), which endorsed the rights of labor and launched the modern tradition of Catholic social teaching. (The document appeared in English under the title, "On the Condition of Workers.") In the United States, observances of the centenary of *Rerum Novarum* were phenomenally widespread. I had never seen anything quite like it in my lifetime. Almost every time I picked up my mail, I learned of another meeting planned to celebrate the anniversary. Some people marked the event with high-level scholarly conferences and seminars at colleges and universities. Other meetings had a more popular thrust, organized by unions, dioceses and social action groups. The gatherings, under whatever auspices, went on all through the year and all over the country. I would wager that American Catholics celebrated the document called the "Magna Carta" of Catholic social teaching more heartily than their counterparts anywhere in the world.

I went to a dozen or more of those gatherings, as speaker and listener, though I had to cancel a swath of engagements scheduled for the latter part of the year, due to hip surgery. What follows in these pages is—compositely— what I said at those meetings and what I might have said at the others.

*   *   *

There are many different ways of observing the centenary of *Rerum Novarum*. I have opted to do so by pulling together informally some of my personal recollections about how the encyclical and follow-up encyclicals of Leo XIII's successors have been received and implemented in the United States. I speak, not as a latter-day part-time academician, but rather in the light of my own experience on the staff of the original National Catholic Welfare Conference and later the United States Catholic Conference.

Looking back fifty years—halfway back to *Rerum Novarum*—I am struck, first of all, by the fact that we now tend to approach the encyclicals and other relevant church documents with a greater sense of historical consciousness. In short, we are less inclined to exegete them talmudically than in the past. My former colleague, Father John F. Cronin, who in years gone by was America's preeminent popularizer of Catholic social teaching, touched upon this point twenty years ago in recalling the reception of Pope Pius XI's 1931 encyclical *Quadragesimo Anno* and related documents. "It never occurred to us," Cronin wrote, "that these documents were both historically and culturally conditioned. We realized that [*Quadragesimo Anno*] was clearly addressed to the major industrial areas of the world. But it did not occur to us how much of the 'mind-set' was Italian and Germanic. Most of us never heard of form criticism. Probably we would not have dared to use it on documents of the magisterium even if we had known what it meant."

If time permitted, I could confirm Cronin's point with examples from my own experience and, more to the point, by citing some of the mistakes that I have personally made in this regard. For present purposes, however, suffice it to say that even a casual survey of scholarly commentaries on *Rerum Novarum* in several different languages clearly validates Cronin's argument. If nothing else, my own reading or rereading in recent months of a representative sampling of these commentaries and historical studies demonstrates that it is impossible to understand Leo's encyclical or any of the more recent encyclicals without examining the historical context within which, and often in response to which, the documents were written. Failure to examine these papal documents in their historical setting has led some to exaggerate their strengths and others to exaggerate their weaknesses. It has also led even scholars of some repute to find a greater degree of unbroken continuity between successive encyclicals than the facts would seem to warrant. A few examples from various points in the ideological spectrum will suffice for present purposes.

It has become rather fashionable in neo-conservative circles to denigrate the social encyclicals and related documents. Some years ago I attended a three-day American Enterprise Institute seminar on social teachings of churches, Catholic and Protestant. Several participants, Catholic scholars among them, repeatedly charged that the encyclicals of Leo XIII and Pius XI and especially those of John XXIII and Paul VI betray a thorough misunderstanding of contemporary capitalist economic theory and practice. Not all went so far in this respect as Professor E. T. Bauer of the London School of Economics, but none of them demurred when Bauer asserted, "The papal letters (on socio-economic problems) . . . can only confuse believers. They are political statements by bogus arguments. . . . (They) are immoral because they are incompetent." Not only that, he said, they also legitimize envy and spread confusion about the meaning of charity.

Bauer and several others complain in particular that these documents pay too much attention to the distribution of wealth and little if any to the need for greater productivity under a system of democratic capitalism. As one of them put it with specific reference to the social documents of the American bishops, "Ethics seems to be confined to workers and their rights and to distribution, without ever considering how and why things are freely produced and distributed."

Some neo-conservatives, mainly Catholics, have taken a different tack. They have rummaged the social documents for anything that may sound like an endorsement of American-style capitalism. A few have gone further by trying to play the popes, especially John Paul II, off against the American bishops in the area of Catholic social teaching.

Father Richard John Neuhaus, recently converted from Lutheranism, brought this game to a new height when John Paul II issued his May 1991 encyclical *Centesimus Annus* ("The 100th Year"), which commemorates the *Rerum Novarum* anniversary. (His article appeared in the *Wall Street Journal* a day before the encyclical was officially released.) Neuhaus wrote that in light of the papal document, "It may be . . . that the controlling assumptions of the American bishops' pastoral letter, *Economic Justice for All*, must now be recognized as unrepresentative of the Church's authoritative teaching." This is the same pastoral letter that Cardinal Agostino Casaroli, one of the pope's most trusted and experienced advisors, went out of his way to praise at a University of Notre Dame conference on *Rerum Novarum*, held just before the Neuhaus decree on American bishops and their social teaching.

Even the more sympathetic writers have felt constrained during the past decade or so to demythologize the social encyclicals in the light of modern scholarship.

To cite but one example, a critique from the left is offered by Father Donal Dorr, in his 1983 book, *Option for the Poor*. "Pope Leo XIII seems to have presumed that socio-economic reform could come without significant political changes and even without major challenge to existing political structures," says Dorr, an Irish missionary priest who has served in various African countries and in Brazil. "I would therefore conclude that what Leo XIII presented as the official Church teaching on socio-political questions did not measure up to the deeply Christian instinct that led him to cry out against mistreatment of the poor."

At the same time, Dorr balances his critique with a realistic assessment of Leo XIII's historical role. "On the other hand it must not be forgotten that *Rerum Novarum* was a major intervention by the pope in defense of the poor. As such it helped to put the Church firmly on their side. The effect was two-fold," he writes. "The encyclical led Church people to make a deeper study of the causes of poverty and to seek more effective means of overcoming them. And at the same time it gave heart to those of the workers and the poor who were able and willing to hear its message; this inspirational effect was quite important, especially when over the years it became apparent that many Church leaders were taking the encyclical seriously."

Curiously, one of the better commentaries on the historical development of Catholic social teaching from Leo XIII until recent times was written two decades ago by a non-Catholic historian, Richard L. Camp (*The Papal Ideology of Social Reform*, 1969). Professor Camp, a sympathetic critic of the encyclicals, starting with *Rerum Novarum*, finds a distinct evolution in papal social teaching that cannot be explained simply as an effort of Leo's successors to bring him up to date. In short, Camp thinks it is naive to exaggerate the strengths of *Rerum Novarum* and equally naive to find too much continuity in Catholic social teaching. On the other hand, his refined sense of historical consciousness prompts him, even when pointing to weaknesses in *Rerum Novarum*, to give due credit to Leo XIII for its strengths.

Specifically, for example, he echoes a point made by the neo-conservative critics of Catholic social teaching—that Leo XIII and some of his successors placed too much emphasis on the distribution of wealth and not enough on the need for greater productivity. But even here his criticism of *Rerum Novarum* is tempered by his understanding of the historical context in which Leo was writing. No one can deny, Camp says, that the distribution of wealth represented a crucial issue of Leo's time, and not only in southern Europe but in the United States, England and other advanced industrial nations. "*Rerum Novarum*," he concludes, "met these issues directly and proposed a balanced, pragmatic blueprint for the regeneration of the proletariat within existing economic institutions which could enable the laborer to take his place as a respected and dignified member of society. . . . He saw the need for the Church to speak for the workingman, and he inspired Catholics to make the laborer's cause their own. Had he done nothing else his place in history as a great pope would still have been secure."

Many other critics of *Rerum Novarum* and more recent papal encycli-

cals have raised the question of wider distribution versus greater productivity. That's fair enough, but by and large these critics are loath to say loud
and clear that even today, as in 1891, the distribution of wealth remains a
serious problem. Indeed, in our own country the falling wages of average
working people and the rising returns of the well-to-do have presented an
economic situation that appears to mock the very idea of distributive justice. (Many commentators have noted that our nation appears to be re-
gressing toward the mal-distribution of the past. Kevin Phillips, a Republican analyst, has argued the point persuasively in his 1990 book *The Politics
of Rich and Poor: Wealth and the American Electorate in the Reagan Aftermath.* Phillips documents a dramatic redistribution of wealth—upward—
during the late 1970s and throughout the 1980s.)

Examining *Rerum Novarum* in its historical context also serves to
remind us that the encyclical had different receptions in different places
because of differing histories and traditions. To cite but one example,
European Catholics in 1891 were badly divided over the issues of "Catholic" or "Christian" vs. "neutral" trade unionism. This debate, which
carried over on the Continent well into the twentieth century, never
caught fire in the United States. For this, credit goes to the leadership of
Cardinal James Gibbons of Baltimore and several of his fellow bishops in
warding off a papal condemnation of the Knights of Labor, the leading
labor federation in the United States in the latter part of the nineteenth
century. From the time of Gibbons to the present, Catholic workers in the
United States have freely joined "neutral" unions and shown no interest in
the formation of a specifically Catholic or Christian labor movement.

As Father John Pawlikowski, professor of social ethics at the Catholic
Theological Union in Chicago has pointed out in his own commentary on
Rerum Novarum, the most direct and lasting effect of the encyclical in the
United States was the impetus it gave to unionization. "Although a few
American bishops like Cardinal Gibbons and Archbishop Ireland had already given their blessing to unionization and Catholics were already active in union leadership, the encyclical opened the doors to a much more
massive and intensive collaboration between American Catholicism and
the labor movement," Pawlikowski writes in his introduction to *Justice in
the Marketplace,* a 1985 collection of Catholic social documents.

This one example, which I will take up again in a moment, can serve to
substantiate Jesuit Father John Coleman's argument in a brilliant essay on
the development of Catholic social teaching. Notwithstanding all of the
theoretical arguments about strengths and limitations of *Rerum Novarum*
and more recent encyclicals, the encyclicals "tended to be read, absorbed
and commented on mainly by socially involved Catholics who generally
gave them a more progressive interpretation than their location in histori-

cal context might have warranted. The encyclicals, then, represent in some sense a genuine unified tradition of sane and humane social thought which we both celebrate today and try to bring forward into the future."

Father Coleman himself is critical of the encyclicals on several scores, but, in the end, he concludes that "ultimately the future of this tradition will depend less on our ability to parrot its significant terms . . . and more on our ability to read the signs of the times in fidelity to the Gospel of human dignity as Leo and his successors tried to do in their times. History will surely unveil all too well our shortcomings. May it also—as it does for this legacy of the popes—show our prophetic vision and courageous action."

I can think of no better way of stating the lesson to be learned today as we go about celebrating the one hundredth anniversary of *Rerum Novarum*.

*   *   *

My second observation has to do with the changing relationship, since and mainly because of Vatican II, between the Holy See and the "local," e.g. American or French or German, churches in the area of Catholic social teaching and Catholic social action. Let me illustrate this point, in an overly simplified manner, by recalling that between 1944 when I first joined the staff of the Social Action Department of the old National Catholic Welfare Conference and the end of Vatican II in 1965, there was literally no contact of any kind between our department and the Holy See. I do not recall that we exchanged at any time even so much as a letter, a cablegram, or a phone call. That is no longer the case, of course. These days, the church in the United States is routinely in contact with the Holy See and its several congregations or offices. The participation of high-ranking Vatican officials in American observances of the centenary of *Rerum Novarum* can serve to symbolize this new and potentially very promising relationship between the local church and the Holy See—a new sense of collegiality in the extended sense of the word.

This changing relationship reflects in its own way a new and better post-Vatican II understanding of ecclesiology. It involves more than simply a new style and new forms of communication, at the bureaucratic level, between the local church and the Holy See. The new collegiality runs deeper than that. It involves the local churches, to some extent at least, in the very process of developing Catholic social teaching. In his apostolic letter of 1971, *Octogesima Adveniens*, Pope Paul VI broke radically new ground in this regard. *Octogesima Adveniens* is written in the form of a familiar dialogue not only with Catholics or with Christians in general, but with all those of good will, and carefully avoids the more pontifical style of teaching which so often characterized similar documents in the not too distant past.

On some matters, of course, Paul VI states his own convictions very firmly, but never in such a way as to force his opinion on the reader or to short-circuit or foreclose the dialogue. On matters which are purely contingent, those open to varying viewpoints which lend themselves to a variety of solutions, he carefully refrains from trying to say—or even leaving the impression that is he is trying to say—the last and final word. Indeed, he goes out of his way to emphasize that it is neither his ambition nor his mission "to utter a unified message and to put forward a solution which has universal validity." His purpose is the more modest one of "confiding" his own thoughts and preoccupations about some, but by no means all, of today's more pressing social problems and of encouraging individual Catholics and groups of Catholics, in dialogue with other Christian brethren and all men of good will, "to analyze with objectivity the situation which is proper to their own country . . ." and, in addition, "to discern the options and commitments which are called for in order to bring about the social, political and economic changes seen in many cases to be needed."

One is reminded here of Pope John XXIII's distinctively pastoral style of teaching. In several different contexts, Pope Paul draws attention to the legitimate variety of options available to men and women of good will. He further underscores the obligation of individual Catholics to form their own conscience on these matters in light of the gospel message but without waiting for directives from their ecclesiastical leaders.

It goes without saying, of course, that the full implications of *Octogesima Adveniens* have yet to be worked out in practice. By way of example, does it follow logically from *Octogesima Adveniens* that there ought to be a more systematic input from the local churches in the drafting of social encyclicals and other universal church documents on Catholic social teaching? This question, even with the best of good will and even under optimum conditions, has no easy answer, given the diversity and complexity of problems confronting a church which today is truly universal in its geographical sweep and spread. In any event, it is an intriguing question and one which, I suspect, will continue to crop up from time to time. It is an old question, of course. Even before Vatican II, it was raised by, among others, the late Father Georges Jarlot, a Jesuit who for many years taught Catholic social teaching at the Gregorian University in Rome. No one could accuse the French priest of prejudice in having complained that the church's pre-Vatican II social teaching was inevitably European and even, like Pope John XXIII's two encyclicals, Italian. His specific reference to John XXIII's two encyclicals, *Mater et Magistra* and *Pacem in Terris*, is somewhat surprising, for, of all the social encyclicals since Leo XIII's *Rerum Novarum*, these two seem the least European or, if you will, the most universal in style as well as in content. Be that as it may, Father Jarlot's overall characterization of the church's social teaching prior to the council is valid.

A German scholar, Phillippe Herder-Dorneigh, went Father Jarlot one better, again before Vatican II, when he said that in addition to appearing too European in content and too "curial" in style, the social encyclicals have also been too theoretical or abstract in their approach to social problems without reflecting the full range of viewpoints within the universal church. The classical period of Catholic doctrine abruptly ended, he said, with the death of Pius XII. The braintrust upon which he had depended and in which German Jesuits played an important role was relegated to the background. New specialists, from different parts of the world, took their place and helped to formulate *Mater et Magistra*. This marked a step in the right direction, in Herder-Dorneigh's view. Yet, he also believed that at the hands of these "new specialists," Catholic social doctrine went to another extreme: from the all-encompassing thing it had once been to a series of individual pronouncements on concrete situations. He exaggerated, of course—recent social encyclicals are hardly a series of concrete recommendations—but, again, the question is still with us.

* * *

My third observation—again at the bureaucratic level—has to do with the Holy See's recent encouragement of local churches to take a more active role in the international arena of social justice and human rights. Again, let me illustrate the point by citing my experience at the old National Catholic Welfare Conference. It is my clear recollection that during my first twenty years on the staff of the old NCWC—i.e. between 1944 and 1965—Rome expected the conference to work exclusively within the continental borders of the United States. I may be stretching the point. A certain amount of significant international work was done by the conference in those days, mainly through the initiative of the late Father Raymond McGowan, one of the unsung heroes of the Catholic social action movement in the United States. But this work was, in a sense, bootleg activity. It was the tolerated exception to the general rule that local churches should leave international affairs to Rome. That's no longer true. Our own National Conference of Catholic Bishops/United States Catholic Conference is now deeply involved in international affairs, with the blessing of the Holy See.

I am speaking here, of course, mainly about changes at the bureaucratic level. The same holds true for the substantive level of social teaching and practice in the church. Before John XXIII, the content of Catholic social teaching was, by and large, concerned with the socio-economic problems of individual nation states. Not so today. More than ever, the church finds itself in dialogue with the various movements of international justice and peace. I will say no more about this, except to add, sociologically speaking and quite apart from any theological considerations, that the role of the Petrine office has taken on, in some respects, greater importance than ever before in modern history. At times this may go down hard with Americans, for, even in our better moments, we are probably more provincial and less cosmopolitan than we are normally willing to admit (witness the unashamedly chauvinistic rhetoric of a typical State of the Union message).

For example, it has become fashionable in some American circles to complain (a bit too peevishly for my taste) that the Holy See has been slow to recognize and absorb the American political and economic experience. There is a certain merit to this complaint, but to overdo it would be to run the risk of being perceived by fair-minded people in other countries, rich and poor alike, as innocents abroad in a very complex world society. In short, I think we would be well advised to take to heart the cautionary words of Cardinal Roger Etchegaray, president of the Pontifical Council on Justice and Peace. He spoke to several hundred delegates attending the U.S. Catholic Conference's observance of the *Rerum Novarum* anniversary. "The entire world," the cardinal said, "cannot be reduced to the United States."

*   *   *

Let me wrap up these random recollections with some summary reflections about a few of what I regard as unresolved problems in carrying out our social teachings.

In my opinion, for whatever it may be worth, we have yet to understand in all of its pertinent implications the principle of *subsidiarity* and the correlative principle of *socialization*. These principles, in tandem, are of central importance in the corpus of modern Catholic social teaching.

First a word about the principle of subsidiarity, which emphasizes the role of non-governmental "mediating structures" in social and economic life. According to this principle, as enunciated by Pope Pius XI in his encyclical *Quadragesimo Anno*, "It is gravely wrong to take from individuals what they can accomplish by their own initiative and industry and give it to the community." It is also "an injustice and at the same time a grave evil and disturbance of right order," Pius XI said, "to assign to a greater and higher association what lesser and subordinate organizations can do."

The principle of subsidiarity holds that government intervention in the economy is justified, and even necessary, when it provides help indispensable to the common good but beyond the competence of individuals or groups. It further holds that family, neighborhood, church, professional and labor groups all have a dynamic life of their own which government must respect.

We have rightly given due prominence to the role of such mediating structures and organizations. Yet we have tended to do so negatively by stressing very one-sidedly their obvious importance as bulwarks against statism. That is to say, we have yet to agree upon a positive and structured role for these organizations in the operation and planning of the economy. We have yet to come to terms, for example, with John Paul's treatment of this subject in his 1981 encyclical, *Laborem Exercens* ("On Human Work"). This encyclical speaks of "a wide range of intermediate bodies," with economic purposes, enjoying "real autonomy" with regard to the public powers and pursuing their aims "in honest collaboration with each other and in subordination to the demands of the common good."

It is my impression that many of those in the United States who rightly stress the importance of these intermediate bodies—neo-conservatives, namely—tend to see them as running parallel to the corporate structures in the domestic and world economies. In other words, they do not really envisage these mediating groups as institutionally involved, as autonomous bodies with economic purposes, in the economic decision-making of either individual nations or the international community.

This limited anti-statist view of intermediate structures may account, at least in part, for the menacing lack of concern in conservative circles about the growing weakness of American unions, one of the more important mediating groups in our society. I regret to say it, but the silence of conservatives on this issue has been deafening in recent years. (I speak here, of course, of those conservatives who do not already oppose unions in principle.)

Robert A. Nisbet is one of the few conservative social and political philosophers who strongly lament the decline of organized labor in the United States. But even he tends to think of unions one-sidedly as powerful forces in support of capitalism and as bulwarks against political invasion of economic freedom. In his book, *The Quest for Community*, first published in 1958 and recently updated, Nisbet writes that "the labor union and co-operative are foremost among new forms of association that have served to keep alive the symbols of economic freedom as such. It should be remarked, they have been the first objects of economic destruction in totalitarian countries. . . . The individual entrepreneur, it may be observed, is less dangerous to the totalitarian than the labor union or co-operative. For in such an association, the individual can find a sense of relatedness to the entire culture and thus become its eager partisan."

Nisbet goes on to say that "the mythology of individualism continues to reign in discussions of economic freedom. By too many partisans of management the labor union is regarded as a major obstacle to economic autonomy and as partial paralysis of capitalism. But to weaken, whether from political or individualistic motives, the social structures of family, local community, labor union, or industrial community, is to convert a culture into an atomized mass. Such a mass will have neither the will, nor the incentive, nor the ability to combat tendencies toward political collectivism."

These are welcome words, coming as they do from a leading American conservative social philosopher. They also come at a time when some of the most influential employer organizations in the United States are insistently calling for a union-free environment and gleefully—as in the case of the United States Chamber of Commerce—predicting the demise of the American labor movement. Now that the iron curtain has come down, it is time for scholars of Nisbet's stature in the conservative community to speak up. They need to defend unions not only as bulwarks against statism but also for their positive role in the proper ordering of economic life in the United States.

I suspect that we have tended to shy away from this problem for fear of being accused of hankering unrealistically and ahistorically for some outmoded form of European "corporativism"—a program of social order outlined by Pope Pius XI in his 1931 encyclical *Quadragesimo Anno*. In his corporativist design Pius XI envisaged: (1) an organized and orderly economic society, with organizations of each industry and profession and a federation of such organizations; (2) an economic society which is self-governing, subject only to the superior power of the state to intervene when the public good demands it; (3) social institutions organized to seek the common good for their members as well as for all economic society; (4) the predominance of such organizations and institutions as the primary means of putting justice into economic life; (5) the rule of the great virtues of justice and charity through the functioning of these organizations.

Unfortunately, corporativism became associated to some extent with Italian, Spanish, and Portuguese forms of fascism or semi-fascism. And this led many critics, particularly on the Continent, to repudiate *Quadragesimo Anno*'s formula for the reconstruction of the social order. That was admittedly an understandable and salutary fear. But, in my opinion, it should not intimidate us from thinking through in very practical and pragmatic American terms the implications of Pope John Paul II's emphasis on the economic role of free and autonomous unions in the economic order.

It might be useful in this regard to revisit John XXIII's encyclical *Mater et Magistra*. Pope John carefully avoided giving his approval to any particular method of organizing or reorganizing economic life. Moreover, even his terminology was somewhat different from that of Pius XI in *Quadragesimo Anno* and in his later encyclical *Divini Redemptoris*. Pius used the terminology of "corporativism" which, in the United States, was freely translated into the so-called Industry Council Plan. (During the 1930s and 1940s, as stated earlier, leaders of U.S. industrial unions as well as the Catholic social action movement pushed the ICP as a means of broadening participation in economic decision-making, through an involved system of labor-management cooperation.) Pope John XXIII, on the other hand, concerned himself mainly with the practical aspects of the problem and carefully avoided using this kind of terminology. He was a pastor and not a jurist. He knew all about the discussions raised by the formulas of Pius XI and Pius XII and the misunderstandings these discussions had caused. So he kept from any formulizing and even went so far as to steer clear of the words "corporation" and "corporative organization."

It would be partially correct, then, to say that John XXIII seemed less interested than Pius XI in the Industry Council Plan. Pope John's approach to the problem of social reconstruction and his terminology was less theoretical—more flexible if you will—than that of Pope Pius XI. But it would be a mistake, I think, to conclude that Pope John had any less interest in the basic principles of social reconstruction underlying the Industry Council Plan. These principles can be summarized as follows:

Economic order will not come naturally. It will not come simply through free competition, free enterprise and free initiative, although a maximum degree of economic freedom must always be safeguarded. Intermediate bodies—e.g. labor unions and professional groups—are natural and necessary if we want to avoid totalitarianism, but not for that reason alone. Institutional cooperation must take place at all levels and among all agents of the economy. Intermediate bodies must cooperate among themselves and with the government in order to play a positive role in the economic order.

While adopting these principles, Pope John did not tell us, in detail, how to put them into practice. His approach, to repeat, was flexible. He opened the doors to all kinds of institutional cooperation among those involved at the different levels of production, strongly insisting that any organization of the economy must take into account the national and international common good. The government has a positive role to play, and it must carry out this role with respect for legitimate autonomies and with the active participation of all involved groups. In substance, proponents of the Industry Council Plan have said this from the beginning. At times, though, their approach and their terminology have appeared rather inflexible. If so, *Mater et Magistra* can serve as a useful corrective. One way of moving in the direction of the Industry Council Plan would be to develop a pragmatic system of American-style co-management or co-determination and new forms of profit-sharing and co-ownership.

In some European countries, following World War II, labor and management did in fact move in this direction. In the United States, however, organized labor showed little if any post-war interest in co-management or co-determination. More recently, in the face of economic dislocation in the United States, one of our major unions demanded and received a limited form of co-determination with the Chrysler Corporation. The United Auto Workers (UAW) reacted pragmatically to the economic crisis in the auto industry. The UAW, with no other choice, agreed to reopen its contract with Chrysler and voted to make drastic wage concessions in a last-ditch effort to keep that near-bankrupt corporation afloat. At the same time, the union demanded in return a seat on the Chrysler Board of Directors and a compensatory share in any future Chrysler profits.

Having addressed the principle of subsidiarity, let me say a word in passing about the related theme of socialization—not socialism, but socialization as the term is used in *Mater et Magistra*. Pope John's thinking on socialization, which favors a positive role by government in promoting social justice, became the most widely publicized and perhaps the most controversial part of *Mater et Magistra*. The pope defined socialization, a word which, to the best of my knowledge, had never before appeared in a papal document, as the "progressive multiplication of relations in society, with different forms of life and activity, and juridical institutions." It finds expression for the most part, not in government programs but in "a wide range of groups, movements, associations, and institutions . . . both within single national communities and on an international level."

John XXIII embraced the phenomenon of socialization—the sum total of these organizational forces, private and public, in a participatory society. "It makes possible, in fact, the satisfaction of many personal rights, especially those of economic and social life, such as, for example, the right to the indispensable means of human maintenance, to health services, to instruction at a higher level, to a more thorough professional formation, to housing, to work, to suitable leisure, to recreation."

There are two likely ways of misinterpreting the concept of socialization: to confuse socialization with socialism, and to equate socialization exclusively with voluntary action by non-government organizations or associations, thus ruling out almost every kind of government action. (It was Pope John's positive view of government intervention in the economy that led William F. Buckley to lampoon *Mater et Magistra,* which means literally, "Mother and Teacher." The headline of an article in Buckley's magazine *National Review* said it all: "Mater Si, Magistra No.")

The neglect of this principle in the corpus of Catholic social teaching accounts in part, I think, for our having gotten bogged down too often in an ideological debate in the United States about capitalism vs. socialism. A prominent American banker, who happens to be a serious and forward-looking student of Catholic social teaching, has taken on the problem in a paper delivered at a major conference on the centenary of *Rerum Novarum* at the University of San Francisco.

Thomas Johnson, former chairman and executive officer of Manufacturers Hanover Trust, says that the breathtaking developments in former communist societies have provided us with an opportunity to take a fresh look at capitalism. This time, he says, we can do so unencumbered by the baggage of the past. By that he means that the examination need no longer involve the issue of capitalism vs. communism. Instead, the examination can sharpen its focus on ways to make market-based economies work better in terms of meeting broad human needs, both material and spiritual.

In a sense, Johnson adds, communism was a rather convenient thing to have around. It served to simplify debate, narrow the options, and discourage rigorous examination. Subtleties were frequently not allowed. Attempts at meaningful discourse were often enfeebled by a hardening of the categories. "In short," he concludes, "with one debate seemingly resolved, we can now focus our energy and our attention on eliminating the significant faults and inadequacies of capitalism that we know to exist, while at the same time preserving those special properties that imbue the markets with their special genius."

I hope he is right about that, for we have been bogged down long enough in an either-or, black-and-white debate about capitalism vs. communism. During the long cold war between the communist east and the capitalist west, we had a plausible excuse for diverting so much of our energy to this debate, even though the debate was often oversimplified and at times reflected national and geo-political rivalries rather than principle. Unfortunately, however, the debate, at least in the United States, turned into an argument not only about Soviet-style communism vs. U.S. capitalism, but also about democratic capitalism vs. democratic socialism (two rather slippery categories that raised the debate to new levels of abstraction). It is regrettable, I think, that the debate so often took such an ideological turn. I say this, among other reasons, because both democratic capitalism and democratic socialism carry so much partisan baggage and are fraught with so much ambiguity that they have become, all too often, little more than shibboleths. And while shibboleths are fun to argue about, they mean a lot less to those in search of answers than to those who seem ideologically stuck with them.

At this stage in our history we need a non-ideological and objective study of the U.S. economy aimed, in the words of Thomas Johnson, at "eliminating the significant faults and inadequacies of capitalism that we know to exist, while at the same time preserving those special properties that imbue the markets with the special genius."

I find reason to rejoice in the fact that this kind of non-ideological, pragmatic reexamination of the U.S. economic system is belatedly underway in the health care field, to cite but one example.

Until a few years ago, debate about health care in the United States was a fruitless exercise in simplistic ideological rhetoric. Any proposal, no matter how modest, to give the government a significant role in the restructuring of the health care system was branded "socialized medicine." Year after year, it was the same old irrelevant debate about free-market capitalism vs. socialism, and all the while the health-care system kept going from bad to worse. Today the system is so flawed that it can only be described as a national crisis.

Fortunately the debate has recently taken a turn for the better. To cite but one highly significant example, *The New York Times* reported (April 8, 1990) on a survey on health care among chief executives of the nation's largest corporations. The survey found that ninety-one percent of them wanted fundamental changes in the health-care system. It also found that seventy-three percent of the executives said that the private sector alone would never solve the problem. They believed that the situation called for some degree of government intervention.

The New York Times carried its report on this survey in its business section. In my opinion, it merited front-page coverage, for its implications for the future are almost revolutionary. Common sense has begun to displace sterile capitalism vs. socialism rhetoric in the debate about the crisis in health care. Skyrocketing costs have convinced the majority of corporate executives that something must be done without delay. After trying to get a grip on medical costs themselves, they have realistically accepted the idea —which they once viewed as heretical—that change must be national, not piecemeal or local. At a minimum, they see an important role for the government in restructuring the system, although, understandably, they do not want the government to run the entire system. Moreover, corporate executives seem willing to cooperate with organized labor and other interested parties in hammering out the details of a viable solution to a problem that has gotten completely out of hand. That is revolutionary and, if I may repeat, cause for celebration.

*   *   *

I take it that one of the purposes of commemorative conferences during the 1991 centenary year was to address in one way or another the challenge put forth by Thomas Johnson and others who want to take a fresh look at the economic order. We will not be alone in doing so, for, contrary to the conventional wisdom of recent decades, we are unexpectedly witnessing a revival of interest in Catholic social teaching. Witness the phenomenally widespread observance here in the United States of the anniversary of *Rerum Novarum*.

I began these reflections by quoting from a 1971 essay by my former colleague, Father John F. Cronin. Let me quote again from that article. "About 1966," Cronin wrote in *The American Ecclesiastical Review*, "there developed a sudden and dramatic turning away from the traditional methods of Catholic social teaching and social action. Encyclical courses were dropped from colleges and seminaries. Even updated books based on the social magisterium ceased to sell." Cronin went on to say, "Prediction is hazardous, but it seems that the golden era of Catholic social teaching, beginning in 1891, has ended by 1971."

I feel certain that Father Cronin, in poor health but still of very sound mind, would be more than happy to concede that history has invalidated this prediction—happy to observe in his declining years that interest in Catholic social teaching, far from having ended in 1971, seems, if anything, on the upswing.

The Leading Role of the Laity

At a forum on the one hundredth anniversary of Pope Leo XIII's encyclical *Rerum Novarum*, I observed in passing that church-related programs in the labor field have, by and large, been on hold, roughly since the period of the Vietnam War. During the question-and-answer period a young woman suggested from the floor that perhaps my definition of "church" in this context was too narrow: too much emphasis on the role of bishops, priests, members of religious orders and other lay church "professionals," not enough on the everyday role of rank-and-file lay people. I thought I had avoided that mistake in my prepared remarks, but in any event the question was well taken. The young woman believed it was up to committed members of the laity to take the lead, on their own initiative, in the field of labor-management relations without waiting for instructions from church "professionals." We, all of us, she emphasized, are the church.

A few years earlier, I encountered a similar sentiment among the laity around the time that the U.S. bishops issued their pastoral letter on Catholic social teaching and the U.S. economy. Organized labor predictably showed a great interest in this document, which deals with workers' needs and problems under several headings. And so I had the opportunity to take part in several seminars on the pastoral letter sponsored by local union coalitions.

At a seminar in San Francisco, one labor leader took to the floor to say that as a regular churchgoer he had never heard a homily or sermon on a labor leader's vocation. In his experience, he said, the word "vocation" was used almost exclusively with reference to priests and to men and women of religious orders. He said that while he did not want to sound holier than thou, he always had thought of his role in the labor movement as a vocation —a call from God to serve his fellow workers. His complaint was echoed by two or three others at the gathering.

Edward Marciniak, president of the Institute of Urban Life in Chicago, has gone a step further in expressing the discontent of certain rank-and-file Catholics. "Among church leaders and their staffs," he said at a conference co-sponsored by the National Center for the Laity, "there lingers an abiding disdain for those Christians who work inside the political and economic system and a predilection for those who are outside or against the system." Educational programs in the church, he said, are weighted in favor of preparation for paid or volunteer positions in church institutions. He asked: What happened to the world of work which so concerns Pope John Paul II in his encyclical on this subject?

This is an old refrain with the National Center for the Laity. Marciniak and others have repeatedly warned of a declining interest in helping the laity to play their indispensable role in the worlds of work, politics and business. Although they sometimes push their point too far, drawing too sharp a distinction between the roles of clergy and laity, their basic argument makes sense and deserves a wide hearing.

They are essentially saying what bishops themselves have said, at least in principle. For example, the U.S. bishops say in their pastoral letter, *Economic Justice for All:* "It is principally through the laity that the Spirit will lead this world to greater love, justice and peace.... Holiness is achieved in the midst of the world. The constant effort to shape decisions and institutions in ways that enhance human dignity and reflect the grandeur and glory of God represents a most important path to holiness."

Cardinal Joseph L. Bernardin, the archbishop of Chicago, seems to have listened carefully to the complaints of the non-professional laity. He has written that "despite today's enormously increased interest in lay ministry, I am convinced that we have scarcely begun to tap its rich potential. Bearing in mind that the primary field for the exercise of lay ministry is in the workaday world, its possibilities within the church are vast. The laity's specific role is not to serve the church in an institutional sense, but the world. . . . They share in Christ's priesthood and are charged with the responsibility of bringing the message of the gospel to the world."

Bishop John Cummins of the diocese of Oakland, California, head of the National Conference of Catholic Bishops' Secretariat on Laity and Family Life, put it graphically when he remarked during a conference, "There isn't much room behind the altar rail." That is to say, the overwhelming majority of lay people will never serve as "lay ministers" in the ecclesiastical sense of the word. They will exercise their ministry, their calling or vocation, not behind the altar rail or within the sanctuary but in and through their respective occupations, be they workers, employers, bankers, professionals, or what have you.

Some may think this is much ado about nothing. I do not agree. At a time when the church puts so much emphasis on the work of catechetical, liturgical and other ministries within the church—and rightly so—we must pay attention also to those who work as Christians in what are sometimes denigrated as purely "secular" tasks—for example, organizing workers into democratic trade unions.

*   *   *

This, in a nutshell, was the message of the highly praised "Chicago Declaration of Christian Concern," a statement issued in 1978 by a group of Chicago area Catholics and directed to the church in the United States. The Chicago Declaration warned that the Catholic Church may have lost a generation of lay leadership because of its preoccupation since Vatican II with internal "churchy" affairs and its consequent devaluation of the laity's social responsibility.

In particular, the statement pointed to three recent developments among American Catholics. The first was the movement to involve lay persons in the church's official ministries; this had the ironic effect of drawing attention away from the secular mission of the laity. The second was the tendency of some clergy members to preempt the role of lay Catholics in social reform. The third was a trend of diminishing interest in Christian social thought as the mediating ground between the gospel and specific political and economic issues. (The latter trend seems, at least at this writing, to have been reversed by the more recent upsurge of interest in Catholic social teaching.)

Drafters of the statement waited "impatiently for a new prophecy, a new word that can once again stir the laity to see the grandeur of the Christian vision for man in society and move priests to galvanize lay persons in their secular-religious role." They point out that in the final analysis, "the church speaks to and acts upon the world through her laity. . . . Without a dynamic laity conscious of its ministry to the world, the church in effect does not speak or act." The Chicago group added: "It would be one of the great ironies of history if the era of Vatican II which opened the windows of the church to the world were to close with the church turned upon herself."

Ecclesiastical chauvinism has no more to recommend it than civic or national super-patriotism. This is by way of saying that a Chicago priest ought to have enough common sense to avoid boasting about his own city or his own archdiocese. Bearing this caution in mind, I will risk saying that the informal committee of Chicago priests, sisters, brothers and lay people —in their call for "a reexamination of present tendencies in the church," in hope of "a new sense of direction"—performed a very useful service to the U.S. Catholic community.

This is not to suggest, nor do its signers pretend, that the Chicago Declaration had the last word on the subject. It did, however, raise many of the right questions. The group's purpose was not to try to answer these questions once and for all but to start a serious dialogue about them among fellow-Catholics not only in Chicago but throughout the nation.

That much it did, at least to some extent, even if the issues pressed by the Chicago Declaration have never made it to the top of the church's agenda in the United States. To add a few remarks to the conversation, I would begin by suggesting that the Chicago Declaration—to which, in the main, I fully subscribe—may have drawn too sharp a distinction between the respective roles of the laity and the clergy in the social ministry of the church. Those who drafted the statement expressed concern that the absence of lay initiative may take us down the road to a new form of clericalism. If this happens, they suggest, the blame would go to many priests, sisters and brothers who "have bypassed the laity to pursue social concerns of their own [and] have sought to impose their own agenda for the world upon the laity."

The point is well taken, but I believe the late great German theologian, Father Karl Rahner, came closer to the truth when he observed that clerics have no monopoly of the new forms of clericalism or clerical triumphalism criticized by the Chicago Declaration. Rahner pointed out that "the same fault, but with the sign reversed, is probably met with just as often among the laity (or among clerics with a lay mentality). They themselves demand from the official church what the clerical triumphalists in fact think can be offered," he writes. "They then reproach the church when the church cannot meet this claim." Indeed, how many times have we read editorials by lay Catholic journalists who set up a problem—say, famine in sub-Sahara Africa—and then rush to the question: What are the bishops going to do about it? To me, however, a more important question is: What are we, the whole church, "the people of God," going to do about it? Rahner describes these lay people as "lay defeatists."

Rahner did not say that clergy should withdraw from the church's social ministry. He said that clerical zeal for social reform, admirable in itself, ought to be coupled with a sense of realism. Clergy should realize that they don't have all the answers to all complicated problems confronting the modern world. The laity should not expect them to provide such answers. More profoundly, Rahner argued that the church and the church's ministry are not exactly the same. He wrote, "The limits of the church's possibilities and those of its official hierarchy are not to be regarded from the outset as identical."

In substance, the Chicago Declaration says the same thing. But Rahner has gone a step further by reminding us that clericalism or clerical triumphalism presents a somewhat more complicated problem than the declaration would suggest. In other words, it is not simply a matter of clergy and religious usurping the role of the laity.

In the late 1980s, the debate resurfaced as bishops around the world gathered for a synod in Rome to address the role of the laity (in all spheres of church and social life). Articles, pamphlets, meetings and at least one book offered a fresh look at the Chicago Declaration. William F. Droel and Gregory F. Augustine Pierce, in their 1987 book *Confident and Competent: A Challenge for the Lay Church,* provided an extended commentary and elaboration on the Chicago Declaration's themes. The authors did not sign the Chicago Declaration, nor were they involved in the consultation leading up to it. Yet they agreed with the statement's thrust and, on the basis of their own experience and in light of subsequent developments, attempted to flesh it out, so to speak, and bring it up to date. They did so convincingly, and in view of the fact that the 1987 synod in Rome dealt with the laity's role, their timing was perfect.

I suggest, however, that while we need such books, what we need more is the living example of lay-initiated programs based on the principles of the Chicago Declaration. The laity have a right to expect the so-called "official" church to respect these principles and to help the laity put them into practice. Droel and Pierce correctly cite "a tremendous need for programs to support the laity in their vocation to job, family and neighborhood." Experience suggests, however, that lay initiative in developing programs of this type is indispensable.

To spend too much time theorizing about the laity's role or lamenting the failure of official church leaders to deal with the problem is to sell the laity short or, worse, to encourage a new form of clericalism, or "lay defeatism." This is not to say that the drafters of the Chicago Declaration fell into this trap. To the contrary, they have played an indispensable role in clarifying the mission of lay Catholics. It would be a mistake, however, to think that statements alone will bring about the changes that they have rightly called for. In short, the time has come for a new burst of lay-initiated action of the type, if I may say, that brought a fleeting measure of fame to Chicago-style Catholicism in the 1940s and 1950s.

*   *   *

At issue here are not only the rights and roles of rank-and-file lay people, but also the church's social mission after Vatican II.

I am persuaded that, proportionately speaking, the justice and peace work of the church has tended to be a bit too clerical, too institutional, or, if you will, too "churchy," for lack of a better word. Before Vatican II, paradoxically, the Catholic social action movement in the United States, though somewhat limited in scope and burdened with an inadequate, top-down type ecclesiology, tended to emphasize more than we do today the laity's independent role, as citizens and members of secular organizations, in helping to solve social problems. At present, despite our greater theological awareness of the church as the "people of God," we tend to emphasize the role of church professionals—be they clerical or lay—in promoting justice and defending human rights.

I raise this question of a "churchy" versus secular social action because I think it has a bearing on the future of the church's involvement in the field of social justice. Is it or should it be the primary—though not exclusive—function of church-related social action organizations to prepare their members to engage in social action on their own initiative in the secular arena? Or, conversely, should it be their primary function to make sure that the institutional church, and, more specifically, the ecclesiastical hierarchy, commits itself publicly to positions of social concern? This strikes me as a timely question and one that deserves careful consideration in any reexamination of the impact of Vatican II.

We should also carefully consider the ways in which we carry out our social ministries. Many of the people involved in social causes before Vatican II saw more clearly than some of today's activists the distinction between social action and "activism." Some of the latter tend to put perhaps too much stock in this or that form of "prophetic witness." They seem less interested in long-range programs of social education and structural reform that do not produce measurable results in the short run.

Finally, we should listen, once again, to those members of the laity who think that the church in the United States has mixed up its priorities in the field of social action. They see the church as devoting too much time, energy and money to the training of church professionals, both clerical and lay, and insufficient time, energy and money to programs aimed at helping the rank-and-file laity—helping lay people prepare themselves to play their own autonomous role as Christians in the temporal order.

As I have said, we have no need to get bogged down in an academic, theoretical debate about the respective roles of the laity and of church professionals in the field of social justice. Theologians can, should and undoubtedly will continue to grapple with this question at their leisure. Nor should we draw too sharp a distinction at the practical level—as the holy father himself has been accused of doing—between the roles of clergy and laity in promoting justice and defending human rights. At the same time, however, we need to review our justice and peace policies and programs at every level to prevent them from becoming top-heavy with church professionals. In more positive terms, we need to concentrate on the formation of authentic and autonomous lay leaders who will exercise their apostolate, not in and through church organizations, but in their secular occupations.

Father John A. Coleman in his 1982 book *An American Strategic Theology*—the best book of its kind that I have seen—has said all of this better than I could hope to do. "The laity are the key social action agents of the church in the world and the critical point of insertion in transforming Christian action in the arenas of economics, politics, etc.," Father Coleman writes. He does not call for a rigid cleavage between all clergy and all laity. In his opinion, "that would be a pastorally disastrous situation." He simply states what appears to him as sociological fact, "namely that the bulk of the clergy and the laity, as a status class, will lack enough tutored expertise in the worldly realm to be the carrier class for a world-transforming mission in and through the arena of work, politics, economics, etc."

*   *   *

What do the church's social-action professionals think about all this?

In February 1991, the U.S. bishops' conference held a major gathering in Washington to commemorate the anniversary of *Rerum Novarum*. Virtually all of the people who attended the meeting work for the institutional church, many of them in social-action offices of dioceses. I told this group that I look forward to a possible future meeting at which they, the professionals, would turn out, but so would an equal number of people in labor, management, the professions and other fields—the people with whom we should be working, the people who will ultimately make a difference in society. And I gently referred to a certain danger that church professionals may take themselves too seriously and exaggerate their role in the church. That is to say, we may look upon Catholic social action as an end in itself, thinking that the church by itself (or together with other religious bodies) will reform society, when our essential mission should be to prepare the faithful to do the work of justice through their own organizations.

My remarks elicited a certain defensiveness, understandable in many respects, on the part of some participants and organizers. And to be fair, I should say that the trends toward a "professional" social action movement in the church may well have been a necessity. The Second Vatican Council, still a relatively recent event in Catholic life, rightly pledged the church to a new engagement with the modern world. The council called for new structures and offices at all levels of the church to promote justice and peace. Those structures and offices had to be staffed. Some of this work remains unfinished.

Yet now that we have the professionals more or less in place, we need to listen to those lay men and women who say: "Wait a minute. You're putting most of your emphasis and spending most of your limited funds on developing social-action professionals under church auspices, but not doing very much for lay organizations of our own choice." The "professional" Catholics in social action have begun to listen. Through their respective offices and organizations, they have begun to look for ways to balance the picture.

Under the extraordinarily far-sighted leadership of Archbishop Rembert Weakland of Milwaukee, the U.S. bishops took a major step in the right direction with their 1986 letter on Catholic social teaching and the American economy. Weakland and his drafting committee adopted an open-ended process of dialogue and consultation with lay people all across the country. (That highly collegial effort has proven one of the most distinctive contributions of the U.S. church to the universal church after Vatican II.) Since then, partly as a result of the pastoral letter, various offices of national church agencies and dioceses have undertaken new efforts to educate parishioners in Catholic social teaching. This helps prepare lay people to take action in the workaday world.

I do not want to play off one against the other—church professionals and the rank-and-file laity. Quite obviously, I am a church professional. John A. Ryan was a church professional, and so were Raymond McGowan and others too numerous to mention. I do, however, want to stress—and restate, in a sharper way—that church professionals must ask themselves: "What is my primary role? Is it to make the church look good in the field of social action? Or is it to help people do the reforming work that needs to be done, through their own organizations?"

How do church professionals go about helping lay people do this work? I do not know of any single way; the answers would vary all over the lot, according to circumstances. One example is a matter taken up by Jesuit Father Walter Burghardt, an expert in the field of homiletics: How do we more effectively preach the word of God, with all of its implications in the social field? (Not easily.) Also worth considering: How do we provide some form of education in Catholic social teaching to union members, managers and people in the professions, if they want it?

Short of organized programs, church professionals have many informal ways of preparing the laity for their social mission. The clergy and other church professionals can offer encouragement to people who labor in the different fields of social action. We can testify to the importance of their work and the goodness of their cause, and help them in various ways. Occasionally we may help them in dramatic ways, as church people marched with the Rev. Martin Luther King, Jr., along the road to Selma, and as many of them picketed with Cesar Chavez in his farm labor movement. The Campaign for Human Development, an arm of the U.S. Catholic Conference, helps people in a rather direct fashion—by funding self-help organizations run by low-income people. The CHD, as an organization, does not make radical changes in society. It helps others. It empowers others, usually in small ways—obviously, funds are limited—but at least in symbolic ways and sometimes in crucial, financial ways.

These and other ways of preparing the laity offer an alternative to the present arrangement, in which the bishops and other church professionals usually take center stage in Catholic social action. The work of CHD is an exception that should be the rule. We can and should help the laity without preempting their leading role in the transformation of society.

A Certain Duty To Organize

In June 1990 I became peripherally involved in a legal dispute centering on a woman who refused to pay her union dues on grounds of religious belief. There was, generally speaking, nothing new about a religious objection to paying dues, or "agency fees" (in return for the services that unions must, by law, give to all workers in a bargaining unit, members and non-members alike). For decades, members of a few Protestant sects that teach against unions and collective bargaining have sought—and received—exemptions from dues' payment in union shops. Unions have generally honored the wishes of labor's religious objectors. In more recent years, courts have granted the same status to people who have no ties to an anti-union church. These objectors need only to demonstrate a sincerely held religious belief against union affiliation. The trend, understandably, is opposed by the labor movement.

The woman in question—a teacher at a public university in Illinois—fits neither description. She was not among the Seventh-Day Adventists who have traditionally won the exemption, nor was she a self-styled biblical exegete who discovered a supposedly anti-union verse in the Bible. The teacher in Illinois took her stand as a member of the Roman Catholic Church.

Joined by an "expert witness" (her husband, another teacher at the school), she argued that Catholic social teaching opposes compulsory dues' payment. In other words, the church aligns itself with the so-called "right to work" movement. As her Exhibit A, she presented *Gaudium et Spes*, a defining document of the Second Vatican Council (also known by its English title, "The Church in the Modern World"). I had a small hand in drafting the passage of *Gaudium et Spes* cited by the teacher and her expert witness. And so, as a witness for the University Professionals of Illinois (UPI), I had to differ with her reading of the text, in my testimony before the Illinois Educational Labor Relations Board.

The hearing served as an occasion to explore the church's view of unions as not simply legitimate, but indispensable. Later on, I will suggest that the church in the United States may stand to lose its tradition of support for workers, among them millions of people in our new "immigrant church." As for now, this is, in essence, what I told the Illinois Board:

*   *   *

During the past century, Catholic social teaching has supported the right of workers to organize into bona fide unions in the strongest possible terms. Plaintiff and her expert witness have cited only two of these documents and have done so very selectively at that. To be sure, they concede that Catholic social teaching affirms the right of workers to organize. In doing so, however, they fail to convey the full flavor of official church teaching on this matter.

First, I will quote briefly, though in context, from the two most recent official church documents on the subject of this hearing—the 1981 encyclical letter of Pope John Paul II, *Laborem Exercens,* and the 1986 pastoral letter of the U.S. Catholic bishops, *Economic Justice for All.*

Under the heading, "Importance of Unions," the encyclical reads in pertinent part as follows:

> All these rights, with the need for the workers themselves to secure them, give rise to yet another right: the right of association, that is, to form associations for the purposes of defending the vital interests of those employed in the various professions. These associations are called labor or trade unions. The vital interests of the workers are to a certain extent common for all of them; at the same time, however, each type of work, each profession, has its own specific character which should find a particular reflection in these organizations. In a sense, unions go back to the medieval guilds of artisans, insofar as those organizations brought together people belonging to the same craft and thus on the basis of their work. However, unions differ from the guilds on this essential point: The modern unions grew up from the struggle of the workers—workers in general but especially the industrial workers—to protect their rights vis-à-vis the entrepreneurs and the owners of the means of production. Their task is to defend the existential interests of workers in all sectors in which their rights are concerned. The experience of history teaches that organizations of this type are an indispensable element of social life, especially in modern industrialized societies. Obviously this does not mean that only industrial workers can set up associations of this type. Representatives of every profession can use them to ensure their own rights. Thus there are unions of agricultural workers and of white-collar workers; there are also employers' associations. All, as has been said above, are further divided into groups or subgroups according to particular professional specializations.

Again, with specific reference to the subject of trade unionism, the U.S. bishops' pastoral letter, *Economic Justice for All*, reads in part:

> The Church fully supports the right of workers to form unions or other associations to secure their rights to fair wages and working conditions. This is a specific application of the more general right to associate. . . . Unions may also legitimately resort to strikes where this is the only available means to the justice owed to workers. No one may deny the right to organize without attacking human dignity itself. Therefore, we firmly oppose efforts, such as those regrettably now seen in this country, to break

existing unions and prevent workers from organizing. Migrant agricultural workers today are particularly in need of the protection, including the right to organize and bargain collectively. U.S. labor law reform is needed to meet these problems as well as to provide more timely and effective remedies for unfair labor practices.

So it is not enough to say, as have the plaintiff and her expert witness, that official Catholic social teaching affirms the right of workers to organize. Catholic social teaching does much more than that. It vigorously supports the free exercise of this right and regards bona fide trade unions as morally necessary or, in the terminology of John Paul II, "indispensable" in contemporary society.

In light of the importance placed on trade unions, a number of the more authoritative commentators on this teaching have argued that some form of guaranteed union security (e.g. dues' collection) is a requirement of social justice. They have further argued that, because unions are morally necessary, there is no denying a certain moral obligation to join a union.

For instance, in their highly regarded, book-length commentary on the entire corpus of Catholic social teaching, *The Church and Social Justice* (1961), Jesuit Fathers Jean Yves Calvez and Jacques Perrin write:

> There is need only to draw out the implications of the reasoning of the popes on the necessity of unionism and on the correlative moral obligation to join a union. The most easily seen argument rests on the fact that, by means of collective bargaining, all those who are employed in an enterprise, even the non-unionists, benefit from the action which the union undertakes in defense of their rights. The individual work contract made by the worker is established with reference to the collective bargain, so he has some sort of tacit engagement and ought to admit to some obligation toward the union. The union, for its part, cannot prosecute its just claims unless it is really representative and even, sometimes, able to appeal to the force of numbers and of finance. There is an even stronger argument, which rests on the moral solidarity of the members of the workers' group. It is certainly never permissible to shut a worker out from work simply because he is out of favor with his union, nor to bring him to severe want simply because he refuses to join. But, on the other hand, it cannot be maintained that workers are absolutely free to refuse to join a union, nor even that they ought not to suffer in some way for not joining.

In *Catholic Social Principles* (1950), Father John F. Cronin identified some of the principles at stake in the view that workers may have an obligation to join a union. Basically, he sees the obligation as growing out of the social nature of human beings.

> In view of the broader functions of unions, many moralists now hold that workers have a duty to join unions. The soundest basis for such an opinion is the obligation of all to participate in group action aimed to infuse a proper order in economic life, so that the institutions of society will be directed toward the common good. This institutional reform cannot be achieved by individual effort alone. It is essentially social. In industrial life, it transcends the boundaries of the single plant or industry. Even where an employer pays good wages and has excellent working conditions, there are common problems of economic society in which labor has both an interest and a duty to participate. If the reason for labor organization were merely the achievement of individual rights, undoubtedly it could be argued that where such rights are adequately protected, unions would not be necessary, much less obligatory. But in the wider pattern of modern life, there are two arguments for unions, even with workers whose employers are imbued with both good will and skill in human relations. The first is the need for positive organization of economic life for the common good. Even unselfish individualism will not achieve such positive order. It may seek good goals, but not in a formal and orderly pattern. Secondly, in view of the power concentration in modern life, there is need of buffer groups to safeguard individual rights. Although a given employer is anxious to protect the rights of his workers, these rights may be invaded as a result of actions taken outside of his sphere of competence. There may be arbitrary action by government or selfish moves by other economic groups. Hence workers in this well-regulated concern would need to act with other workers to protect interests common to all.

In citing the Calvez-Perrin and Cronin commentaries, I do not mean to argue that all workers, always and everywhere, are obliged to join a union. I simply wish to reemphasize that Catholic social teaching does much more than simply state that workers have a right to organize. If I may repeat, it vigorously supports the exercise of this right. Further, as Calvez and Perrin have pointed out, it favors some form of guaranteed union security that would require workers to contribute their "fair share" to the cost of administering a legally constituted union. For this reason, and with very few exceptions, authoritative U.S. commentators on Catholic social teaching have strongly opposed so-called "right-to-work" legislation that prohibits even the limited form of union security known as the "union shop."

Let me turn to plaintiff's brief citations from two, and only two, of the numerous church documents on this subject.

From the first of these two documents, the Second Vatican Council's *Gaudium et Spes* (known in English as the "Constitution on the Church in the Modern World"), the plaintiff cites three paragraphs. The last of these is the most, if not the only, pertinent part of the passage:

> Among the personal rights of the human person must be counted the right of freely founding labor unions. These unions should be truly able to represent the workers and contribute to the proper arrangement of economic life. Another such right is that of taking part freely in the activity of these unions without the risk of reprisal.

Plaintiff interprets these two sentences to mean, in her words, "that while there exists the right of workers to form unions, there also exists a separate right . . . which ensures the freedom to take part and, if this right of freedom exists, also the freedom not to take part in the union without reprisal whether that reprisal be made by the employer or the union."

With all due respect, I must challenge plaintiff's interpretation of this passage.

Please forgive the personal reference, but it so happens that I served as an official consultant to the commission of the Second Vatican Council which drafted this section of *Gaudium et Spes*. I took an active part in every meeting of the commission during the lengthy drafting process. On the basis of that experience, I can state without fear of contradiction that plaintiff has misinterpreted the part of the document which affirms the right of workers to take part in unions without fear of reprisal. The passage refers not to alleged reprisals by the union (e.g. by requiring members to pay a fair share of the cost of administering the union) but, rather, to reprisals by employers or by authoritarian governments. The drafters had in mind, for example, the then fascist regime in Spain which prohibited the free exercise of the right to organize and to participate in free trade unions.

The most authoritative of all the scholarly commentaries on *Gaudium et Spes* fully reinforces my memory in this regard. The commentary, by

world-renowned German Jesuit scholar Father Oswald von Nell-Breuning
(who has since passed on), explains the meaning of the sentences cited by
plaintiff:

> The next paragraph deals with trade unions. The right to found
> them freely is passionately proclaimed and it is emphasized that
> to take part in the activity of a union must be "*sine ultionis peri-
> culo,*" i.e. must involve no sanctions either from employers or the
> State. In conditions such as ours, employers will scarcely be
> tempted to blacklist workers who are active in their unions, but
> in authoritarian and completely or semi-Fascist states, coercive
> measures by the State authorities against active trade unionists
> are still the order of the day. The optimism of the Council re-
> garding the activity and anticipated future development of trade
> unions, especially their growth to ever greater responsibility, is
> perhaps wishful thinking, and is in remarkable contrast to the
> pessimism of some Catholic sociologists and theorists regarding
> the state and future prospects of trade unionism (*Commentary on
> the Documents of Vatican II*, 1968).

So the purpose of this section of *Gaudium et Spes* was to uphold the
right of workers to take part freely in autonomous unions—not the right to
opt out by refusing to pay their share of the cost of administering that
union. (In light of labor's downward slide in recent years, Nell-Breuning's
remarks at the end of this passage have the ring of prophecy.)

Plaintiff's one-sentence citation from the encyclical letter of Pope
John XXIII's *Pacem in Terris* is, in my judgment, even less persuasive than
her interpretation of the pertinent section of *Gaudium et Spes*. The sentence which she cites from *Pacem in Terris* reads as follows:

> If we turn our attention to the economics sphere, it is clear that
> man has a right by the natural law not only to an opportunity to
> work, but also to go about his work without coercion.

According to the plaintiff's brief, this means that the requirement to
pay her "fair share" of union maintenance is a form of coercion prohibited
by Catholic social teaching. I have already addressed this argument indirectly in my discussion of why the overwhelming majority of authoritative
commentators on Catholic social teaching favor some form of union security (e.g. the union shop) and why they oppose so-called "right-to-work"
laws which prohibit the union shop. I do not know of a single authoritative
commentator on Catholic social teaching who would agree with plaintiff's

argument that this sentence provides her with a religiously-based conscientious objection to having "fair share" deductions made from her salary to the UPI. To the contrary, the overwhelming majority would argue, as already cited, that there is no denying a certain moral obligation to belong to and support a union.

I must respectfully ask plaintiff and her expert witness to forgive me for saying, in conclusion, that, in my judgment, they have misread Catholic social teaching on the subject of trade unionism. They have done so by selectively citing only two of the official church documents on this subject. More to the point, they have cited even these two documents out of context and without due regard for their legislative history and for the judgment of the overwhelming majority of scholarly commentators on this subject.

*   *   *

As one could imagine, the idea that people have a certain duty to organize may not go down well in an age of "union-free" environments. Apparently it was a hard swallow for the Illinois Educational Labor Relations Board. The board later ruled that the teacher had a sincerely held belief against coming up with her dues money. Nonetheless, the point of my testimony bears repeating: Catholic social teaching holds that unions are not only legitimate but indispensable, especially in modern industrialized societies. To this extent, at least, the church sends out a counter-cultural message.

Marking the one hundredth anniversary of Pope Leo XIII's *Rerum Novarum*, Pope John Paul II renewed this message in his encyclical *Centesimus Annus*. John Paul II pays tribute to the labor movement in various regions of the world for its leadership during the past century in promoting the kinds of reform advocated by Leo XIII in 1891. He further points to the continuing need for a strong and effective labor movement, not only in the third world, but also in economically developed countries. Unions, he says, have a crucial role not only in negotiating labor contracts, but also as "places where workers can express themselves. They serve the development of an authentic culture of work and help workers to share in a fully human way in the life of their places of employment."

In a related context, the pope—as he had previously done in *Laborem Exercens*—lends support to the efforts of workers "to obtain full respect for their dignity and to gain broader areas of participation in the life of industrial enterprises so that, while cooperating with others and under the direction of others, they can in a certain sense 'work for themselves' through the exercise of their intelligence and freedom." This is a clear call for new experiments in co-management and co-ownership and, in general, for a broader definition of the role of trade unions over and above their somewhat limited role in traditional collective bargaining.

In response to these and other statements of support for trade unionism, some commentators have charged that Catholic social teaching writes out a blank check of support for organized labor. But this complaint misses the point.

The bishops' pastoral letter, for instance, is not a partisan pro-union document. In stressing the need for strong and effective unions and opposing efforts to thwart the free exercise of labor's right to organize, the pastoral is not suggesting that labor stands above criticism. Moreover, the pastoral is not siding against management, much less pitting labor against management. To the contrary, it explicitly states that workers have obligations to their employers and that trade unions and their counterparts in management jointly "have duties to society as a whole." The pastoral, calling for "an imaginative vision of the future that can help shape economic arrangements in critical new ways," strongly emphasizes the representative and coordinating role of organized labor and management, jointly assisted by the government, in developing new forms of bona fide partnership for the public good.

Yet even this balanced view of labor-management relations runs counter to the anti-union currents in our culture. In late 1990 a clash between a leading U.S. bishop and a leading U.S. business newspaper offered an illustration of how far the church had drifted from the mainstream. At the time the U.S. Senate subcommittee on labor held a field hearing on legislation to ban the permanent replacement of strikers. The hearing in New York coincided with steps taken by the New York *Daily News* to put strikers out of their jobs. In his testimony, Cardinal John J. O'Connor spoke of the church's traditional support for the right of workers to withhold their labor, without fear of reprisal, and strongly endorsed the legislation.

"It is useless to speak glowingly in either legal or moral terms about the rights to bargain and to strike as a last resort, or even the right to unionize, if either party, management or labor, bargains in bad faith, or in the case of management, with the foreknowledge of being able to permanently replace workers who strike, on the primary basis of the strike itself," the New York prelate said in his remarks to the Senate panel. "In my judgment, this can make a charade of collective bargaining, and a mockery of the right to strike."

The cardinal's testimony drew a response from the nation's leading business newspaper. *The Wall Street Journal* (December 12, 1990) predictably smirked (I almost said sneered) at the cardinal's alleged innocence and naiveté. Another periodical, *Crain's New York Business,* went *The Wall*

Street Journal one better. Whereas the *Journal* was content to trivialize the argument by talking down to Cardinal O'Connor in a rather flip and patronizing tone, *Crain's* response was deadly serious. A December 17, 1990 editorial in *Crain's* pronounced the cardinal "anti-business" and lacking in "any real understanding of the economic issues involved."

Why all this huffing and puffing about the cardinal's testimony? Where had the editors of the *Journal* and of *Crain's* been hiding all these years? Surely they must have known that, in defending the right of workers to exercise their right to strike without losing their jobs, the cardinal was being faithful to the letter and spirit of official Catholic teaching in this area. (In fact, the *Journal* had branded Pope Paul VI's 1967 encyclical *Populorum Progressio* as "warmed-over Marxism.") And surely they must also have known that the pernicious practice of breaking a strike by hiring permanent replacements is a recent aberration in the field of labor-management relations in the United States.

For his part, Cardinal O'Connor has offered steady leadership in the drive to reclaim the right to strike without fear of reprisal. (The legislative effort continued at this writing.) Comparisons are often said to be odious, but I would argue that the cardinal is the best friend organized labor has had in the American Catholic hierarchy in recent years. More power to him.

What the cardinal always keeps in mind, and his critics at times seem to ignore, is that we are dealing here not only with purely technical innovations in labor-management-government relations. We are dealing also with ethical and profoundly human problems of great significance for the future of our society. This point can be summarized as follows:

—The United States is a leader among nations, not only economically, but morally as well. We serve as models in matters of social and human justice for our developing and developed neighbors. We have the responsibility to achieve a just balance between economic needs and human needs.

—Workers are the linchpin to our economic survival. Their right to employment security is basic in an advanced and humane society.

—We must develop mechanisms for the worker to participate in and contribute fully to the economic success of the enterprise through participation and involvement. In other words, we must tap the creativity and talents of our workers. In an increasingly global economy, no longer can we ignore their potential contributions.

—We must make technological advances serve not only business but the worker as well. Technology, when used responsibly, should enhance rather than undermine the contribution of the worker. We, as a society, should not sacrifice our workers to the age of technology; rather we should make it possible for all to benefit from new technology and fully participate in its development.

—We need to think about competitiveness in a way that does not sacrifice a segment of our population. As a society we cannot and must not abandon workers whose skills or industries have become obsolete. We have a moral obligation to provide them with the mechanisms necessary to once again become productive and make their own contributions to the economy.

—We need not be trapped by the frameworks of the past. We need, instead, to learn from them and create new opportunities and approaches consistent with our values. Through applying creativity and ingenuity in meaningful ways we can effectively mesh our economic realities and our human values.

Put another way, every person is made in the image and likeness of God and endowed with a special dignity, which is not dependent upon accidental characteristics such as social status. This dignity finds expression in a set of basic human rights, economic as well as political. Thus, in delineating human rights, Pope John Paul II has consistently looked to the economic realm. Speaking to the United Nations in 1979, he said, "Permit me to enumerate some of the most important human rights that are universally recognized: the right to life, liberty, and security of the person; the right to food, clothing, housing, sufficient health care . . . all these human rights taken together are in keeping with the substance of the dignity of the human person."

Human rights are not mere abstract realities. They are realized in the concrete conditions of personal, social, economic, and political life. They imply a set of minimum conditions of material well-being which must be met if human dignity is to be protected and human beings are to grow and develop fully. Nothing less is satisfactory. "The economic challenge of today," as the bishops say in their letter, "has many parallels with the political challenge that confronted the founders of our nation. In order to create a new form of political democracy they were compelled to develop new ways of thinking and political institutions that had never existed before. . . . We believe the time has come for a similar experiment in securing economic rights: the creation of an order that guarantees the minimum conditions of human dignity in the economic sphere for every person."

*   *   *

Where do we go from here?

As I have said in another context, it would be fatuous to talk theoretically about new forms of labor-management cooperation—or even a "new American experiment" in economic democracy—without a consensus that strong and effective labor unions are indispensable in our society. At present, no such consensus exists in the United States. So the question remains: How should we respond to labor's moment of crisis?

One option is to throw up our hands and indulge in a bit of despair, if we are so inclined. Another is to simply forget about the labor problem and move on to more fashionable causes. Neither one of these, however, offers a real option for Catholics who hold to the church's social teaching. Forgetting or despairing over the labor problem would amount to a betrayal of our American Catholic heritage, an abandonment of the tradition begun over a century ago by Cardinal James Gibbons of Baltimore (the seat of American Catholicism in those days). We used to think of our church in the United States as a church of immigrants, and so it was. In his day, Cardinal Gibbons spoke to and for an overwhelmingly immigrant population of Catholics in the United States. And it was only natural, in a sense, that he would come to their defense when they took up the struggle to secure their rights as workers.

Our record in supporting their economic rights and, specifically, their right to organize into effective unions was, if not always glorious, at least creditable—better perhaps than the performance of the church in any other industrialized nation from the end of the nineteenth century until the middle of the twentieth century. In my opinion, we have placed ourselves in danger of misreading the demography of today's Catholic population.

It is no secret that many of our second and third generation Catholics, descendants of earlier immigrants, have moved up the social and economic ladder. Upon hearing the story of the American church's sympathy for the worker, they often reply: "But that's ancient history. We're no longer an immigrant nation or an immigrant church." But we are, of course. Recent years have brought some of the largest waves of immigration in the nation's history. And as in the nineteenth and early twentieth century, a significant number of these immigrants, if not most of them, are at least marginally Catholic. In our so-called "upwardly mobile" church, this is top secret: that we are still a church of immigrants—millions of newcomers, principally from Asia and Latin America, who need the support for their economic rights that the church gave to our European forebears.

In a sense, these millions of immigrants have less protection than the German, Italian, Polish, Irish and other immigrants of the past: they are low on skills in a high-tech society. The early immigrants, too, had few skills, generally speaking. Yet in those days, the immigrant worker could start at the bottom and eventually work himself into a steady job, in part because our mass production economy counted on the skills of a blue-collar worker. Today, most of the good jobs call for a level of skill and education that would have kept the immigrant families of the 1930s and 1940s out of the middle class. In the 1980s and 1990s, too many immigrant families find themselves in a prolonged state of poverty or near-poverty.

Along with these newcomers, we also face another kind of immigrant in the American workplace—women, many of whom have become the sole or primary wage-earners in their families. We, as a church, need to find ways of helping women workers develop their own leaders and organizations.

It would be a tragedy of the first order if the church were to walk away from its tradition of sympathetic support for workers and their unions, which started in the Gibbons era. If we lose the Gibbons tradition in this generation, we may lose it forever. That is no exaggeration. And we would do so with the patently false and myopic assurance that the challenges faced by the church of Gibbons no longer confront the church of today.

Even if the new immigrants and the great mass of women workers in the labor market were reasonably well off (and they are not, of course), we would still need a strong and effective labor movement and a church to keep alive the Gibbons tradition of support for the movement. But why? What difference would it make if the American labor movement were to go into permanent decline?

I take my answer from the writings of the late great Msgr. John A. Ryan, first director of the Social Action Department of the old National Catholic Welfare Conference. At the beginning of the Great Depression, Ryan offered words of encouragement to a labor movement so weakened that it seemed on the verge of oblivion. I ended a previous chapter with Ryan's words, and I will do the same in closing here, because they give direction to the Catholic social action movement during another period of labor decline.

"Effective labor unions are still by far the most powerful force in society for the protection of the laborer's rights and the improvement of his or her condition," Ryan said. "No amount of employer benevolence, no diffusion of a sympathetic attitude on the part of the public, no increase of beneficial legislation, can adequately supply for the lack of organization among the workers themselves."

Neither, may I add, can the great proliferation of church-related "justice and peace" programs adequately supply for the lack of organization among the workers themselves.

Selected Bibliography

1. American Catholic Social Thought and Social Action

Abell, Aaron I. *American Catholicism and Social Action: The Search for Social Justice.* Garden City: Hanover House, Doubleday, 1960. 306 pp.

Betten, Neil. *Catholic Activism and the Industrial Worker.* Gainesville: University Presses of Florida, 1976. 191 pp.

Blantz, Thomas E., C.S.C. *A Priest in Public Service: Francis J. Haas and the New Deal.* Notre Dame: University of Notre Dame Press, 1982. 380 pp.

Broderick, Francis R. *Right Reverend New Dealer: John A. Ryan.* New York: Macmillan, 1963. 290 pp.

Browne, Henry J. *The Church and the Knights of Labor.* Washington, D.C.: The Catholic University of America Press, 1949. 415 pp.

Coleman, John A. *An American Strategic Theology.* New York/Ramsey: Paulist Press, 1982. 296 pp.

Costello, Gerald M. *Without Fear or Favor: George Higgins on the Record.* Mystic: Twenty-Third Publications, 1984. 293 pp.

Curran, Charles E. *American Catholic Social Ethics: Twentieth-Century Approaches.* Notre Dame: University of Notre Dame Press, 1982. 353 pp.

Haughey, John C., S.J., ed. *The Faith That Does Justice: Examining the Christian Sources of Social Change.* New York/Ramsey: Paulist Press, 1977. 295 pp.

Hollenbach, David. *Justice, Peace and Human Rights: American Catholic Social Ethics in a Pluralistic Context.* New York: Crossroad, 1988. 260 pp.

Maida, Adam J., ed. *Issues in the Labor-Management Dialogue: Church Perspectives*, St. Louis: The Catholic Health Association of the United States, 1982. 273 pp.

Marx, Paul B., O.S.B. *Virgil Michel and the Liturgical Movement*. Collegeville: The Liturgical Press, 1957. 466 pp.

Miller, William D. *Dorothy Day: A Biography*, San Francisco: Harper and Row, 1982. 527 pp.

Murray, John Courtney, S.J. *We Hold These Truths: Catholic Reflections on the American Proposition*. Kansas City, Missouri: Sheed and Ward, 1960. 336 pp.

National Conference of Catholic Bishops. *Economic Justice for All: Pastoral Letter on Catholic Social Teaching and the U.S. Economy*. Washington, D.C.: United States Catholic Conference, 1986. 188 pp.

Novak, Michael. *The Spirit of Democratic Capitalism*. New York: Simon and Schuster, 1982. 433 pp.

O'Brien, David J. *American Catholics and Social Reform: The New Deal Years*. New York: Oxford University Press, 1968. 287 pp.

Piehl, Mel. *Breaking Bread: The Catholic Worker and the Origin of Catholic Radicalism in America*. Philadelphia: Temple University Press, 1982. 296 pp.

Ryan, John A. *Distributive Justice*. New York: The Macmillan Company, 1942. 357 pp.

————. *Social Doctrine in Action: A Personal History*. New York: Harper and Brothers Publishers, 1941. 297 pp.

2. Labor

Bok, Derek C. and Dunlop, John T. *Labor and the American Community*. New York: Simon and Schuster, 1970. 542 pp.

Craypo, Charles. *The Economics of Collective Bargaining*. Washington, D.C.: Bureau of National Affairs, 1986. 259 pp.

Dubofsky, Melvin and Tine, Warren Van, eds. *Labor Leaders in America*. Urbana and Chicago: University of Illinois Press, 1987. 396 pp.

Dulles, Foster Rhea and Dubofsky, Melvin. *Labor in America: A History*, 4th ed. Arlington Heights: Harlan Davidson, 1984. 425 pp.

Filippelli, Ronald L. *Labor in the USA: A History*. New York: Alfred A. Knopf, 1984. 315 pp.

Geoghegan, Thomas. *Which Side Are You On? Trying To Be for Labor When It's Flat on Its Back*. New York: Farrar, Straus and Giroux, 1991. 287 pp.

Kerr, Clark and Staudohar, Paul D., eds. *Industrial Relations in a New Age*. San Francisco: Jossey-Bass, 1986. 419 pp.

Kochan, Thomas A., ed. *Challenges and Choices Facing American Labor.* Cambridge: The MIT Press, 1985. 356 pp.

Kochan, Thomas A., Katz, Harry C., and McKersie, Robert B., eds. *The Transformation of American Industrial Relations.* New York: Basic Books, 1986. 287 pp.

Levy, Jacques. *Cesar Chavez: Autobiography of La Causa.* New York: W. W. Norton and Company, 1975. 546 pp.

Lipset, Seymour Martin, ed. *Unions in Transition: Entering the Second Century.* San Francisco: Institute for Contemporary Studies Press, 1986. 505 pp.

Marshall, Ray. *Unheard Voices: Labor and Economic Policy in a Competitive World.* New York: Basic Books, 1987. 339 pp.

Taylor, Ronald B. *Cesar Chavez and the Farm Workers: A Study in the Acquisition and Use of Power.* Boston: Beacon Press, 1975. 333 pp.

Weiler, Paul C. *Governing the Workplace: The Future of Labor and Employment Law.* Cambridge: Harvard University Press, 1990. 317 pp.

3. Commentaries on Church Documents

Baum, Gregory. *The Priority of Labor: A Commentary on Laborem Exercens.* New York/Ramsey: Paulist Press, 1982. 152 pp.

Calvez, Jean-Yves, S.J. *The Social Thought of John XXIII: Mater et Magistra.* Chicago: Henry Regnery Company, 1964. 121 pp.

Calvez, Jean-Yves, S.J., and Perrin, Jacques, S.J. *The Church and Social Justice.* London: Burns and Oates, 1961. 466 pp.

Camp, Richard L. *The Papal Ideology of Social Reform.* Leiden: E. J. Brill, 1969. 180 pp.

Charles, Rodger, S.J., with MacLaren, Drostan, O.P. *The Social Teaching of Vatican II: Its Origin and Development.* Oxford: Plater Publications, and San Francisco: Ignatius Press, 1982. 569 pp.

Coleman, John A., S.J., ed. *One Hundred Years of Catholic Social Thought.* Maryknoll: Orbis Books, 1991. 364 pp.

Curran, Charles E., and McCormick, Richard A., S.J. *Readings in Moral Theology No. 5: Official Catholic Social Teaching.* New York/Mahwah: Paulist Press, 1986. 459 pp.

Dorr, Donal. *Option for the Poor: A Hundred Years of Vatican Social Teaching.* Dublin: Gill and Macmillan, and Maryknoll: Orbis Books, 1983. 328 pp.

Douglass, R. Bruce, ed. *The Deeper Meaning of Economic Life: Critical Essays on the U.S. Catholic Bishops' Pastoral Letter on the Economy.* Washington, D.C.: Georgetown University Press, 1986. 223 pp.

Gannon, Thomas M., ed. *The Catholic Challenge to the American Economy:*

Reflections on the U.S. Bishops' Pastoral Letter on Catholic Social Teaching and the U.S. Economy, New York: Macmillan Company, 1987. 296 pp.

Hollenbach, David, S.J. *Claims in Conflict: Retrieving and Renewing the Catholic Human Rights Tradition.* New York/Ramsey/Toronto: Paulist Press, 1979. 219 pp.

Kammer, Fred, S.J. *Doing Faithjustice.* Mahwah: Paulist Press, 1991.

McShane, Joseph M., S.J. *"Sufficiently Radical": Catholicism, Progressivism, and the Bishops' Program of 1919.* Washington, D.C.: The Catholic University of America Press, 1986. 307 pp.

Schuck, Michael J. *That They Be One: The Social Teaching of the Papal Encyclicals 1740–1989.* Washington, D.C.: Georgetown University Press, 1991.

Vorgrimler, Herbert, ed. *Commentary on the Documents of Vatican II, Volume Five.* New York: Herder and Herder, 1968. 415 pp.

4. Collections of Church Documents

Benestad, J. Brian, and Butler, Francis J., eds. *Quest for Justice: A Compendium of Statements of the United States Catholic Bishops on the Political and Social Order, 1966–1980.* Washington, D.C.: United States Catholic Conference, 1981. 487 pp.

Byers, David M., ed. *Justice in the Marketplace: Collected Statements of the Vatican and the United States Catholic Bishops on Economic Policy, 1891–1984.* Washington, D.C.: United States Catholic Conference, 1985. 521 pp.

Gremillion, Joseph, ed. *The Gospel of Peace and Justice: Catholic Social Teaching since Pope John.* Maryknoll: Orbis Books, 1976.

O'Brien, David J. and Shannon, Thomas A., eds. *Catholic Social Thought: The Documentary Heritage.* Maryknoll: Orbis Books, 1992.

———. *Renewing the Earth: Catholic Documents on Peace, Justice and Liberation.* Garden City: Image Books, 1977.

Walsh, Michael and Davies, Brian, eds. *Proclaiming Justice and Peace: Papal Documents from Rerum Novarum through Centesimus Annus.* Mystic: Twenty-Third Publications, 1991. 522 pp.

Index